MW00634326

NUMBER IN SCRIPTURE:

ITS SUPERNATURAL DESIGN AND SPIRITUAL SIGNIFICANCE.

BY

E. W. BULLINGER.

THIRD EDITION, REVISED.

"The works of the Lord are great,
Sought out of all them that have pleasure therein."

Ps. cxi. 2.

LONDON:
EYRE & SPOTTISWOODE (BIBLE WAREHOUSE) LTD.,
33, PATERNOSTER ROW, E.C.
1913.

First Edition, 1894.
Second Edition, 1895
Third Edition, 1913

PREFACE

TO THE FIRST EDITION.

MANY writers, from the earliest times, have called attention to the importance of the great subject of Number in Scripture. It has been dealt with, for the most part, in a fragmentary way. One has dealt with some particular number, such as "seven"; another has been content with a view of the primary numbers, and even when defining their significance, has given only one or two examples by way of illustration; another has confined himself to "symbolical numbers," such as 10, 40, 666, etc.; another has taken up such symbolical numbers in their relation to chronology or to prophecy; another has collected examples, but has dealt little with their meaning.

There seemed, therefore, to be room, and indeed a call, for a work which would be more complete, embrace a larger area, and at the same time be free from the many *fancies* which all, more or less, indulge in when the mind is occupied too much with one subject. Anyone who values the importance of a particular principle will be tempted to see it where it does not exist, and if it be not there will force it in, in spite sometimes of the original text. Especially is this the case when chronology is dealt with, the greater uncertainty of dates lending itself more readily to the author's fancy.

The greatest work on this subject, both chronological and numerical, is not free from these defects. But its value is nevertheless very great. It is by the late Dr. Milo Mahan, of New York. His work *Palmoni*,* which was republished among his collected works, has long been out of print. It greatly increased my interest in this subject, and led me to further study, besides furnishing a number of valuable illustrations.

It is too much to hope that the present work should be free from these defects, which are inseparable from human infirmity. From one point of view it is a subject which must prove disappointing, at any rate to the author, for illustrations are continually being discovered; and yet, from another point of view, it would be blasphemy to suppose that such a work could be complete; for it would assume that the wonders of this mine could be exhausted, and that its treasures could be all explored!

I must, therefore, be content with the setting forth of general principles, and with giving a few examples from God's Word which illustrate them, leaving others to extend the application of these principles and search out illustrations of them for themselves.

May the result of this contribution to a great subject be to stimulate the labours of Bible students; to strengthen believers in their most holy faith; and to convince doubters of the Divine perfection and inspiration of the Book of Books, to the praise and glory of God.

E. W. BULLINGER.

Bromley, Kent,
November 1894.

This Third Edition has been revised in one or two important particulars. See pages 128, 129, and 159–163.

E. W. B.

"Bremgarten," Golder's Hill,
Hampstead, N.W. *May*, 1913.

---

* Not the anonymous *Palmoni* by an English author, published in London.

CONTENTS.

PART I.
SUPERNATURAL DESIGN.

CHAPTER I.
THE WORKS OF GOD.

CHAPTER II.
THE WORD OF GOD.

PART II.
SPIRITUAL SIGNIFICANCE.

NUMBER IN SCRIPTURE.

PART I.

Its Supernatural Design.

CHAPTER I.

DESIGN SHOWN IN THE WORKS OF GOD.

"Who hath measured the waters in the hollow of His hand;
And meted out heaven with a span;
And comprehended the dust of the earth in a measure,
And weighed the mountains in scales,
And the hills in a balance?" (Isa. xl. 12.)

"The works of the LORD are great,
Sought out of all them that have pleasure therein." (Ps. cxi. 2.)

THERE can be neither works nor words without number. We can understand how man can act and speak without design or significance, but we cannot imagine that the great and infinite Creator and Redeemer could either work or speak without both His words and His works being absolutely perfect in every particular.

"As for God His WAY is perfect" (Ps. xviii. 30). "The Law of the LORD is perfect" (Ps. xix. 7). They are both perfect in power, perfect in holiness and righteousness, perfect in design, perfect in execution, perfect in their object and end, and, may we not say, perfect in *number*.

"The LORD is righteous in all His ways: and holy in all His works" (Ps. cxlv. 17).

All His works were (and are) done, and all His words were spoken and written, in the right way, at the right time, in the right order, and in the right number. "He telleth the number of the stars" (Ps. cxlvii. 4). He "bringeth out their host by number" (Isa. xl. 26). "He weigheth the waters by measure" (Job xxviii. 25).

We may, therefore, say with David: "I meditate on all Thy works; I muse on the work of Thy hands" (Ps. cxliii. 5).

In all the works of God we find not only what we call "Law," and a Law-maker, but we observe a Law *enforcer*. We speak of laws, but they are nothing in themselves. They have no being; they possess no power; they cannot make themselves, or carry themselves out. What we mean when we speak of law in nature is simply this: God in action; God not merely giving or making laws, but carrying them out and enforcing them.

As He is perfect, so His works and His words also must be perfect. And when we see number used not by chance, but by design; not at haphazard, but with significance; then we see not merely so many works and words, but the Living God working and speaking.

In this first part of our subject we are to speak only of *design* in the use of number; and in the second part, of *significance*. In this first chapter we will confine our thoughts to design as it is seen in the *works* of God; and in the second, as it is seen in the *Word* of God.

When we see the same design in each; the same laws at work; the same mysterious principles being carried out in each, the conviction is overwhelming that we have the same great Designer, the same Author; and we see the same Hand, the same seal stamped on all His works, and the same signature or autograph, as it were, upon every page of His Word. And that, not an autograph which may be torn off or obliterated, but indelible, like the water-mark in the paper; so impressed upon and interwoven with it that no power on earth can blot it out.

Let us turn first to

THE HEAVENS.

Here we see number displayed in a remarkable manner. The 12 signs of the Zodiac, each with three constellations, making 36 in all, which together with the 12 signs make a total of 48. There must be a reason, therefore, why the number 12 should thus pervade the heavens. Why should 12 be the predominating factor? Why should it not be 11, or 13, or 7, or 20?

Because 12 is one of the four perfect numbers, the number of *governmental perfection*; hence it is associated with the *rule* of the heavens, for the sun is given "to rule the day," and the moon "to govern the night." The significance of this, however, must be deferred till we come to consider the number "twelve" under this head. It is enough for us now to notice the fact here, upon the threshold of our subject, that we have one common measure, or factor, which is seen in the 12 signs of the Zodiac, the 36 (3 × 12) constellations,* the total 48 (4 × 12); the 360 (12 × 30) degrees, into which the great circle of the heavens is divided. No one can tell us why the number of degrees was first fixed at 360. It has come down to us from ancient times, and is used universally without a question.† And it is this division of the Zodiac which gives us the 12 months of the Zodiacal year. This is called also the Prophetic year, for it is the year which is used in the prophecies of the Bible.‡

Here, then, is an example of number as it is used in the heavens. *Twelve* is the pervading factor.

CHRONOLOGY.

It is not necessary to go into the intricacies of this vast part of our subject. Notwithstanding the fact that God gave to man these heavenly time-keepers, he has so misused the gift (as he has every other gift which God has ever given him) that he cannot tell you now what year it

---

* There are other modern constellations now: Hevelius (1611–1687) added twenty-two; Halley (1656–1742) added fifteen. But every one knows how different these are from the ancient constellations, both in their names, their character, and their utter absence of all significance. See *Witness of the Stars.*

† It probably arises from the product of the four numbers, 3, 4, 5, 6, which arise out of the phenomena which lie at the root of Geometrical and Arithmetical Science. 3 × 4 × 5 × 6 = 360, while 360 × 7 = 2520.

‡ There are different or relative kinds of years, according as we reckon the revolutions of the sun in relation to certain objects, *e.g.:* (1.) In relation to the *equinoctial points.* The time taken by the sun to return to the same equinoctial point is called the *Solar* year (also the *Civil*, or *Tropical* year), and consists of 365·2422414 solar days (or 365 days 5 hours 48 minutes 49·7 seconds). (2.) In relation to the *stars.* The time taken by the sun to return to the same fixed star is called the *Sidereal year*, and consists of 365·2563612 solar days (or 365 days 6 hours 9 minutes 9·6 seconds). (3.) In relation to his own orbit. The time taken by the sun to return to the same point in his own orbit is called the *Anomalistic year*, and consists of 365·2595981 solar days (or 365 days 6 hours 13 minutes 49·3 seconds). The word "Anomalistic" means *irregular*, and this kind of year is so called because from it the first irregularities of planetary motion were discovered.

really is! No subject is in more hopeless confusion, made worse by those who desire the dates to fit in with their theories of numbers, instead of with the facts of history.

We shall, therefore, avoid man's use of numbers. Our only concern in this work is with God's use of them. Here we shall find both design and significance. Here, therefore, we shall find that which is certain and full of interest.

The first natural division of time is stamped by the Number *seven.* On the *seventh* day God rested from His work of Creation.

When He ordained the ritual for Israel which should show forth His work of Redemption, *seven* is again stamped upon it in all its times and seasons. The *seventh* day was the holy day; the *seventh* month was specially hallowed by its number of sacred festivals; the *seventh* year was the Sabbatic year of rest for the land: while 7 x 7 years marked the year of Jubilee (Lev. xxv. 4, 8).

Thirty jubilees bring us from the Exodus to the opening of Christ's ministry, when, opening Isa. lxi. 2, He proclaimed "the acceptable year of the Lord" in a *seven*-fold prophecy (see Luke iv. 18-21).

The great symbolical divisions of Israel's history, or rather of the times of God's dealings with them, are marked by the same number; and if we confine ourselves to *duration* of years rather than to the succession of years and chronological *dates;* with καιρός (*kairos*), season, a definitely limited portion of time, rather than with χρόνος (*chronos*), time, *the course of time in general* * (hence our word "chronology"),—we shall have no difficulty.

God's dealings with His people have to do with actual *duration* of time rather than with specific *dates;* and we find that His dealings with Israel were measured out into four periods, each consisting of 490 (70 times 7) years. Thus:—

The 1st. From Abraham to the Exodus.
The 2nd. The Exodus to the Dedication of Temple.
The 3rd. From the Temple to Nehemiah's return.
The 4th. From Nehemiah to end of 70 weeks.

---

* In *modern* Greek καιρός has come to mean *weather*, and χρόνος, *year*, thus preserving the essential distinction between the two words.

It is clear that these are periods of duration having regard only to Israel, and to Jehovah's immediate dealings with them. For in each one there is a period of time during which He was not immediately governing them, but in which His hand was removed, and His people were without visible tokens of His presence with them.

	Years.
1. From the birth of Abraham to the Exodus was *actually* (Gen. xii. 4; xvi. 3; and xxi. 5) *	505
But deducting the 15 years while Ishmael was Abram's seed, delaying the seed of promise	15
Leaving the *first* 70 × 7 of years	490

2. From the Exodus to the foundation of the Temple, according to Acts xiii. 20: †

	Years.	Years.
In the Wilderness	40	
Under the Judges	450	
Saul	40	
David	40	
Solomon (1 Kings vi. 1, 37)	3	
		573

* Abraham was 75 years old when the promise (Gen. xii. 4) was made to him. The Law was given 430 years after (Exod. xii. 40; Gal. iii. 17). But 430 and 75 make 505 years, or 15 years over the 490. How are we to account for this gap of 15 years as forming part of the 505 years? The answer is that at Abraham's departure into Canaan (xii. 4) he was 75 years old, Ishmael was conceived 10 years after (xvi. 3), therefore Abraham was 85 at Ishmael's conception. But he was 100 years old when Isaac was born (xxi. 5). Therefore it follows that there were 15 years (100 *minus* 85=15) during which Ishmael was occupying and usurping the place of the "promised seed"; and 15 from 505 leaves 490. Here then we have the first of the seventy-sevens of years, and the first "gap" of 15 years.

† The actual number of years was 573, according to Acts xiii. 20. But 1 Kings vi. 1 says: "It came to pass in the four hundred and eightieth year after the children of Israel were come out of Egypt . . . . he began to build the house of the LORD." Therefore commentators immediately conclude that the book is wrong. It never seems to dawn on them that *they* can be wrong. But they are, because the number is *ordinal*, not *cardinal*, and it does not say four hundred and eighty years, but "**eightieth** year." The 480th from or of what? Of the *duration* of God's dealings with His people, deducting the 93 years while He had "sold them" into the hands of others. Thus there is no discrepancy between 1 Kings vi. 1 and Acts xiii. 20. In the Acts the *actual* number of years is stated in a *cardinal* number; while

But from these we must deduct the Captivities under		
Chushan (Judg. iii. 8)	8	
Eglon (Judg. iii. 14)	18	
Jabin (Judg. iv. 3)	20	
Midianites (Judg. vi. 1)	7	
Philistines (Judg. xiii. 1) *	40	
		93
Leaving		480
To this we must add the years during which the Temple was in building, for the finishing of the house (1 Kings vi. 38)		7
And *at least* for the furnishing and ending of all the work (1 Kings vii. 13-51) † ...		3
Making altogether the *second* 70 × 7 of years =		490
3. From the Dedication of the Temple to Nehemiah's return in the 20th year of Artaxerxes (Neh. ii. 1)		560
Deduct the 70 years' Servitude in Babylon (Jer. xxv. 11, 12; Dan. ix. 2)		70
Leaving the *third* 70 × 7 of years		490
4. From Nehemiah's return to "cutting off" of "Messiah the Prince" (Dan. ix. 24-27)		
The "Seven weeks" (7 × 7)	49	
The "Threescore and two weeks" (62 × 7)	434	
		483

in the Kings a certain reckoning is made in an *ordinal* number, and a certain year in the order of God's dealings with His people is named. And yet by some, the inspiration of Acts xiii. 20 is impugned, and various shifts are resorted to, to make it what man thinks to be correct. The R.V. adopts an ancient punctuation which does not after all remove the difficulty; while in the *Speaker's Commentary* the words in 1 Kings vi. 1 are printed *within brackets*, as though they were of doubtful authority.

* The 18 years of Judg. x. 8 were part of the joint 40 years' oppression; on the one side Jordan by the Philistines, and on "the other side Jordan in the land of the Amorites" by the Ammonites.

† For in 1 Kings viii. 2 it was *dedicated* in the *seventh* month, though it was *finished* in the eighth month. Therefore it could not have been the same year; and it may well have required three years for the completion of all the interior work described in 1 Kings vii. 13-51

"After" this, Messiah was to be "cut off," and then comes this present interval, the longest of all, now more than 1890 years, to be followed, when God again deals with His people Israel, by "One week"* 7

490

Thus the number *seven* is stamped on "the times and seasons" of Scripture, marking the *spiritual perfection* of the Divine Prophecies.

Nature.

We see the same law at work in various departments of nature. Sometimes one number is the dominant factor, sometimes another. In nature *seven* is found to mark the only possible mode of classification of the mass of individuals which constitutes the special department called science. We give the *seven* divisions, with examples from the animal and vegetable kingdoms. The one specimen of an *animal* (the dog) and one specimen of a *flower* (the rose).

I.	Kingdom	Animal	Vegetable.
II.	Sub-Kingdom ...	Vertebrata ...	Phanerogamia.
III.	Class	Mammalia ...	Dicotyledon.
IV.	Order	Carnivora ...	Rosifloræ.
V.	Family	Canidæ	Rosaciæ.
VI.	Genus	Dog	Rosa.
VII.	Species	Spaniel	Tea-rose.

* This "one week" must be future, because since Messiah was "cut off" no prince has come and made a covenant with the Jews and in the "midst of the week" caused "the sacrifice and the oblation to cease." This is specially stated to be the work of "the Prince that shall come." See Dan. viii. 11, where it is done by "the little horn"; xi. 31, where it is the work of "the vile person" (different names for the same person); and xii. 11. All these four passages are the work of the same person, and that person is not Christ, but Antichrist. Besides, Messiah was "cut off" after the "threescore and two weeks," *i.e.*, at the end of the *second* of these three divisions. This cannot be the same event as that which is to take place "in the midst" of the *third* of these three divisions. In a prophecy so distinct, that the very distinction is the essential part of it, it is impossible for us to introduce such confusion by violently taking an event declared to take place "after" the *end* of the *second* period and say it is the same event which is spoken of as taking place in the *middle* of the *third*; and at the same time, out of four distinct descriptions

THE VEGETABLE KINGDOM.

Here all is law and order. Number comes in, in many cases determining various classifications. In the Endogens (or inside-growing plants) *three* is a prevailing number; while in Exogens (or outside-growing plants) *five* is a prevailing number.

The grains in Indian corn, or maize, are set in rows, generally straight, but in some cases spirally. These rows are always arranged in an *even number*. Never odd! They range from 8, 10, 12, 14, 16, and sometimes as high as 24. But never in 5, 7, 9, 11, 13, or any odd number of rows. The even number is permanent. Mr. H. L. Hastings tells of one farmer who looked for 27 years and could not find a "cob" with an *odd* number of rows. A slave was once offered his freedom if he found a corn-cob with an odd number, and one day he found one! But he had found it also some time before, when it was young; carefully cut out one row, and bound it up, so that the parts *grew together* as the corn-cob developed, and finally presented the phenomenon of having an odd number of rows. This exception proves the rule in an interesting manner.

If we notice how the leaves grow upon the stem of a plant, not only is *law* seen in classifying their nature and character, but *number* is observed in their arrangement and disposition. Some are placed alternately, some opposite, while others are arranged *spirally*. But in each case all is in perfect order. After a certain number of leaves one will come immediately over and in the same line with the first:—

In the apple it is the fifth leaf,
In the oak it is the fourth,
In the peach, etc., it is the sixth,
In the holly, etc., it is the eighth; but it takes *two turns* of the spiral before the eighth leaf stands immediately over the first.
In the larch it is the twenty-first leaf; but it is not until after *eight turns* of the spiral that the twenty-first leaf stands directly over the first.

---

of the latter event to make one refer to the former and three to the latter—this is simply trifling with the Word of God. A system of interpretation which requires such violent and unwarranted treatment of God's Word stands self-condemned.

Examples might be multiplied indefinitely were *design in nature* our only subject. We are anxious to search the Word of God, and therefore can touch merely the surface of His works, but sufficiently to illustrate the working of Law and the presence of the Law-enforcer.

PHYSIOLOGY

offers a vast field for illustration, but here again the grand impress is seen to be the number *seven*. The days of man's years are "Three-score years and ten" (7 × 10). In *seven* years the whole structure of his body changes: and we are all familiar with "the seven ages of man."

There are *seven* Greek words used to describe these *seven* ages, according to Philo :—

1. Infancy (παιδίον, *paidion*, child).
2. Childhood (παῖς, *pais*, boy).
3. Youth (μειράκιον, *meirakion*, lad, stripling).
4. Adolescence (νεανίσκος, *neaniskos*, young man).
5. Manhood (ἀνήρ, *anēr*, man).
6. Decline (πρεσβύτης, *presbutēs*, old man).
7. Senility (γέρων, *gerōn*, aged man).

The various periods of *gestation* also are commonly a multiple of *seven*, either of days or weeks.

With INSECTS the *ova* are hatched from *seven* half-days (as the wasp, bee, etc.) ; while with others it is *seven* whole days. The majority of insects require from 14 (2 × 7) to 42 (6 × 7) days; the same applies to the *larva* state.

With ANIMALS the period of gestation of—

The mouse is 21 (3 × 7) days.
The hare and rat, 28 (4 × 7) days.
The cat, 56 (8 × 7) days.
The dog, 63 (9 × 7) days.
The lion, 98 (14 × 7) days.
The sheep, 147 (21 × 7) days.

With BIRDS, the incubation of—

The common hen is 21 (3 × 7) days.
The duck, 28 (4 × 7) days.

With the *Human* species it is 280 days (or 40 × 7).

Moreover, man appears to be made on what we may call the *seven*-day principle. In various diseases the *seventh*, fourteenth, and twenty-first are critical days: and in others *seven* or 14 half-days. Man's pulse beats on the *seven*-day principle, for Dr. Stratton points out that for six days out of the *seven* it beats faster in the morning than in the evening, while *on the seventh day it beats slower.* Thus the number *seven* is stamped upon physiology, and he is thus admonished, as man, to rest one day in *seven*. He cannot violate this law with impunity, for it is interwoven with his very being. He may say "I will rest when I please,"—one day in ten, or irregularly, or not at all. He might as well say of his eight-day clock, "It is mine, and I will wind it up when I please." Unless he wound it at least once in eight days, according to the principle on which it was made, it would be worthless as a clock. So with man's body. If he rests not according to the Divine law, he will, sooner or later, be compelled to "keep his sabbaths," and the rest which he would not take at regular intervals, at God's command, he has to take at the command of man *all at once!* Even in this case God gives him more rest than he can get for himself; for God would have him take 52 days' rest in the year, and the few days' "change" he is able to get for himself is a poor substitute for this. It is like all man's attempts to improve on God's way.

It is not always *seven,* however, which is the predominant factor in physiology or natural history.

In the case of the BEE, it is the number *three* which pervades its phenomena—

In three days the egg of the queen is hatched.
It is fed for nine days (3 × 3).
It reaches maturity in 15 days (5 × 3).
The worker grub reaches maturity in 21 days (7 × 3),
And is at work three days after leaving its cell.
The drone matures in 24 days (8 × 3).
The bee is composed of three sections,—head and two stomachs.
The two eyes are made up of about 3,000 small eyes, each (like the cells of the comb) having six sides (2 × 3).
Underneath the body are six (2 × 3) wax scales with which the comb is made.
It has six (2 × 3) legs. Each leg is composed of three sections.

The foot is formed of three triangular sections.

The antennæ consist of nine (3 × 3) sections.

The sting has nine (3 × 3) barbs on each side.

Is this design? or is it chance? Why should it be the number *three* instead of any other number? No one can tell. We can only observe the wondrous working of supernatural laws, and admire the perfection of design.

CHEMISTRY.

Here we are met with a field of research in which constant discoveries are being made. Chemistry is worthy of the name *Science*. Here are no theories and hypotheses, which deprive other so-called sciences of all title to the name. Science is *Scientia*, knowledge, that which we *know*, and what we know is *truth* which can never alter. Chemistry, for example, is not like geology, whose old theories are constantly being superseded by new ones. If we *know* the action of a certain substance, then our knowledge never changes. But side by side with this unchangeable truth there is the constant discovery of new truths.

All matter is made up of certain combinations of various elements, which are its ultimate, indecomposable constituents. Not that these elements are absolutely simple, but that hitherto they have not been decomposed. Some of these have been known from the most ancient times, while others are of quite recent discovery. Hence their number is slowly being increased. In 1874 there were 64; now there are about 70.

But though their total number cannot yet be known, the law by which they are arranged has been discovered. This law is complex, but perfect.

1. All the elements when magnetized fall into two classes. One class immediately ranges itself east and west, at *right angles* to the line of magnetic force (which is north and south), and is hence called *Diamagnetic* (*i.e.* through or across the magnet); while the other immediately ranges itself by the side of and parallel to the magnetic pole (*i.e.* north and south), and is called *Paramagnetic* (*i.e.* by the side of the magnet).

2. Further, it is observed that these elements have other properties. Some combine with only *one* atom of another element, and are called *Monads;* some combine with only

two atoms of another element, and are called *Diads;* some combine with only *three*, and are called *Triads:* while those that combine with *four* are called *Tetrads*, etc.

3. Now when the elements are arranged, first on the two sides of the dividing line, according to their *Diamagnetic* and *Paramagnetic* characters; and then placed on lines according to their properties as *Monads, Diads*, etc.; and further, are arranged in the order of their *atomic weights*,* the result is seen in the accompanying illustration, which exhibits the presence and working of a wonderful law.

On carefully examining this table it will be seen,—

1. That on either side of the central or neutral line, there are alternate groups of *seven* elements, and that these *seven* fall into the form of an introversion, *Monad* answering to *Monad, Diad* to *Diad*, etc., thus:—

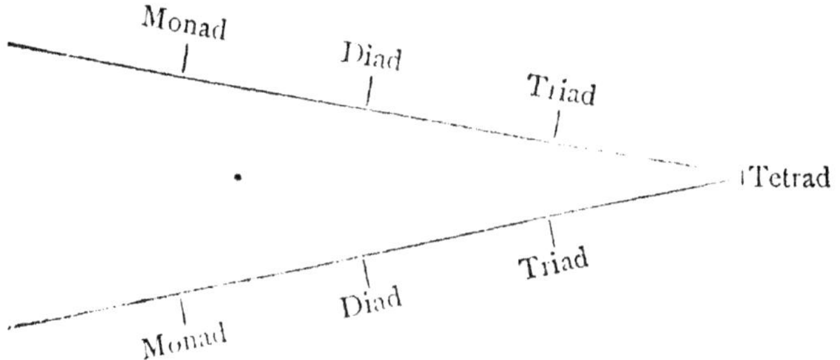

Then, on the other side, the group of *seven* is arranged in the opposite way, but in a corresponding manner:—

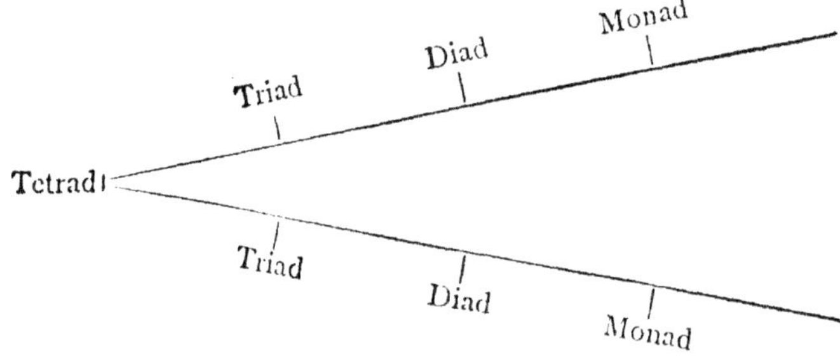

Thus we have an introversion of *seven* elements *alternated* throughout the entire series.†

* The atomic weight is the smallest weight according to which different elements combine.

† Since the First Edition many new elements have been discovered—helium, argon, radium, etc. An improved and very beautiful form of the curve is given by Professor J. Emerson Reynolds, in his Presidential Address to the Chemical Society, in 1902. See the Transactions, Vol. 81.

Reynold's Curve of the Elements. according to the Newlands-Mendelejeff Periodic Law.

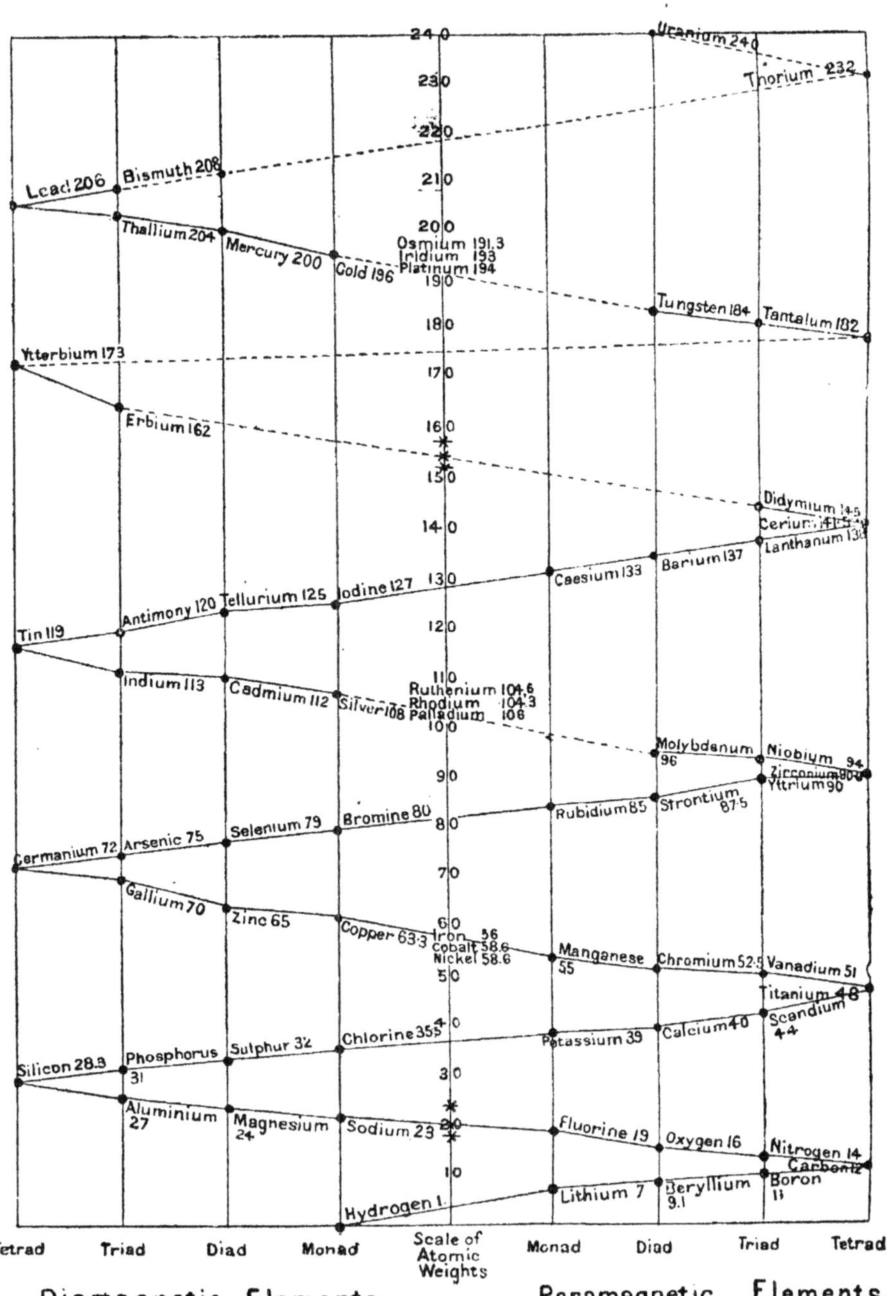

2. Next observe that each time the line crosses upward from *right to left* there is a group of *three* neutral elements that occur together, near the *atomic weights* of 60, 100, and 190. So perfect is the law that the discoverers believe that about the points 20 and 155 there are yet two sets of three elements to be discovered for the places marked ✻ ✻ ✻.

3. Also observe that when the lines pass upward from *left to right* there are *no* elements whatever on this neutral line, and therefore we do not expect any to be discovered.

4. Further, that there are others which will yet be discovered to fill in the gaps that are left vacant, above the weights 145. A few years ago the number stood at 64. The present list contains 69. Some newly-discovered elements have been brought under notice while writing these words. They are Cerium, 141·5; Neodymium, 140·8; Praseodunium, 143·6; and "Ytterbium," 173. These with others that may yet be discovered will fill up some of the gaps that remain.

5. There is an element whose atomic weight is a multiple of 7 (or very nearly so) for every multiple up to 147, while the majority of the others are either square numbers (or multiples of a square number), multiples of 11, or cube numbers. Indeed we may say that every *important* element is a multiple of either 4 or 7; *gold,* the most valuable, for example, being 196 (4×7^2); *iron,* the most useful, 56 (7×2^3); *silver* being 108 (4×27, or $2^2 \times 3^3$), *copper* 63 (7×9), *carbon* 12 (3×4), *mercury* 200 (4×50), *bismuth* 208 (4×52), etc.*

6. Note that all the parts of the image which Nebuchadnezzar saw in his dream are here, and they are all on the left or *diamagnetic* side; that is to say, they are at *cross* purposes with the line of Divine government! The three which are pure and unmixed are all on the same line of *monads*—"gold," "silver," and "copper,"—while the fourth, "iron," is neutral, neither for nor against, like the fourth power, which is both religious and at the same time antichristian. The heaviest is at the top and the lightest at the bottom,

* Where the others are not *exact* multiples of these numbers, they are so nearly exact that the slight uncertainty in the accepted weights might account for some of the differences.

as though to show us that the image being top-heavy is not destined to stand. Three have already passed away; the fourth is approaching its end; and presently, the "power" which was committed to the Gentiles shall be given to Him "whose right it is," and the fifth monarchy (illustrated by the Rock out of which all the others proceed) shall swallow all up when the kingdoms of this world shall become the kingdom of our Lord and of His Christ.

Thus the very elements of matter are all arranged according to number and law. When this law was first spoken of, it appeared to some chemists to be as absurd as suggesting that the alphabetical arrangement could be the scientific or natural order.

But here we have a natural, or rather, we should say, a Divine order. For the elements, when arranged according to the weights and properties which God has given to them, are found to fall into this wondrous order. Here there can be no room for human fancy, but all is the result of knowledge, or science truly so called.

Sound and Music.

Sound is the impression produced on the ear by the vibrations of air. The *pitch* of the musical note is higher or lower according as these vibrations are faster or slower. When they are too slow, or not sufficiently regular and continuous to make a musical sound, we call it *noise*.

Experiments have long been completed which fix the number of vibrations for each musical note; by which, of course, we may easily calculate the difference between the number of vibrations *between* each note.

These were finally settled at Stuttgart in 1834. They were adopted by the Paris *Conservatoire* in 1859, but it was not till 1869 that they were adopted in England by the Society of Arts. The following is the scale of *Do* showing the number of vibrations in a second under each note and the differences between them :—

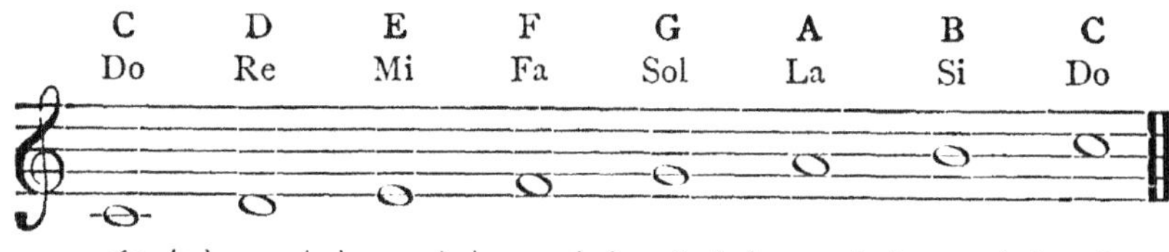

In the upper row of figures, those immediately under each note are the number of vibrations producing such note. The figures in brackets, between these numbers, show the difference between these vibrations. The figures in the lower line are merely the *factors* of the respective numbers.

On examining the above it will be at once seen that the number *eleven* is stamped upon music; and we may say *seven* also, for there are *seven* notes of the scale (the eighth being the repetition of the first).

The number of vibrations in a second, for each note, is a *multiple of eleven*, and the difference in the number of vibrations between each note is also a multiple of eleven. These differences are not always the same. We speak of tones and semitones, as though all tones were alike, and all semitones were alike; but this is not the case. The difference between the *semitone Mi* and *Fa* * is 22; while between the other semitone, *Si* and *Do*, it is 33. So with the *tones:* the difference between the tone *Do* and *Re*, for example, is 33; while between *Fa* and *Sol* it is 44; between *Sol* and *La* it is 44; and between *La* and *Si* it is 55.

The ear can detect and convey these vibrations to the brain only within certain limits. Each ear has within it a minute organ, like a little harp, with about ten thousand

* In using this notation it is worth recording and remembering, in passing (though it is hardly relevant to our subject), the origin of what is now called *Solfeggio.* It arose from a Mediæval hymn to John the Baptist which had this peculiarity that the first six lines of the music commenced respectively on the first six successive notes of the scale, and thus the first syllable of each line was sung to a note one degree higher than the first syllable of the line that preceded it :—

Ut *queant laxis*
Re-*sonare fibris*
Mi-*ra gestorum*
Fa-*muli tuorum*
Sol-*ve polluti*
La-*bii reatum*
Sancte Iohannes.

By degrees these syllables became associated and identified with their respective notes, and as each syllable ended with a vowel they were found to be peculiarly adapted for vocal use. Hence *Ut* was artificially replaced by "*Do.*" Guido of Arezzo was the first to adopt them in the 11th century, and Le Maire, a French musician of the 17th century, added "*Si*" for the seventh note of the scale, in order to complete the series. It might have been formed from the initial letters of the two words in this line, *S* and *I.*

strings. These organs were discovered by an Italian named Corti, and hence have been named "the organs of Corti." When a sound is made, the corresponding string of this little harp vibrates in sympathy, and conveys the impression to the brain. The immense number of these little strings provides for the conveyance of every conceivable sound within certain limits. In the scale, as we have seen, there is a range of 264 vibrations. There is a difference between each one, so that there are practically 264 notes in the scale, but the ear cannot detect them. The ear of a skilled violinist can detect many more than an ordinary untrained ear. The mechanical action of a pianoforte can record only twelve of these notes. The violin can be made to produce a much larger number, and is therefore more perfect as an instrument, but not equal in this respect to the human voice. The wonderful mechanism of the human voice, being created by God, far excels every instrument that man can make.

There are vibrations which the ear cannot detect, so slow as to make no audible sound, but there are contrivances by which they can be made *visible to the eye.* When sand is thrown upon a thin metal disc, to which a chord is attached and caused to vibrate, the sand will immediately arrange itself in *a perfect geometrical pattern.* The pattern will vary with the number of the vibrations. These are called "Chladni's figures." Moist plaster on glass or moist water-colour on rigid surfaces will vibrate at the sound, say, of the human voice, or of a cornet, and will assume forms of various kinds—geometrical, vegetable and floral; some resembling ferns, others resembling leaves and shells, according to the pitch of the note.

The "Pendulograph" is another contrivance for rendering these vibrations visible to the eye; and for exhibiting depths of sound which are totally inaudible to the ear. The pen is attached to one pendulum and the paper to the other, and these are made to oscillate at right angles with each other. When each pendulum is set at *the same* length (making the same number of vibrations in the same time), the figure made by the pen will be a perfect circle. But when these lengths (or vibrations) vary, the patterns that are described are as exquisite as they are marvellous, and almost infinite in their variety and design.

Even the organs of Corti are limited in their perception, notwithstanding the many thousands of minute vibrating chords. When these organs are perfect or well formed there is what is called "an ear for music." But in many cases there is "no ear for music." This means that these organs are defective, not fully developed, or malformed, in the case of such persons; and that the sounds are not accurately conveyed to the brain.

There is a solemn and important truth therefore in the words, "HE THAT PLANTED THE EAR"! (Ps. xciv. 9). What wondrous planting!

Not every one has this peculiar (musical) "ear." And no one has by nature that ear which can distinguish the things of God. The spiritual ear is the direct gift and planting of God. Hence it is written, "He that hath an ear," *i.e.*, only he that hath that divinely-planted, God-given ear can hear the things of the Spirit of God. "An ear to hear" those spiritual things is a far greater reality, and an infinitely greater gift, than an ear for music!" Oh wondrous ear! It is the Lord that gives "the hearing ear" (Prov. xx. 12). He wakeneth the ear to hear (Isa. l. 4); It is the Lord that openeth the ear (Isa. l. 5). The natural ear does not hear spiritual sounds; it cannot discern them (Isa. lxiv. 4 and 1 Cor. ii. 9). Thus nature and grace illustrate each other, and reveal the great fact that there is a secret ear, more delicate than any "organs of Corti," that can detect sounds invisible as well as inaudible to the senses, and which enables those who possess it to say:—

"Sweeter sounds than music knows
Charm me in Emanuel's name;
All her hopes my spirit owes
To His birth, and cross, and shame."

COLOUR.

One more step brings us to colour, which is caused by the vibrations of *light*, as sound is caused by the vibrations of *air*. There is a relation between the two, so that a particular colour corresponds to a particular note in music.

Hence there are seven colours answering to the seven musical sounds, and it is found that sounds which harmonize, correspond with colours that harmonize. While discords in colour correspond with discords in music.

The *seven*, both in music and colour, are divided into three and four. Three primary colours and four secondary, from which all others proceed, answer to the three primary sounds called the Tri-chord, or common chord, and four secondary.

The subject is too abstruse to enlarge further upon here. Sufficient has been said to show that in the works of God all is perfect harmony, order and symmetry, both in number and design; and one corresponds with the other in a real and wonderful manner.

The one great question now is, May we not expect to find the same phenomena in that greatest of all God's works, viz., His Word? If not the greatest in some senses, yet it is the greatest in its importance to us. For if we find in it the same corresponding perfection in design, then we see throughout the whole of it the same mysterious autograph. And its truths, and promises, and precepts come to us with increased solemnity and power; for the words of the book say with the stars of heaven

"The hand that made us is divine."

CHAPTER II.

DESIGN SHOWN IN THE WORD OF GOD.

WE now come to the Word of God, which is the greatest, and, to us, most important of all God's works. May we not look for, and expect to find, number used not only with the same wondrous design, but, here, with *significance* also? If there be design, there must be significance. We may not always see the reason for the latter in the works of creation; but we cannot fail to do so in the great work of Divine Revelation.

In Dan. viii. 13 we read, "Then I heard one saint speaking, and another saint said unto that certain saint which spake, How long shall be the vision concerning the daily sacrifice, and the transgression of desolation," etc.? Here, a revelation of a certain future prophetic event was made to Daniel, by a certain saint or holy one, *i.e.*, a holy angel; and "another" angel asked a question concerning *numbers*—"How long," etc.? The name of "that certain saint" is given in the Hebrew, and is placed in the margin, with its meaning. His name is "PALMONI," and it means "*the numberer of secrets*, or *the wonderful numberer*."

So that there is one holy angel, at least, whose function has to do with *numbers*. Numbers, therefore, and their secrets, hold an important place in the words as well as in the works of God. "A wonderful numberer" ("PALMONI") presides over them, and has his place in making known the things of God.

This certainly looks like design; and, if so—if not only the "days" in which revealed events shall take place are numbered, but the *words* also themselves are numbered—then we shall have a great and wondrous proof of the Divine, verbal, and even literal inspiration of the Word of God.

"It is the glory of God to conceal a thing: but the honour of kings is to search out a matter" (Prov. xxv. 2). In searching out, therefore, the secrets of the Word of God, we are doing not only a royal, but an honourable work.

"The works of the LORD are great: sought out of all them

that have pleasure therein" (Ps. cxi. 2). This is quite different, of course, from trying to find out what God calls His "secret things."

"The secret things belong unto the LORD our God; but those things which are revealed belong unto us and to our children for ever" (Deut. xxix. 29). Our searching must be confined to what is *revealed*. With what God has been pleased not to reveal, but to keep secret, not only have we nothing whatever to do, but we are guilty of the sin of presumption in even speculating about it. If a child of God is observed to be much occupied with God's "secret things," he will be found to be one who neglects the study of the things which God has *revealed*.

We can have neither words nor works without "number." The question which we have to answer is—Is number used with design or by chance? Surely if God uses it, it must be with infinite wisdom and with glorious perfection. And so it is. Each number has its own significance; and its meaning is found to be in moral harmony and relation to the subject matter in connection with which it stands. This harmony is always perfect. Every word of God's Book is in its right place. It may sometimes seem to us to be deranged. The lock may be in one place, and the key may sometimes be hidden away elsewhere in some apparently inadvertent word or sentence.

A volume might be written in illustration of this fact; and it would be a profitable Bible-study to search out these little seemingly unimportant keys.

For example: In Gen. xi. and xii., we see how Abram came out of Ur of the Chaldees, but instead of going on at once to Canaan, he stops a long time in Haran. The explanation of this delay is not given there. It is hidden away in Acts vii. 4, where we read, "from thence (*i.e.* from Haran) *when his father was dead*." From which we learn that Terah was the hindrance; and we are taught by the fact, thus emphasised, how earthly relationships may sometimes hinder our complete obedience.

Another example is Isa. lii. 4: "My people went down aforetime into Egypt to sojourn there; and the Assyrian oppressed them without cause." Here is a very difficult lock. This verse has greatly puzzled commentators, who assume that two oppressions are spoken of, one in Egypt and the other in Assyria. They are therefore at a loss to understand and explain why these two oppressions are mentioned together in one verse, as though they were closely connected, when in fact they were separated by more than seven centuries. The key is hidden away in one little word in Acts vii. 18, "There arose *another* king." The word here translated "another" is not ἄλλος, *another* of the same kind; but it is ἕτερος, *another* of a different kind; showing us that it was a *different dynasty* altogether: and the monuments now prove that it was a new Assyrian dynasty.*

Many other examples might be given to show how a name, or a word, or a genealogy, or a date, may be found, which is seemingly of little or no importance in its context, and yet may throw wondrous light on a passage written elsewhere, and be a key to a difficulty, otherwise inexplicable. "But all these worketh that one and the self-same Spirit," whose infinite wisdom is seen inspiring the whole of Divine revelation and securing a uniformity in results which would be absolutely impossible in a work written separately by different writers.

Let us defer for the present the subject of *significance*, and look at a few facts which show a manifest *design* pervading the whole Bible, by which various agents, writing at different intervals, and thus separated both by place, and time, and circumstance, are yet made to use certain words a definite number of times.

The actual number depends upon the special significance of the word; for the significance of the word corresponds with the significance of the number of the times it occurs.

---

* The last king of the XVIIIth dynasty, Amenhotep IV., was succeeded by a new race of kings which is called the XIXth dynasty, commencing with RAMESES I. and his son Seti I., who reigned together, Seti I. surviving as the Pharaoh of the "Oppression" (Exod. i. and ii.) and dying (Exod. ii. 23). His mummy is now in the Boulak Museum. He was succeeded by RAMESES II., and his successor Menephtah was the Pharaoh who was drowned in the Red Sea. The change to this new dynasty is clearly seen in the monuments, in the great difference between the round faces, flat noses, and thick lips of the XVIIIth or Egyptian dynasty, and the long face, high cheekbones, and aquiline nose of the Assyrian of the XIXth dynasty. Josephus speaks of "the crown being come into *another* family" (*Ant.* ii. 9). The same is implied in the words "a new king" (Exod. i. 8); note חדש and קום. See Deut. xxxii. 17; Judg. v. 8; Dan. ii. 31, 39, 44; iii. 24.

Where there is no such special significance in the meaning or use of the word, there is no special significance in the number of its occurrences.

But where there is a *general importance* in the word, apart from its direct *significance*, then the word occurs according to law.

All such general and important words—*i.e.*, such words on which the Holy Spirit would have us place special emphasis, or would wish us to lay special stress—occur a certain number of times. These are either—

(1) A *square* number, or
(2) A *cube*, or
(3) A multiple of seven, or
(4) A multiple of eleven.

It is interesting to notice why these numbers should be thus associated together. They are significant in themselves, for *seven* is one of the four so-called perfect numbers, 3, 7, 10 and 12, as we shall see below.

3 is the number of *Divine* perfection.
7 „ „ *Spiritual* perfection.
10 „ „ *Ordinal* perfection.
12 „ „ *Governmental* perfection.

The product of these four perfect numbers forms the great number of *chronological perfection*, $3 \times 7 \times 10 \times 12 = 2520$, the times of Israel's punishment, and the times of Gentile dominion over Jerusalem.*

The association of the numbers 11 and 7 connects this arithmetical law with the geometrical, and calls our attention to the phenomena presented by the sides of the four primary rectilineal forms—

In the *plane*,
The triangle has 3 sides }
The square has 4 „ } = 7.

In the *solid*,
The pyramid has 5 sides }
The cube has 6 „ } = 11.

The number 18 (the sum of these, 7 + 11) in Scripture and in nature is usually thus divided into 7 and 11, or 9 and 9.

---

* See *The Witness of the Stars* (Part II.), by the same author.

As 7 is to 11, so is the height of a pyramid (whose base is a square) to the length of its base.

It is also the expression of the ratio between the diameter of a circle and its semi-circumference; or between a semi-circle and its chord.

Further, as 18 in Scripture and in nature is divided into 7 and 11, so 7 is divided into 3 and 4 (3 + 4 = 7), and 11 is divided into 5 and 6 (5 + 6 = 11).

These numbers, 3, 4, 5, and 6, are related by a perfect arithmetical progression, whose difference is unity (1). Their product gives us the well-known division of the circle into 360 degrees (3 × 4 × 5 × 6 = 360).* No one can tell us why the great circle of the heavens (the Zodiac) should be divided into 360 parts, instead of any other number, for apart from this it appears to be perfectly arbitrary. This is the number, however, which gives us the great Zodiacal, Prophetic, and Biblical year of 360 days, which was given originally to Noah, and employed by the Babylonians and Egyptians.

It is the multiplication of *seven* of these great Zodiacal circles, or years, by *seven*, which gives us the great number expressive of *chronological perfection* (360 × 7 = 2520).

The number 2520 is, perhaps, the most remarkable of all others, for

(1) It is the summary of all the primary rectilinear forms.

(2) It is the product of the four great numbers of completion or perfection, as shown above (for 3 × 7 × 10 × 12 = 2520).

(3) It is the Least Common Multiple (L.C.M.) of all the ten numbers from which our system of notation is derived; for the L.C.M. of 1, 2, 3, 4, 5, 6, 7, 8, 9, 10, is 2520.

Finally, in the musical scale, as we have already seen, we again meet with these numbers *seven* and 11 as the expression of the *seven* primary notes and the 11 semitones.

What there is of design or chance in all this we must leave to the judgment of our readers.

---

* The number 360 is divisible without a remainder by all the nine digits except *seven*.

It is sufficient for our purpose now, merely to note that these two numbers, *seven* and 11, have been specially selected to play so important a part;* and that there is such a remarkable relation between them must be due to design.

Why should it be these two numbers *seven* and 11? Why not any other two numbers? or why two at all? Why not three? We may or may not be able to explain why, but we cannot close our eyes to the fact. We are now merely observing phenomena and noting the working of laws. Let us look first at

THE BOOKS OF THE BIBLE.

The Old Testament.

The Authorised Version, and indeed all printed Bibles, contain and reckon 39 separate books in the Old Testament.

The Alexandrian Jews and early Christian Fathers reckoned 22 (2 × 11) books. This number was arbitrarily and artificially made by putting certain books together in order to make the number of the books agree with the number of letters in the Hebrew alphabet.†

But all these reckonings are of no value, none of them being based on any authority, and all of them being against the authority of the Hebrew MSS., which is all that we have to guide us in the matter. In other words, the number and order of the books of the Bible come to us on precisely the same authority as its facts and doctrines.

In the Hebrew MSS. Ezra and Nehemiah are always reckoned as one book, with the one name, Ezra. Each of the double books is reckoned as one book (*e.g.* 1 and 2 Sam., 1 and 2 Kings, and 1 and 2 Chron.), and all the minor prophets are also reckoned as one book. This makes 24 books in all. This is 8 × 3, both factors stamping the number with the seal of Divine perfection. (See under the numbers *Three* and *Eight*.) ‡

* Why they should have been so selected we cannot tell. That there must be a peculiar adaptation in certain numbers and certain things is clear, even according to man's usage of them. Man speaks of "three cheers" and "forty winks," but why no other number would do no one can tell.

† This number 22 they obtained by arbitrarily reckoning Judges and Ruth together as one book, and Jeremiah and Lamentations together, in addition to reckoning the double books as one, and Ezra-Nehemiah as one.

‡ For further information on this interesting subject see a pamphlet on *The Names and Order of the Books of the Old Testament*, by the same author.

The New Testament.

The New Testament contains 27 separate books ($3\times3\times3$ or 3^3).

Of these 27 books, 21 (3×7) are Epistles.

THE WRITERS.

If we take the agents employed, we have 28 writers (4×7) in the Old Testament, and 8 (2^3) in the New Testament; or together, 36 (6^2).

Of the 21 Epistles of the New Testament 14 (2×7) are by Paul, and *seven* by other writers.

In this we have an argument for the Pauline authorship of the Epistle to the Hebrews; an argument which is confirmed by the numbers of verbal occurrences shown below. (See pages 37–41.)*

Not only do we find these phenomena in the books and the writers of the Bible, but in the occurrences of important words and phrases.

WORDS IN THE OLD TESTAMENT.

"Mercy seat"	occurs	27	times	(3^3).
"The candlestick"	,,	27	,,	(3^3).
The "wave offering" †	,,	28	,,	(4×7).
The "heave-offering" ‡	,,	28	,,	(4×7).

"Frankincense" occurs { in Lev. 7, elsewhere 14 } 21 (3×7).

"Tenth deal," 28 times (4×7).

"Shittim wood," שִׁטָּה and שִׁטִּים, 28 times (4×7).

---

* The following logical reasoning also supports the Pauline agency. There are four steps in the argument:—

1. Peter wrote his First Epistle to the Διασπορά, *the Dispersion.* See 1 Pet. i. 1.
2. His Second Epistle was addressed to the same dispersed of Israel. See 2 Pet. iii. 1.
3. To these same he says (2 Pet. iii. 15) "our beloved brother Paul . . . hath written unto YOU."
4. Where is this Epistle if it be not the one which is addressed to "the Hebrews"?

† Only in Exod. and Lev. the A.V. does not translate "wave" uniformly.

‡ In its sacrificial character.

"Living" (חי, *Chai*):

Chaldee	... ...	7	175 (7 × 25).
Hebrew	Lev. ...	35 (5 × 7)	
	Num. ...	7	
	Deut. ...	21 (3 × 7)	
	Sam. ...	49 (7 × 7)	
	Solomon	56 (7 × 8)	

"Manna," מָן, occurs 14 times (2 × 7).

Qoheleth, קֹהֶלֶת, "preacher," *seven*, all in Ecclesiastes:

3 at the beginning (i. 1, 2, 12).
1 in the middle (vii. 27).
3 at the end (xii. 8, 9, 10).

"Little children," טַף:

In Deut.	7	42 (6 × 7).
Rest of Pentateuch	21	
Elsewhere ...	14	

In God's covenant with Noah (Gen. ix.) the word ברית *Berith*, "covenant," is used *seven* times; with Abraham (Gen. xv. and xvii.) 14 times.

N'ginah (נְגִינָה, "*a song*," etc.):

In Psalm titles	7	14.*
Elsewhere	7	

"Chief Musician" (מנצח, *M'natstsach*): †

In Psalms ...	55 (5 × 11)	56 (7 × 8).
Hab. iii. 19 (R.V.)	1	

"Blessed" (אשרי, *ashrey*): ‡

Psalms	25 (5^2)	44 (4 × 11).
Rest of Old Testament	19	

---

* *Seven* times in singular:—one in Psalms (lxi.), and six elsewhere. *Seven* times in plural (*Neginoth*):—six in Psalms (iv., vi., liv., lv., lxvii., lxx.), and one elsewhere (Hab. iii. 19), thus making a double-sevenfold arrangement within another!

† The verb occurs 9 times (3^2) with other meanings.

‡ This word is masculine plural construct, and means literally, ***O the blisses of! O the happinesses of!*** It is never used in the singular, to show that God's blessings cannot be numbered. It is translated 17 times "happy" and 27 times "blessed."

"Vision":

חזו, *Cheh-zev* (Chald.) 11
חזון, *Chah-zon* ... 35 (5×7)
חזיון, *Chiz-zah-yohn* ... 9 (3^2)
} 55 (5 × 11).

"Branch":

נצר, *Neh-tzer* * 4 (2^2)
צמח, *Tsemech* † 12 (3 × 2^2)
} 16 (4^2).

פסח, *pah-sach*, the verb used of *the Passover*, *seven* times.

כתנת, *k'thōh-neth*, and *koot-toh-neth*, "coats," 28 times (1st occ. Gen. iii. 15).

לשן, (*lish-shahn*) (Chald.), *languages*, 7 times—all in Daniel.

זרע, (*zeh-ragh*), *seed*, 224 (7 × 32).

WORDS IN THE NEW TESTAMENT.

"The Father" occurs in	Matt.	...	44	times	(4 × 11).
,, ,,	Mark ‡	...	22	,,	(2 × 11).
,, ,,	Luke	...	16	,,	(4^2).
,, ,,	John	...	121	,,	(11^2).
,, ,,	Rest of N.T.		77	,,	(7 × 11).

"The Lamb," a peculiar word ἀρνίον (*arnion*) as used of Christ, 28 times § (4 × 7).

φῶς (*phōs*), *light*, occurs 72 times (3^3 × 6) if we add with R.V. Eph. v. 9 and Rev. xxii. 5.

ἅπαξ (*hapax*), *once*, or *once for all*, 14 times (2×7), omitting 1 Pet. iii. 20 with R.V. This is a word used especially of Christ's sufferings and death.

ἀνάστασις (*anastasis*), *rising again* 1
resurrection 39
raised to life again (with ἐκ) 1
the first that should rise (with πρῶτος ἐξ) ... 1
} 42.

* From נָצַר (*Nahtsar*), *to preserve*, which occurs 63 (7 × 9) times.

† *Tsemech* is used of Christ *the Branch* 4 (2^2) times.

‡ One passage (xi. 26) is disputed, and is omitted in the R.V. The above numeration is an argument for its retention.

§ The Concordance gave 29; but, on examination, one of these was found to belong to Antichrist, Rev. xiii. 11.

ἄφθαρτος (*aphthartos*), *not corruptible* ... 1
incorruptible ... 4
uncorruptible ... 1
immortal ... ... 1 } 7.

"Israelites" (pl.), 7.

Κόκκος (*kokkos*), *grain* 6
corn 1 } 7.

Κυριεύω (*kurieuō*), *be Lord of* 1
lord 1
exercise lordship over ... 1
have dominion over ... 4 } 7.

Ὠδή (*Odee*), *a song*, 7.

ψαλμός (*psalmos*), *a psalm*, 7.

Ναζαρέθ, ρετ (*Nazareth*) occurs 12 times ($2^2 \times 3$)
Ναζωραῖος, (*Nazarethan*) " 13 " * } 25 (5^2).

There is another word Ναζαρηνός (*Nazarene*), which seems to have not so much a local reference, but *a moral sense.* This word occurs six times,† and partakes of the moral significance of the number *six.* This shows that the other two words refer to the city and its inhabitants, as noun and adjective; and therefore, that Ναζωραῖος, in Matt. ii. 23, has special reference to the inhabitants of the *city*, and means "He shall be called a *Nazarethan.*" (See "the first fulfilment of prophecy in the New Testament," under the number "*One*," p. 63.)

σύνεσις (*sunesis*), *understanding* ... 6
knowledge ... 1 } 7.

σπέρμα (*sperma*), *seed*, 44 (4 × 11).

μεθερμηνεύω (*methermeeneuō*), *interpret* 5
be by interpretation 2 } 7.

---

* This is omitting Mark x. 47 and Luke xxiv. 19, where the reading is Ναζαρηνός (*Nazarene*), according to Lachmann, Tischendorf, Tregelles, Alford, Westcott and Hort. For the significance of this number, see under "*Thirteen.*"

† Adding the two passages in the above note, they are Mark i. 24; x. 47; xiv. 67; xvi. 6; Luke iv. 34; xxiv. 19.

"Verily" is shown to be a weighty word. It occurs 49 times (7^2) in the first three Gospels* and 25 times in John (5^2). In the Gospel of John, however, it is always used double ("Verily, verily"), making 50 altogether in John, and 49 in the other three, or 99 in all ($3^2 \times 11$).

If we separate those which were spoken to the *Disciples* and those spoken to *others*, we have

		Spoken to the Disciples.	Spoken to others.
Matthew	...	20 ($2^2 \times 5$)	10 (2×5)
Mark	...	9 (3^2)	4 (2^2)
Luke	...	4 (2^2)	2
		—	—
		33 (3×11)	16 (4^2)
John	...	10 (2×5)	15 (3×5)

"Moses" occurs 80 times in the New Testament ($4^2 \times 5$) (or $2^3 \times 10$). The Concordance gave only 79, overlooking Heb. xi. 23.

The names of the Apostles conform to this law:—

Peter	occurs	245	times	($7^2 \times 5$)
Simon † (used of Peter)	„	50	„	($5^2 \times 2$)
James (the great)	„	21	„	(3×7)
James (the less)	„	21	„	(3×7)
John	„	49	„	(7^2)
Simon Zelotes	„	4	„	(2^2)
Matthew	„	8	„	(2^3)
Philip	„	16	„	(4^2)
Paul	„	160	„	($4^2 \times 10$)
Saul (Apostle)	„	25	„	(5^2)

Seven were called before the whole Twelve were appointed:—

John	John i.	35–39
Andrew	„	40
Peter	„	41, 42
Philip	„	43
Nathanael (Bartholomew) ...	„	47–51
James (son of Zebedee) ...	Matt. iv.	21
Matthew	„	ix. 9.

* Omitting Matt. vi. 11 and Luke xiii. 35 with R.V.

† The Concordance gave in this case one too many, viz., 51, but this was found to include Mark iii. 18, which is another Simon (the "Canaanite").

Then the Twelve appear to have been called at *seven* different times:—

1. Andrew and John, John i. 35-39 ...
2. Peter, John i. 41 ... ...
3. Philip, John i. 43 ... ... } 4 } 7
4. Nathanael (Bartholomew), John i. 47-51)
5. James (son of Zebedee), Matt. iv. 21 ...
6. Matthew, Matt. ix. 9 ... ... } 3
7. The remaining five, Luke vi. 13-16 ...

Here the *seven* is divided as usual into 4 and 3. Four being recorded in John's Gospel, and three in the other Gospels.

It is probable also that they belonged to *seven* different families, but the relationships are too uncertain for us to speak positively. At any rate *seven* were brothers:—Peter and Andrew; James and John; James (the less), Judas (Lebbæus or Thaddæus), and Simon (Zelotes).

Side by side with this *seven*-fold order, marking the number of the Apostles, there is a three-fold division of the twelve into fours.

Altogether there are four (2^2) lists of the Apostles' names; three in the Gospels and one in the Acts. In each list the order of the names varies, but with this remarkable agreement, that the first name in each group is the *same* in each list, while the other three, though they are in a different order, are never in a different group, thus:—

	Matt. x. 2—4.	Mark iii. 16—19.	Luke vi. 14—16.	Acts i. 13.
1	PETER			
2	and Andrew	and James	and Andrew	and James
3	James	and John	James	and John
4	and John	and Andrew	and John	and Andrew
5	PHILIP			
6	and Bartholomew *	and Bartholomew *	and Bartholomew *	and Thomas
7	Thomas	and Matthew	Matthew	Bartholomew
8	and Matthew	and Thomas	and Thomas	and Matthew
9	JAMES (son of Alphæus)			
10	and Lebbæus †	and Thaddæus †	and Simon‡ (Zelotes)	and Simon ‡ (Zelotes)
11	Simon ‡ (Can.)	and Simon ‡ (Can.)	& Judas† (br. of Jas).	& Judas † (br. of Jas.)
12	and Judas (Iscariot)	and Judas (Iscariot)	and Judas (Iscariot)	Vacant.

* A *patronymic* for Nathanael. See John i. 44-46, where he is joined with Philip as here, and John xxi. 2.

† Judas the brother of James, to distinguish him from Judas Iscariot. He was called Lebbæus or Thaddæus, words which have a similar meaning, *courageous*.

‡ Canaanite, not a Gentile name, but an Aramaic word meaning the same as *Zelotes*.

Note (1) that 4 hold the same place in each list, Judas Iscariot being always last.

(2) That in Matthew and Luke the *first* four are arranged in pairs according to their *calling* and *sending* out; while in Mark and Acts they are placed individually according to their pre-eminence.

(3) The *second* four are given in Matthew, Luke, and Acts, in *pairs;* while in Mark they are given *individually*.

(4) The *third* four are in Matthew, again given in *groups;* while in Mark, Luke, and Acts the order is *individual*.

(5) That each group furnished a penman of the N.T.: from the first Peter and John; from the second Matthew; from the third James and Jude.

The illustrations of the working of this law might be indefinitely extended. We have given merely a selection from our lists, which contain a large number of examples. Let us turn to

The Apocalypse.

In the Book of the Revelation of Jesus Christ, *seven* seems to be the predominating number, not only used as a numeral, but in the occurrences of the important words:—

"Jesus" occurs 14 times (2 × 7) (*seven* times alone, and *seven* times with "Christ").

"Lord"* occurs 21 times (3 × 7).

"Spirit," 14 times, Πνεῦμα, i. 10; ii. 7, 17, 29; iii. 1, 6, 13, 22; iv. 5; v. 6; xi. 11; xiv. 13; xxii. 17.

ἄξιος (*axios*), *worthy*, iii. 4; iv. 11; v. 2, 4, 9, 12; xvi. 6.

ὑπομονή (*hupomonee*), *patience*, i. 9; ii. 2, 3, 19; iii. 10; xiii. 10; xiv. 12.

σάρξ (*sarx*), *flesh*, xvii. 16; xix. 18 (five times), 21.

δέκα κέρατα (*deka kerata*), *ten horns*, xii. 3; xiii. 1 (twice); xvii. 3, 7, 12, 16.

προφήτεια (*propheeteia*), *prophecy*, i. 3; xi. 6; xix. 10; xxii. 7, 10, 18, 19.

* This word κύριος gave some trouble. For the Concordance gave 22. This was good enough, being 2 × 11. But being in the Apocalypse we expected a multiple of *seven*, and this led to a more careful examination. We found that the R.V. omitted κύριος, on due authority, in Rev. xvi. 5 and xix. 1, while it inserted it in xi. 4 instead of the word "God," thus leaving exactly 21 as above.

σημεῖον (*seemeion*), *sign*, xv. 1.
wonder, xii. 1, 3; xiii. 13.
miracle, xiii. 14; xvi. 14; xix. 20.

ἀστήρ (*asteer*), *star*, i. 16, 20 (twice); ii. 1, 28; iii. 1; vi. 13; viii. 10, 11, 12; ix. 1; xii. 1, 4; xxii. 16 (14 times in all).

ψυχή (*psuchee*), *life*, viii. 9; xii. 11.
soul, vi. 9; xvi. 3; xviii. 13, 14; xx. 4.

καιρός (*kairos*), *time* (*i.e.* season), i. 3; xi. 18; xii. 12, 14 (3 times); xxii. 10.

σεισμός (*seismos*), *earthquake*, vi. 12; viii. 5; xi. 13 (twice), 19; xvi. 18 (twice); seven times elsewhere in N.T., making 14 in all.

ἑτοιμάζω (*hetoimazō*), *make ready*, xix. 7.
prepare, viii. 6; ix. 7, 15; xii. 6; xvi. 12; xxi. 2.

βασιλεύω (*basileuo*), *reign*, v. 10; xi. 15, 17; xiv. 6; xx. 4, 6; xxii. 5; 14 occurrences elsewhere, making 21 in all.

ἱμάτιον (*himation*), *garment*, iii. 4; xvi. 15.
raiment, iii. 5, 18; iv. 4.
vesture, xix. 13, 16.

ἄβυσσος (*abussos*), *bottomless*, ix. 1, 2.
bottomless pit, ix. 11; xi. 7; xvii. 8; xx. 1, 3.

νεφέλη (*nephelee*), *cloud*, i. 7; x. 1; xi. 12; xiv. 14 (twice), 15, 16.

τέταρτος (*tetartos*), *fourth*, iv. 7; vi. 7 (twice); viii. 12; xvi. 8; xxi. 19.
fourth part, vi. 8.

δρέπανον (*drepanon*), *sickle*, xiv. 14, 15, 16, 17, 18 (twice), 19.

τόπος (*topos*), *place*, ii. 5; vi. 14; xii. 6, 8, 14; xvi. 16; xx. 11.

μακάριος (*makarios*), *blessed*, i. 3; xiv. 13; xvi. 15; xix. 9; xx. 6; xxii. 7, 14.

ὀξύς (*oxus*), *sharp*, i. 16; ii. 12; xiv. 14, 17, 18 (twice); xix. 15.

θύμος (*thumos*), *wrath* (God's), xiv. 10, 19; xv. 1, 7; xvi. 1.
fierceness, xvi. 19; xix. 14.

οὐαί (*ouai*), *woe*, 8 } 14* (2 × 7).
alas, 6 }

βρονταί (*brontai*), (Nom. pl.), *thunders*, x. 3, 4; xvi. 18.
thunderings, iv. 5; viii. 5; xi. 19; xix. 6.

ἀκολουθέω (*akoloutheō*), *to follow*, vi. 8; xiv. 4, 8, 9, 13; xix. 14.
reach, xviii. 5.

πίπτω (*piptō*), *to fall down* (in worship of God), iv. 10; v. 8, 14; vii. 11; xi. 16; xix. 4, 10.

These are some examples, among many others, from one book.

PHRASES OF THE BIBLE.

אֵלֶּה תּוֹלְדוֹת (*aleh tol'doth*), *these are the generations*, *i.e.*, these are the events that time brought forth to one; (from ילד (*yalad*), *to bring forth*); or these are the things or persons produced by him. This phrase occurs 14 times in the Bible, 13 times in the Old Testament and once in the New Testament.

Genesis	...	11 times, of the Patriarchs, etc.
Numbers (iii. 1)		1 of Aaron and Moses.
Ruth (iv. 18)	...	1 of Pharez (David).
		13
Matthew (i. 1)		1 of Jesus.
		14

The first and last are used only of the "first Adam" and of the "last Adam." But these have the additional formula, "*This is the book of*," etc. (Gen. v. 1 and Matt. i. 1).

While the total number is 14, Genesis has 11, which divide the book into twelve sections. The first section being the Introduction, and the rest consisting of these eleven "*Tol'doth*," making twelve divisions in all, in Genesis.

The eleven *Tol'doth* in Genesis are as follows:—

1. ii. 4—iv. 26. The Heavens and the Earth.
2. v. 1—vi. 8. Adam.
3. vi. 9—ix. 29. Noah.

* There is another *seven*-fold arrangement in connection with this word; for while Bruder's Concordance gives 14 times in Revelation as *noun* and *interjection*, the word occurs 42 times elsewhere as interjection only.

4. x. 1—xi. 9. The Sons of Noah.
5. xi. 10—26. Shem.
6. xi. 27—xxv. 11. Terah (not Abraham's!)
7. xxv. 12—18. Ishmael.
8. xxv. 19—xxxv. 29. Isaac.
9. xxxvi. 1—8. Esau.
10. xxxvi. 9—xxxvii. 1. Esau's posterity.
11. xxxvii. 2—l. 26. Jacob (not Joseph's).

The Massorah calls attention to the fact that the word *Tol'doth,* in the Old Testament, is spelt in two ways. The *first* and the *last* occurrences (Gen. ii. 4 and Ruth iv. 18) are spelt with two *Vaus,* (תּוֹלְדוֹת); the other eleven are spelt with one *Vau* (תּוֹלְדֹת). Various fanciful explanations of the phenomena are indulged in by Jewish Commentators. But the simple reason seems to lie in the fact, that the spelling of the first and last is called *plenè, i.e.,* full or complete; while the spelling of the other eleven is called *defectivè.* Thus the *eleven* which relate to Adam and his posterity (v. 1, &c.) are stamped with *defect:* while the *first,* which relates to the heavens and the earth, tells of the perfection in which they were created; and the *last,* which relates to Pharez (Ruth iv. 18), contains the first mention of the name of DAVID, and tells of the Perfect One—David's Son and David's Lord, who shall restore perfection to His people as well as to the new heavens and the new earth.

It is instructive to notice these divine divisions, and see how different they are from either man's chapters, or man's theories as to the Jehovistic and Elohistic sections, according to which some editor is supposed to have pieced together a number of separate documents by two different authors, one of whom used the word *Elohim* (God), and the other *Jehovah* (LORD).

As a matter of fact, if we take these divinely marked sections, five of them contain *both* titles (*viz.,* the 2nd, 3rd, 6th, 8th, and 11th); four of them contain *neither* (the 5th, 7th, 9th, and 10th); only the first has the combined title *Jehovah Elohim* (the LORD God); and only the Introduction has *Elohim* alone; while "Jehovah" is used by nearly all the speakers, except the Serpent, Abimelech (to Abraham, not to Isaac), the sons of Heth, Pharaoh, Joseph, and his brethren.

D 2

Thus, this simple fact to which we are led by the consideration of design in the employment of numbers, entirely explodes the elaborate theories of the so-called "higher critics" concerning the Book of Genesis.

"In all the land of Egypt" (בכל ארץ מצרים):—

7 times in Genesis.
13 times in Exodus.
1 time in Jeremiah.
—
21 in all (3 × 7).

"His mercy endureth for ever" (לעולם חסדו):—

6 times in Chronicles.
1 time in Ezra.
34 times in Psalms.
1 time in Jeremiah.
—
42 in all (6 × 7).

"A jealous God," 7.
"The ends of the earth," אפסי ארץ (*aphse eretz*), 14.
"Behold (or Lo), the days come," 21.
"Thus saith the Lord God (or the Lord)," 126 (7 × 18).
"As I live, saith the Lord God," 14 (all in Ezek.).
"Daughter (or Daughters) of Jerusalem," 7 in singular; 7 plural.
"The tree of life":

3 times in Genesis.
4 times in Proverbs.
—
7

"This is a faithful saying," πιστὸς ὁ λόγος (*pistos ho logos*), 7 (all in Timothy and Titus); 1 Tim. i. 15; iii. 1; iv. 9, 12 †; 2 Tim. ii. 11; Tit. i. 9; iii. 8.
"These things saith . . ." (τάδε λέγει ὁ . . .), 7 in Revelation.
"Children of Israel," 14 times in New Testament.
"Son of David," used of Christ, 14 times; with slightly different wording,* 7 „ } 21 (3 × 7).

---

* Matt. xxii. 42; Luke i. 32; John vii. 42; Rom. i. 3; 2 Tim. ii. 8; Rev. v. 5; xxii. 16. † πιστῶν ἐν λόγῳ.

"And thou shalt know that I am the LORD" occurs 7 times (1 Kings xx. 13; Isa. xlix. 23; Ezek. xvi. 62; xxv. 7; xxii. 16; xxxv. 4, 12).

We must not, however, multiply these *seven*-fold occurrences, because they properly come under our head of "significance," and belong to the many illustrations of this number of *spiritual perfection*. We shall treat them more fully under the number "*Seven*." We will close these few specimens, selected from a long list of over one hundred, with the phrase, thus shown to be important:—

"As it is written"* (καθὼς γέγραπται, and ὡς γέγραπται):

Matthew ...	1	24 with καθώς ($2^2 \times 6$).
Mark ...	2	
Luke ...	1	
Romans ...	14	
Acts ...	2	
1 Corinthians	2	
2 Corinthians	2	
Mark ...	2	4 with ὡς (2^2).
Luke ...	1	
1 Corinthians	1	
	28 ($2^2 \times 7$)	

Of these 28, note, that 7 are in the Gospels, and 21 in the rest of the New Testament; a *seven*-fold arrangement within the square numbers.

EVIDENCE AS TO AUTHORSHIP.

This law, affecting the occurrence of important words, may be used in evidence as to authorship. For example, if we take certain words in Paul's Epistles alone, we do not find the law operating unless we include the Epistle to the Hebrews. If we add the occurrences in Hebrews to those in the other Pauline Epistles, the harmony is at once restored. Omitting those numbers which have their own special significance, such as 2, 3, 4, 5, 6, 8, 9, 10, 12, 13, etc.,

* The tense is perfect, and refers not to the act of writing, or to the fact that it was once written, but to the truth that *it standeth written*.

let us note the following examples of squares, cubes, 7, and 11:—

The Pauline Epistles.

	Paul's Epistles.	Hebrews.	Total.
ἀγαπητός (*agapeetos*), *beloved* ...	27	1	28 (4 × 7)
ἄγγελος (*angelos*), *angel* ...	14	13	27 (3^3)
ἀγγέλους (*angelous*), *angels* (acc. pl.)	5	2	7
ἐπαγγέλλειν (*epangellein*), *to announce*	5	4	9 (3^2)
ἀπέιθεια (*apeitheia*), *unbelief* ...	5	2	7
ἄγειν (*agein*), *to do*	7	1	8 (2^3)
ἄξιος (*axios*), *worthy*	8	1	9 (3^2)
ἁγιασμός (*agiasmos*), *sanctification*	8	1	9 (3^2)
αἷμα (*haima*), *blood*	12	21	33 (3 × 11)
ἀπιστία (*apistia*), *unbelief* ...	5	2	7
ἐπαισχύνεσθαι (*epaischunesthai*), *to be ashamed*	5	2	7
παραιτεῖσθαι (*paraiteisthai*), *to shun*	4	3	7
αἰώνιος (*aiōnios*), *eternal* ...	21	6	27 (3^3)
ἀκούειν (*akouein*), *to hear* ...	34	8	42 (6 × 7)
ἄλλος (*allos*), *another* ...	31	2	33 (3 × 11)
ἀρνεῖσθαι (*arneisthai*), *to deny*	6	1	7
ἄρτος (*artos*), *bread*	10	1	11
διάβολος (*diabolos*), *the devil* ...	8	1	9 * (3^2)
βασιλεύς (*basileus*), *king* ...	4	8	12 † (2^2 × 3)
γεννᾶν (*gennān*), *to beget* ...	7	4	11
γῆ (*gee*), *earth*	14	11	25 (5^2)
ὄνομα (*onoma*), *name*	21	4	25 (5^2)
γράφειν (*graphein*), *to write* ...	62	1	63 (7 × 9)
δέσμιος (*desmios*), *prisoner* ...	5	2	7
δεσμός (*desmos*), *bond, fetter* ...	8	1	9 (3^2)

* The number of *judgment.*

† The number of *governmental* perfection.

	Paul's Epistles.	Hebrews.	Total.
ἐνδείκνυσθαι (*endeiknusthai*), *to demonstrate*	9	2	11 *
δικαίωμα (*dikaiōma*), *righteous act* or *requirement* † ...	5	2	7
δέχεσθαι (*dechesthai*), *to receive*	13	1	14 (2 × 7)
ἀποδίδομαι (*apodidomai*), *to pay*	8	3	11
εὐδοκεῖν (*eudokein*), *to seem good*	11	3	14 (2 × 7)
ἐξουσία (*exousia*), *authority* ...	27	1	28 (4 × 7)
ἐλέγχειν (*elenchein*), *to convict*	8	1	9 (3^2)
ἔρχεσθαι (*erchesthai*), *to come*...	72	5	77 (7 × 11)
εἰσέρχεσθαι (*eiserchesthai*), *to enter*	4	17	21 (3 × 7)
ἔσχατος (*eschatos*), *last* ...	6	1	7
προσεύχεσθαι (*proseuchesthai*), *to pray*	20	1	21 (3 × 7)
ἀνέχεσθαι (*anechesthai*), *to endure*	10	1	11
προσέχειν (*prosechein*), *to attend to*	5	2	7
ζητεῶ (*zeeteō*), *to seek*	20	1	21 (3 × 7)
Θεός (*theos*), *God*	548	68	616 (7 × 88)
ἀφιέναι (*aphienai*), *to send away*	5	2	7
ἀνιστάναι (*anistanai*), *to raise up*	5	2	7
καθιστάναι (*kathistanai*), *to set down*	3	4	7
καθαρίζειν (*katharizein*), *to purify*	3	4	7
ἐπικαλεῖσθαι (*epikaleisthai*), *to invoke*	6	1	7
κληρονομία (*kleeronomia*), *inheritance*	5	2	7
κοινωνία (*koinōnia*), *fellowship*	13	1	14 (2 × 7)
εὐλογεῖν (*eulogein*), *to praise, bless*	8	6	14
διαλογίζεσθαι (*dialogizesthai*), *to deliberate*	34	1	35 (5 × 7)
λοιπός (*loipos*), *remaining* ...	27	1	28 (4 × 7)

* Only in these Epistles. † See under the number *Nine* (p. 241, note)

	Paul's Epistles.	Hebrews.	Total.
μάρτυς (*martus*), *witness* ...	9	2	11
ἁμαρτία (*hamartia*), *sin* ...	63	25	88 (8 × 11)
νόμος (*nomos*), *law*	119	14	133 (19 × 7)
ἀνομία (*anomia*), *lawlessness* ...	5	2	7
μετάνοια (*metanoia*), *repentance*	4	3	7
ὁρᾷν (*horān*), *to see*	4	3	7
ὄρος (*oros*), *mountain*	3	4	7
ἀπειθεῖν (*apeithein*), *to disbelieve*	5	2	7
ἀπιστία (*apistia*), *unbelief* ...	5	2	7
πιστεύειν (*pisteuein*), *to believe*	54	2	56 (7 × 8)
πρᾶγμα (*pragma*), *deed* ...	4	3	7
πολύς (*polus*), *many*	81	7	88 (8 × 11)
πούς (*pous*), *foot*	10	4	14 (2 × 7)
πρῶτος (*prōtos*), *first*	12	9	21 (3 × 7)
ῥίζα (*rhiza*), *root*	6	1	7
ἀσθένεια (*asthencia*), *sickness* ...	12	4	16 (4^2)
σημεῖον (*seemeion*), *sign* ...	8	1	9 (3^2)
σπέρμα (*sperma*), *seed*	18	3	21 (3 × 7)
σταυρός (*stauros*), *stake (cross)*	10	1	11
ἀπόστολος (*apostolos*), *apostle* ...	34	1	35 (5 × 7)
σωτηρία (*sōteeria*), *salvation* ...	18	7	25 (5^2)
ἐπιτελεῖν (*epitelein*), *to accomplish*	7	2	9 (3^2)
Υἱός (τοῦ) Θεοῦ (*huios (tou) Theou*), *Son of God*	4	4	8 (2^3)
τελειόω (*teleioō*), *to perfect* ...	2	9	11
ἀθετεῖν (*athetein*), *to nullify* ...	6	1	7
θεμέλιος (*themelios*), *foundation*	7	2	9 (3^2)
πρόθεσις (*prothesis*), *setting forth*	6	1	7
τοσοῦτος (*tosoutos*), *so great* ...	2	5	7
τύπος (*tupos*), *a type*	8	1	9 (3^2)
υἱός (*huios*), *a son*	40	24	64 (8^2)
" " (applied to Christ)	17	11	28 (4 × 7)
ὑστερεῖν (*husterein*), *to lack* ...	8	3	11
φωνή (*phōnee*), *voice*	6	5	11
φέρειν (*pherein*), *to bear* ...	2	5	7
χωρίζειν (*chōrizein*), *to separate*	6	1	7
Ἰσαάκ (*Isaak*), *Isaac*	3	4	7

This list might be greatly extended, especially if we included groups of words *from the same root.*

When we consider the same phenomena with regard to the other numbers according to their own peculiar significance,* the evidence is overwhelming as to the so-called Pauline authorship of the Epistle to the Hebrews. Without it the Epistles of St. Paul are only *thirteen* in number, with it they are 14 (2 × 7). This principle governs the occurrences and use of words.

The same test may be applied to

The two Epistles of Peter.

	1st Epistle.	2nd Epistle.	Total.
ἅγιος (*hagios*), *holy*	8	6	14 (2 × 7)
ἁμαρτία (*hamartia*), *sin* ...	6	1	7 †
ἀπό (*apo*), *from*	5	2	7
πίστις (*pistis*), *faith*	5	2	7
ἵνα (*hina*), *that*	13	1	14 (2 × 7)
δόξα (*doxa*), *glory*	11	5	16 (4^2)
εἴδω (*eidō*), *to see*	5	3	8 (2^3)
ἔσχατος (*eschatos*), *last* ...	2	2	4 (2^2)
ἔχω (*echō*), *to have*	4‡	5	9 (3^2)
καλέω (*kaleō*), *to call*	6	1	7
Κύριος(*kurios*), *Lord*	8	13§	21 (3 × 7)
νῦν (*nun*), *now*	5	2	7
οὖν (*oun*), *therefore*	6	1	7 ‖
περί (*peri*), *for, or concerning*	5	2	7
ποιέω (*poieō*), *do, make* ...	3	4	7
ὑπό (*hupo*), *by*	2	5	7

The Old and New Testaments Combined.

In the same way we may take both Old and New Testaments together, and see how marvellously *thirty-six* writers

* *E.g.* κατέχειν (*katechein*), *to hold fast*, 10 + 3 = 13. See under significance of 13 and the use of this word in connection with the Apostasy.

† Reading ἁμάρτημα (*harmarteema*) instead of ἁμαρτία (*hamartia*) in 2 Pet. i. 9 with G., T., Tr., W. and H.

‡ Reading κρίνοντι (*krinonti*) with W. H., instead of ἔχοντι κρῖναι (*echonti krinai*), 1 Pet. iv. 5.

§ Omitting 2 Pet. iii. 9, with L., T., Tr., A., W. H., and R.V.

‖ Omitting with R.V. 1 Pet. ii. 13, and 2 Pet. iii. 11, and adding it in 1 Pet. v. i.

so use their words that when all are taken together we find the same law at work! This would be absolutely impossible if "one and the self-same Spirit" had not inspired *the whole* so as to produce such a harmonious result. The instances are very numerous, and the following words and phrases are given merely as examples:—

"Hallelujah":
24* in Psalms ($2^2 \times 6$) } 28 ($2^2 \times 7$).
4 in Revelation (2^2) }

"Hosanna":
1 in Old Testament † } 7.
6 in New Testament }

"Shepherd," used of God or of Christ:
(רעה), 12 ‡ in Old Test. ($2^2 \times 3$) } 21 (3×7).
(ποιμήν) 9 § in New Test. (3^2) }

"Jehovah Sabaoth," translated variously "the LORD of Hosts," "the God of hosts," etc.:
Old Testament, 285 } 287 (7×41).
New Testament, 2 }

"Corban," an offering:
Old Testament (קרבן) ... ... 82 }
New Test. (κορβᾶν, Mark vii. 11) 1 } 84 (7×12).
" (κορβανᾶς, Matt. xxvii. 6) 1 }

"Milk":
Old Testament (חלב), 44 (4×11) } 49 (7×7).
New Testament (γάλα), 5 }

---

* Viz., in *seven* Psalms, once each; in *seven* Psalms, twice each; in *one* three times, making 24 in all. Besides this *seven*-fold arrangement within the square numbers, the total of the squares yields a *seven*-fold result (28).

† Psalm cxviii. 25.

‡ Gen. xlix. 24; Ps. xxiii. 1; lxxx. 1; Isa. xl. 11; Jer. xxxi. 10; Ezek. xxxiv. 12, 23 (twice); xxxvii. 24; Zech. xi. 16; xiii. 7 (twice).

§ Matt. xxvi. 31; Mark xiv. 27; John x. 11 (twice), 14, 16; Heb. xiii. 20; 1 Pet. ii. 25; v. 4.

"Isaac":

In Deuteronomy	7	7 × 18.
Rest of Pentateuch ...	91 (7 × 13)	
Elsewhere in Old Test. ...	14 (2 × 7)	
New Test., Luke and Acts	7	
" Paul's Epistles *	7	

"Aaron":

In Old Testament	443	448 (4^3 × 7).
In New Testament	5	

"Abaddon" (*Destruction*):

In Old Testament	6	7.
In New Testament	1	

Christ spoken of at the right hand of God:

Old Testament	2 (Ps. cx. 1, 5)	21 (3 × 7).
New Testament	19	

"After the order of Melchizedek": †

Old Testament	1	7.
New Testament	6	

"The stone which the builders refused is become the head of the corner": ‡

Old Testament	1	7.
New Testament	6	

"Thou shalt love thy neighbour as thyself":

Old Testament (Lev. xix. 18)	1	7.
New Testament	6 §	

"Uncircumcision of the heart":

Old Testament ...	6 ‖	7.
New Testament ...	1	

The half of the important Prophetic period (the one week, and its separate divisions, Dan. ix. 27) is mentioned

* Including the Epistle to the Hebrews.

† Ps. cx. 4, quoted in Heb. v. 6, 10; vi. 20; vii. 11, 17, 21.

‡ Ps. cxviii. 22, quoted in Matt. xxi. 42; Mark xii. 40; Luke xx. 17; Acts iv. 11; 1 Pet. ii. 4, 7.

§ Matt. xix. 29; xxii. 39; Mark xii. 31; Rom. xiii. 9; Gal. v. 14; James ii. 8.

‖ Lev. xxvi. 41; Deut. x. 16; Jer. iv. 4; ix. 26; Ezek. xliv. 7, 9; Acts vii. 51.

seven times. This, perhaps, ought to be reserved and considered in its significance under the number "seven." The point, however, now is the manner in which this *seven* is made up; for though the period is given in *three* different languages, *two* Testaments, and *three* forms (years, months, and days) the number is still *seven*:—

Dan. vii. 25, Chaldee, "Time, and times, and the dividing of time"	1
Dan. xii. 7, Hebrew, "Time, times, and an half"	1
Rev. xii. 14, Greek, "Time, and times, and half a time"	1
Rev. xi. 2; xiii. 5, "Forty and two months" ...	2
Rev. xi. 3; xii. 6, Twelve hundred and sixty days	2
	7

Have we not in all this a design which is far beyond nature? A supernatural design? Numbers must occur; and the only question is, Shall they be used by design or by chance? In order, or disorder? According to law, or without law? In the works of God they are used always in perfect order. Surely then we ought to look for the same order in His Word; and be surprised if we do not find it.

If we look at a window of coloured glass, made after the modern fashion, with pieces of various colours put in at haphazard, we see at once that there is no design. But if we observe another window in which the pieces of glass are arranged in a perfect and intricate geometrical pattern, or with human or other forms, we immediately acknowledge *design*, and say that the hand that formed that window must have been guided by a head that designed the whole!

This is our conclusion, then, as to the works and Word of God. Neither Moses nor any other person could have secured the above results. Moses used a certain word by Divine inspiration, not knowing, in all probability, how many times he had used it. It is inconceivable that, even had he known, he could have told Joshua how many times he was to use it; and that Joshua could have arranged with another; and that this could have gone on for fifteen centuries and ensured that the last writer should use the word only a certain definite number of times so as to secure a particular result! Impossible! No! Each writer must have been ignorant as to this final result; but each wrote "as he was moved by the Holy Ghost"; and hence, each contributed such a part as should end in perfecting the original design.

This sweeps away as with a flood, all the puny attempts of man either in attacking or defending the inspiration of the Word of God; for that word has suffered almost as much from the unwise defences of its friends, as from the malignant attacks of its enemies.

"The Law of the LORD is perfect."

We take the high ground of making everything else submit to it. Instead of making the Bible agree with science, science must agree with the Bible. If it does not, it is only because it is "science falsely so-called," and not real science. *Scientia* is the Latin word for *knowledge.* Whereas very much of what goes by the name of "science" to-day is not science at all. It is only *hypothesis!* Read man's books on this so-called science, and you will get tired of the never-ending repetition of such words as "hypothesis," "conjecture," "supposition," etc., etc. This is the reason that such theories, which are falsely dignified by the name of *science,* are constantly changing. We talk of the "Science of Geology," or of "Medical Science"; but read books on geology or medicine, for example, written fifty years ago, and you will find that they are now quite "out of date." But *truth* cannot change. Truth will never be "out of date." What we *know* can never alter! This of itself proves that the word *science* is wrongly used when it is applied only to *hypotheses,* which are merely invented to explain certain phenomena.

It is not for such *theories* that we are going to give up facts. It is not for *conjectures* that we are going to abandon truth. Man must offer us something better than *his own* thoughts if he wants us to give up the thoughts of God. In the Bible we have got something certain and something perfect. Every fact and truth which is discovered only helps to prove its truth and to exhibit its perfection. No monument that has ever been dug up—no manuscript that has ever been discovered, has ever been other than *an evidence of Bible truth!* We are not afraid of any phenomena which may be observed in the rocks, or of any monuments or tablets which may be dug up from beneath them. These are not, and never have been, contrary to the Word of God. It is only *man's interpretation* of them which is against that Word, because it is only his *thoughts* which oppose it.

"The Law of the LORD is perfect."

Man, and all his thoughts are imperfect; so imperfect that he has failed even to take proper care of God's perfect Word.

Like a beautiful stained glass window which has suffered from accident, or fire, or siege, and which man has endeavoured to "restore." We can see how exquisite are its colours and patterns; how perfect it once was. Here and there is a tiny piece wanting, or misplaced. But it does not hinder us from discerning the perfection of the original geometrical figure, or from admiring the delicacy of the features of the figure pourtrayed. The window is indeed marred. And one man has done much to repair the injury caused by the negligence of another. We can see the defect of the repairs; but we can see also that the *design* was originally perfect, and we praise and admire the wisdom of the designer.

So it is with the Word of God. Nothing can hide the perfection displayed in its design. Man has been false to his trust. He has not preserved it with the faithfulness which should ever characterise a steward. But because man has been unfaithful, we are not going to question the faithfulness of God! Because man has not properly cared for this precious gift of God, we are not going to question the perfection of that gift!

But this is what man has done and is doing;—he is charging upon God the result of his own sin, neglect, and folly!

God has given man this "bread of life," and he is analysing it instead of eating it! God has given man His Word, and he is criticising it instead of believing it! This is the "wisdom" of man "up to date." This is the highest flight of his wisdom—"higher criticism"! Truly "the world by wisdom knew not God" (1 Cor. i. 21). It never did and never will. Human wisdom ever leads *from* God. It is so with nineteenth century wisdom! It may seem very clever, very daring, very wise, for man to criticise the Word of God, but it is still true, as it is written (1 Cor. iii. 19),

"THE WISDOM OF THIS WORLD IS FOOLISHNESS WITH GOD."

Then away with man's wisdom! we do not want it. What we want is God's truth, and if man's science does not agree with God's Book, then so much the worse for his science.

We will come to God's Word as those who are foolish in the eyes of the world, because we desire to be made wise unto salvation (2 Tim. iii. 15); and because we remember the words of the Lord Jesus, how He said, "Ye do err, not knowing the Scriptures" (Matt. xxii. 29).

Whence but from Heaven could men unskilled in arts,
In several ages born, in several parts,
Weave such agreeing truths? or how, or why,
Should all conspire to cheat us with a lie?
Unasked their pains, ungrateful their advice,
Starving their gain, and martyrdom their price.—*Dryden.*

PART II.

Its Spiritual Significance.

INTRODUCTION.

HAVING thus shown and established the ***supernatural design*** in the use of number, both in the works of God and in the Word of God, we now come to the *spiritual significance* of the numbers themselves.

We propose to take them in order, and to give under each not merely *lists* of passages or things, but first to define and explain the significance of the number, and then to illustrate its meaning, and show its teaching, as applied to its use, to numbers of things that are mentioned, the numbers of occurrences of words and things, the numbers of words used for a thing, and the numbers formed by the letters of the words themselves. This last is called by the ancients *Gematria.* This is the use of the letters of the alphabet instead of figures. Arabic numerals being a comparatively modern invention were not, of course, known to, and could not have been used by, the more ancient nations.

The Hebrews and Greeks, therefore, used their alphabets as follows :—

THE HEBREW ALPHABET

consists of 22 (2 × 11) letters, so the 5 finals were added to make up three series of 9, or 27 in all, but are not used in Gematria.

Aleph	א	= 1	Yod	י	= 10	Koph	ק	= 100	
Beth	ב	= 2	Kaph	כ	= 20	Resh	ר	= 200	
Gimel	ג	= 3	Lamed	ל	= 30	Shin	ש	= 300	
Daleth	ד	= 4	Mem	מ	= 40	Tau	ת	= 400	
He	ה	= 5	Nun	נ	= 50	Kaph	ך	= 500	Finals.
Vau	ו	= 6	Samech	ס	= 60	Mem	ם	= 600	
Zayin	ז	= 7	Ayin	ע	= 70	Nun	ן	= 700	
Cheth	ח	= 8	Pe	פ	= 80	Pe	ף	= 800	
Teth	ט	= 9	Tsaddi	צ	= 90	Tsaddi	ץ	= 900	

THE GREEK ALPHABET.

The Greek letters were 24, and the required number, 27, was made up by using the final "ς" or ϛ (called *Stigma*) for 6, and adding two arbitrary symbols called respectively *Koppa*, for 90, and *Sampsi*, for 900.

Alpha	α	= 1	Iota	ι	= 10	Rho	ρ	= 100
Beta	β	= 2	Kappa	κ	= 20	Sigma	σ	= 200
Gamma	γ	= 3	Lambda	λ	= 30	Tau	τ	= 300
Delta	δ	= 4	Mu	μ	= 40	Upsilon	υ	= 400
Epsilon	ε	= 5	Nu	ν	= 50	Phi	φ	= 500
Stigma	ϛ *	= 6	Xi	ξ	= 60	Chi	χ	= 600
Zeta	ζ	= 7	Omicron	ο	= 70	Psi	ψ	= 700
Eta	η	= 8	Pi	π	= 80	Omega	ω	= 800
Theta	θ	= 9	*Koppa*	ϙ	= 90	*Sampsi*	ϡ	= 900

* This letter ς (called *Stigma*) is used for the number 6. Why this letter and number should be thus associated we cannot tell, except that both are intimately connected with the ancient Egyptian "mysteries." The three letters S S S (in Greek Σ Σ Σ) were the symbol of *Isis*, which is thus connected with 666. Indeed the expression of this number, Χξς, consists of the *initial* and *final* letters of the word Χριστός (*Christos*), Christ, viz., Χ and ς, with the symbol of the serpent between them. Χ – ξ – ς.

ONE.

There can be no doubt as to the significance of this primary number. In all languages it is the symbol of *unity*. As a cardinal number it denotes *unity;* as an ordinal it denotes *primacy*. Unity being indivisible, and not made up of other numbers, is therefore independent of all others, and is the source of all others. So with the Deity. The great First Cause is independent of all. All stand in need of Him, and He needs no assistance from any.

"*One*" excludes all difference, for there is no second with which it can either harmonise or conflict.

When it is written: "Hear, O Israel, the LORD thy God is one LORD," it does not deny the Doctrine of the Trinity, but it excludes absolutely *another* Lord: it excludes, therefore, all idolatry.

Hence the First Commandment declares "Thou shalt have NO OTHER GODS" (Exod. xx. 3).

It asserts that there is in God a *sufficiency* which needs no other; and an *independence* which admits no other.

It marks the *beginning*. We must begin with God. All our words and works must be characterised by the *first* words of the Bible: "In the beginning GOD." Nothing is right that does not begin with Him. "God first" is the voice of Scripture. "Seek ye first the kingdom of God and His righteousness; and all these things shall be added unto you" (Matt. vi. 33) is the testimony of Christ. "God first" is the great proclamation. The angels sang: "Glory to God in the highest." This was the beginning of their song. And it was after this that they sang of "good-will" towards man. This, too, must be the great principle governing all our testimony and our work. We cannot give "glory to God" without doing good to men. And there is no real good-will for men which does not spring from a desire to glorify God. The rapid declension, which is the great mark of these last days, comes from an ignoring of this great principle. God is shut out, and man is exalted. Hence "the gospel of God" (Rom. i. 16) is being rapidly and almost universally superseded by the gospel of man, which is a gospel of sanitation, and indeed is now openly called "*Christian Socialism.*" But it is a socialism *without Christ.* It does not begin with the glory of God, and it will not and cannot end in any real good to man. It begins with man; its object is to improve the old nature apart from God, and to reform the flesh; and the measure of its success is the measure in which man can become "good" without "God."

Man's ways and thoughts are the opposite of God's. God says, "Seek *first.*" *Man* says, "Take care of number one." He is in his own eyes this "number one," and his great aim is to be independent of God.

Independence, in God, is His glory. Independence in man, is his sin, and rebellion, and shame.

In the Word of God, therefore, God is *first*, and before all.

> "Thus saith the LORD, the King of Israel,
> And his redeemer the LORD of hosts:
> I am the first, and I am the last;
> And beside Me there is no God." (Isa. xliv. 6.)

> "Hearken unto Me, O Jacob, and Israel My called;
> I am He; I am the first, I also am the last.
> Mine hand also hath laid the foundation of the earth,
> And My right hand hath spanned the heavens."
> (Isa. xlviii. 12, 13.)

> "Before Me there was no God formed,
> Neither shall there be after Me.
> I, even I, am the LORD;
> And beside Me there is no Saviour." (Isa. xliii. 10, 11.)

> "I am Alpha and Omega,
> The first and the last." (Rev. i. 11, 17; ii. 8; xxii. 13.)

Thus Jehovah emphasises this great foundation truth. All must be confusion where man refuses to recognise it. All must be peace where it is owned.

The *first* is the only one. There cannot be *two* firsts. Man ignorantly speaks of the "two first," or the "three first," when he really means the first two, or the first three, etc. The Word of God does not thus ignorantly speak. He is the only one. He is first in priority of time. He is first in superiority of rank, and He is first in absolute supremacy.

Redemption and salvation began with God. His was the *word* which first revealed it (Gen. iii. 15). His was the *will* which first purposed it (Heb. x. 7). His was the power that alone accomplished it. Hence "Salvation is of the LORD" (see Exod. xiv. 13; 2 Chron. xx. 17; Jonah ii. 9; etc.). His is the will from which it all proceeds. "Lo, I come to do Thy will," said the Redeemer (Ps. xl. 7, 8; Heb. x. 7) when He came to do that "will."

THE FIRST RECORDED WORDS OF THE LORD JESUS are full of significance.

Here is another illustration of the significance of number in Scripture. The Lord Jesus must have spoken from the time that all children spoke; but not one syllable that He uttered has the Holy Spirit been pleased to record in the Scriptures, until He was twelve years of age. And then only this *one* utterance from His birth till He entered on His ministry at His baptism. Only one sentence out of all those twenty-nine years. Surely words thus singled out by the Holy Spirit must be full of significance. What were they? They are written down for us in Luke ii. 49: "WIST YE NOT THAT I MUST BE ABOUT MY FATHER'S BUSINESS?" Solemn words! Significant words! Especially in the light these *first* words throw upon His *last* words, "IT IS FINISHED." What was finished? "The Father's business." Yes, it was the Father's will. "Lo, I come to do Thy will, O My God." "This is the Father's will which hath sent Me, that of all which He hath given Me I should lose nothing, but should raise it up again at the last day" (John vi. 39). Salvation was no afterthought with God. It was part of His "eternal purpose." It originated in His "will." It was not merely for the good of man, but for the glory of God in a thousand ways which we see not now or yet. Hence it is that when Jesus was delivering up His work back into the Father's hands, He could say: "I have glorified Thee on the earth: I have finished the work which Thou gavest Me to do" (John xvii. 4).

We may find another illustration of the significance of the number "one" or "first" in noticing

THE FIRST MINISTERIAL WORDS OF THE LORD JESUS.

At His baptism (Matt. iii. 13-17) He was anointed for His ministry, and immediately after we read: "THEN was Jesus led up of the Spirit into the wilderness to be tempted of the Devil." For forty days He fasted and was tempted. Not a word that escaped His lips during those forty days is written down. But the very first recorded words of His ministry are: "It is written." Three times over: "It is written;" "It is written;" "It is written."

His official ministry closed with His High-Priestly prayer to the Father in John xvii., for at its close He went out into the Garden of Gethsemane to His betrayal, and within a few hours His death. In those last words of His ministry there is the same threefold reference to the Word of God: *v.* 17, "Thy word is truth;" *v.* 14, "I have given them Thy word;" and *v.* 8, "I have given unto them the words which Thou gavest Me."

What does this fact say to us? If we have ears to hear, it says *The beginning and end of all ministry is the Word of God.* Yea, it is the whole sum and substance of ministerial testimony. The Lord thus exalted the Word of God, and by the significance of His *first* ministerial words He impresses upon us this great lesson.

The First Book

of the Bible also affords us another illustration. In Genesis we see Divine sovereignty and supremacy. Sovereignty in Creation, in giving life, and in sustaining life.

The name by which God specially revealed Himself to the Patriarchs, He says (Exod. vi. 3), was El-Shaddai (God Almighty). This Title occurs

In Genesis 6 times
Rest of Pentateuch 3 times } = 9 (3^2),

nine times in all; the square of *three*, the number of Divine perfection.

The *first* occurrence of the name "Almighty" is also full of instruction, but we shall consider it under the number "*five*."

All through this *first* Book we see this Divine supremacy and sovereignty—sovereignty of will in election and calling: calling Abram and no other (Acts vii. 2); choosing Isaac and not Ishmael (Gen. xvii. 18-21); Jacob and not Esau (*ibid.* xxv. 23, etc.); Ephraim and not Manasseh (*ibid.* xlviii. 19; Heb. xi. 21).

This *first* book is the *one* book. It contains all the other books in embryo, and has been well called "the seed plot of the Bible." Its Divine title is "THE BEGINNING," *i.e.* the first: "In the beginning God," *i.e.*, God first. Here is the beginning of life, the beginning of prophecy (Gen. iii. 15). The woman's seed foretold, and the beginning of the enmity between her seed and the seed of the serpent.

The covenant made with Abraham (Gen. xv.) was unconditional, because there was only *one* contracting party. The Law had a mediator, therefore there were *two* parties to that covenant. "But a mediator is not of one [*contracting party* *], but God is one" (Gal. iii. 20). God alone made this covenant, hence it is called "the covenant of PROMISE."

Then we have the sufferings of Christ, and the glory which should follow, foreshown in Joseph. His death as a substitute is foreshown in Isaac's ram. "The way of Cain" and the way of God are seen in Cain's fruits and Abel's lamb, showing the true and only ground of access to and worship of God.

Thus in the forefront of revelation we are shown that man cannot be saved by works, but by grace alone. The foundation of all truth is here. Gospel truth shines brightly here. All is in *one* book, and that the *first*.

THE FIRST COMMANDMENT.

"This is the first and great commandment," Matt. xxii. 37, 38, or in Mark xii. 29, 30, "Hear, O Israel; the LORD our God is one LORD: thou shalt love the LORD thy God with all thy heart, and with all thy soul, and with all thy mind, and with all thy strength."

The reference is to Deut. vi. 4. This is "first" in order, first in time, and first in importance. This is therefore the "greatest" in necessity, in extent, and in nature. The first in the Law, and the greatest in the Law, and hence it was one of the four passages written on the phylacteries of the Jews.

The Hebrew words may be variously rendered, but the quotation of the Lord Jesus, written by the Holy Spirit in

---

* The ellipsis is wrongly supplied in Gal. iii. 20. It is not the word *mediator* which is to be repeated, but the *contracting party* from *v.* 19.

the Gospels, fixes the meaning of the words. In the Hebrew the order is, "Hear, O Israel, Jehovah our Elohim, Jehovah One." The Jews repeat it to-day thus, "Hear, O Israel, the LORD our God, the LORD is One," and the whole congregation repeat the word "One" for several minutes.*

If the Lord had not supplied the verb which fixes the meaning, we might well have read it as the Jews do, for this fixes (unconsciously to them) the doctrine of the Trinity. For the three Persons are named, and then it is declared that they are *one:* "The Lord, our God, The Lord, is one," *i.e.*, the three, *Father*, *Son*, and *Spirit*, are one.

But there is a further peculiarity in this passage. In all the MSS. and printed texts the last letters of the first and last words are always written and printed *majuscular*, *i.e.*, larger than the others; thus:

"Shem**A** Israel, Jehovah, Elohenu, Jehovah, Echa**D**."

In the Hebrew the first of these two larger letters is ע (*ayin*), and the second is ד (*daleth*). Rabbi Bochin has this remark, "It is possible to confess one God with the mouth, although the heart is far from Him. For this reason ע and ד are *majuscula*, from which, with *tsere* subscribed, עֵד '*a witness*,' is formed, that every one may know, when he professes the unity of God, that his heart ought to be engaged and free from every other thought, because God is a *witness* and knows all things." † What may be the true reason, however, for these two letters being larger, we do not know. The real sense of the words, according to their meaning, is, Hear, O Israel, Jehovah (the ever-existing One) our Elohim (our Triune God), Jehovah "is one."

What is here predicated of Jehovah is not the *unity* of God at all, but that it is to Him that the name Jehovah rightfully belongs, that He is the one and only God, and that there can be no other. It is equally opposed to all forms of *Theism* and *Deism*, which are the creations of man's ideas, as well as to *polytheism* on the one hand, and national or local deities on the other. The whole statement has regard to *revelation*. Israel alone could say, Jehovah is "*our* God,"

---

* As "Elohim" is plural we might with much more reason repeat "Elohenū" for several minutes!

† J. H. Mich., *Bibl. Hebr.*

because He had made Himself known—"His ways unto Moses, and His acts to the children of Israel" (Ps. ciii. 7).

With this agrees the choice of the word *Echad*, which is used for "one." In the Hebrew there are two words in use for the number "one." אֶחָד (*Echad*), "one," *unus;* and יָחִיד (*Yacheed*), "an only one," *unicus*.

The latter, *Yacheed* (יָחִיד), means absolute unity, or uniqueness, an *only one*. It occurs only twelve times in the Old Testament (3×2^2), viz.:

Pentateuch, 3.
Rest of Old Testament 9 (3^2).

Gen. xxii. 2, "Take now thy son, *thine only* son Isaac."

Gen. xxii. 12 and 16, "Hast not withheld thy son, *thine only* son."

Judg. xi. 34, "She was his *only child*."

Ps. xxii. 20, "Deliver . . . my darling" (marg. *only one*).

Ps. xxv. 16, "I am *desolate* and afflicted."

Ps. xxxv. 17, "Rescue . . . my darling (marg. *only one*) from the lions."

Ps. lxviii. 6, "God setteth *the solitary* in families."

Prov. iv. 3, "I was . . . tender and *only* beloved in the sight of my mother."

Jer. vi. 26, "Mourning as for an *only son*."

Amos viii. 10, "I will make it as the mourning of an *only son*."

Zech. xii. 10, "As one that mourneth for his *only son*."

These are all the occurrences of the word *Yacheed*, and here therefore we see the meaning of the word. *But this is not the word which is used in* Deut. vi. 4, and it is never used of Jehovah. It is used of the Lord Jesus as the only begotten Son; but never of Jehovah—the Triune God.

But אֶחָד (*Echad*) *is so used* because it does not mean absolute unity, but a compound unity. Always one of others which make up the one. Its first occurrence is:—

Gen. i. 5, "The first day" (of *seven*).

Gen. ii. 11, "The name of *the first* is Pison" (*i.e.* one of four).

Gen. ii. 21, "He took one of his ribs."

Gen. ii. 24, "They two shall be *one* flesh."

Hence when it is used twice, the word being repeated, "one, one," it is translated both *one* and *the other;* but it is always *one* where there are others. (Hence sometimes *each,* as in Num. vii. 85.)

Gen. xlix. 16, "*As one of* the (twelve) tribes of Israel."

Num. xiii. 23, "A branch with *one* cluster of (many) grapes."

We even have the plural *Echadim* (like *Elohim*), *ones.* In speaking of the two sticks representing the houses of Israel and Judah, it says, Ezek. xxxvii. 19, "They shall become *ones* in Thine hand."

Ps. xxxiv. 20, "He keepeth all his bones, not *one* of them is broken."

In all these and other places *Echad* is *composite.* It is one of others, and hence it is the word used in Deut. vi. 4. Jehovah (the Father), Elohim (the Son), and Jehovah (the Spirit) is *Echad*:—One Triune God.

This is the teaching of the number *one* as applied to this *first* commandment. There is only one Lord, consequently there is no other to divide the heart. Therefore thou shalt love the Lord with all thy heart. Thus the ground of the claim is first mentioned, and then this first and great commandment is given, based upon it.

But this leads to another illustration in Zech. xiv. 9.

The One Millennial Rule.

"And the LORD shall be King over all the earth;
In that day shall there be one LORD, and His name one."

There will in that glorious day be no one to dispute Jehovah's rule. There will be no difference of law, or will, or rule, then. All will be harmony, unity, and agreement. This is the secret of Millennial peace. In the Lord's Prayer the two are placed together, one being consequent upon the other.

"Thy kingdom come."

"Thy will be done on earth as it is in heaven."

Where there are more wills than one, there can be no peace, no rest. There must necessarily be conflict and confusion.

This is the secret of all disturbance in families, parties, and nations.

We sometimes hear of a "Dual Control," but it is a fiction. It exists only in words, not in reality!

This is the secret of rest for the heart now—"*One will.*" As long as there are two wills there can be no peace. As long as our will is not subject to God's will, we cannot know what rest is.

This is where the Lord Jesus, as man, found rest in the midst of His rejection. In Matt. xi., John the Baptist doubts, *vv.* 2, 3; the people of that generation reject Him, *vv.* 16-19; the cities which saw His mightiest works do not believe, *vv.* 20-24. Then we read in the next verses (25, 26), "AT THAT TIME Jesus answered and said, I THANK THEE, O FATHER, Lord of heaven and earth, because Thou hast hid these things from the wise and prudent, and hast revealed them unto babes, EVEN SO FATHER; for so it seemed good in Thy sight." And then turning to His weary servants, the subjects of similar trials and disappointments, He says, "Come unto Me, all ye that labour and are heavy-laden, and I will give you rest."

In other words, *rest* is to be found only in subjection to the Father's will. This is the secret of present rest for our souls. This is the secret of Millennial peace and blessing for the earth.

How simple! and yet what strangers we are to this rest! How the Lord's servants are rushing hither and thither to find this great blessing, and yet do not enter into it! Why is this? It is because *we do not believe that His will is better than our own.* If we were occupied with the Lord instead of with ourselves, with the Blesser instead of with our "blessing," we should soon have such a sense of His grace and glory and power as would convince us that His will is better than ours; and then, instead of being busy with ourselves and enquiring how we are to give up our will, we should see that His is so good that we really loathe our own, and desire only His.

This blessing is not gained by any "act of surrender" or "act of faith," but our own will simply vanishes in the contemplation of His will as we see it to be all-gracious and all-good.

Man's modern methods all begin at the wrong end. They begin with ourselves, they occupy us with ourselves, and hence the failure. The Divine method puts "God First," and thus the end is assured.

It is when our hearts are so before God and so with God, that we learn the wondrous wisdom of His way, and the perfection, sweetness, and blessedness of His will. We yearn to possess it, we long for it, and desire to come into its joy; and our own will vanishes without an effort, and without our knowing it, until we discover afterwards what has happened by a happy experience.

In Millennial days this will be the blessing of the whole earth. For in that day there shall be one King, one will, "one Lord, and His name one."

The Unity of the Spirit.

This is the unity of the members of the one body of Christ, who are all animated by the same Spirit. It is a unity which we cannot *make*. It is made for us in Christ. We can only preserve it, and live in the power of it by the Holy Spirit, who is "the bond of peace." It needs indeed carefully preserving, for it is opposed to all man's ideas of unity in churches and sects. It is a spiritual unity.

In Eph. iv. 4–6 this unity of the body and its members is set forth. And note the *seven*-fold nature of it. It is set forth in an *Epanodos, i.e.*, the sentences are arranged in an introversion, where the first answers to the last, the second to the next to the last, etc. The Lord is exalted by being placed in the centre of the whole.

A | There is one BODY,
  B | and one SPIRIT,
    C | Even as ye are called [also] in one HOPE of your calling:
      D | ONE LORD,
    C | One FAITH,
  B | One BAPTISM,
A | One God and Father of all [*the members of this Body*], who is above [or *over you*] all, and through [or *with you*] all, and in you all.

Here note, then, in A and *A*, we have the one Body. In B and *B*, we have the Spirit and His Baptism. In C and *C*, the graces of "faith" and "hope"; while in D the Lord stands out as the great head of this one Body, the keystone of this arch of Divine truth.

FIRST OCCURRENCES OF WORDS.

These are always important. The ancient Jewish commentators call special attention to them, and lay great stress upon them as always having some significance. They generally help us in fixing the meaning of a word or point us to some lesson in connection with it.

Take for example the word—

"*Hallelujah.*"

Where does it first occur? Ps. civ. 35:—

"Let the sinners be consumed out of the earth,
And let the wicked be no more.
Bless thou the LORD, O my soul,
HALLELUJAH."

And where is the first occurrence in the New Testament? Rev. xix. 1–3, "I heard a great voice of much people in heaven, saying ALLELUIA;* salvation, and glory, and honour, and power† unto the Lord our God; for true and righteous are His judgments; for He hath judged the great whore, which did corrupt the earth with her fornication, and hath avenged the blood of His servants at her hand, and again they said ALLELUIA."‡

In both these cases, in the Old Testament and in the New, the first occurrence of the word "Hallelujah" stands in connection with *judgment.* It is for this that praise is given to God. This does not accord with the teachings of the false charity and the traitorous toleration of the present day. The servants of Jehovah, who are imbued with the spirit of the Scriptures, are to, and can, praise Him for the destruction of His and their enemies.

---

* This is the Greek spelling of the Hebrew word "Hallelujah."

† The repetition of this word "and" is an example of the figure of *Polysyndeton.*

‡ This is an example of the figure of Repetition called *Epanadiplosis,* where the same word that begins the sentence is repeated at the end, for the sake of emphasis, and to call our attention to some important lesson in connection with it.

"Prophet."

The first occurrence of this word stands in connection with Abraham, Gen. xx. 7. God says to Abimelech king of Gerar, concerning Abraham and his wife, "Now therefore restore the man his wife: for he is a PROPHET, and he shall pray for thee and thou shalt live."

We learn from this that the word *Prophet* does not mean merely one who *foretells*, but one who witnesses for God as His spokesman.* The Hebrew word occurs in Exod. vii. 1, "Aaron thy brother shall be thy *prophet*"; while Exod. iv. 16 gives as the equivalent, "he shall be thy *spokesman*." This is exactly what it means; and the man who spoke for God was recognised by the people as God's man, *i.e.*, "A man of God."

"Holy."

The first occurrence of קדש (*Ko-desh*), *holy*, is in Exod. iii. 5. Not in the Book of the Beginning (Genesis); not until Exodus is opened—the Book of Redemption, which records how God came down to redeem His people out of Egypt (Exod. xv. 13). The *creature* cannot understand anything about *holiness* except on the ground of *redemption*.

"Bride."

The first occurrence of the word "bride," כלה (*Kalah*), as applied to the Bride of Jehovah, is in Isa. xlix. 18. This fixes the meaning of the term as applying only to Israel, and not to the Church, which is "the Body of Christ," part of "Christ mystical"; in other words, part of the Bridegroom. We are thus pointed to the fact that Israel is the Bride. Compare Isa. l. 1; liv. 1, 4, 6; lxi. 5, 10; lxii. 4, 5.†

"The Day of the Lord."

This important expression occurs first in Isa. ii. 12, and if we read the description of it as there given to us by the Holy Spirit, and note its character and object, as well as the purpose of it, we shall have a clear understanding of its meaning.

---

* See *The Man of God*, by the same author.

† See *The Mystery*, by the same author.

It is the day when the LORD ariseth to shake terribly the earth; when man shall be humbled and brought low; and when God alone shall be exalted.

Read the whole passage Isa. ii. 10–22, and note how it is emphasised, and how its importance is further shown by being stamped throughout with two figures, which run side by side,—*Polysyndeton,* the word "and" being used twenty times in nine verses, and *Synonymia, i.e.,* where different words of similar meaning are heaped together and repeated. Here there are *seven* words and twenty repetitions of them in order to show the *loftiness* of man's natural pride, and the *depth* to which it shall be brought down and humbled in "the Day of the LORD."

This is the first occurrence of the expression:—

> "For the day of the LORD of hosts shall be upon every one
> that is proud and lofty,
> And upon every one that is lifted up; and he shall be
> brought low . . .;
> And the LORD alone shall be exalted in that day." (*v.* 11.)

THE FIRST QUESTIONS

of the Old and New Testaments are also full of instruction.*

Gen. iii. 9, "Where art thou?"

This question was put by God to the sinner who is hiding from His holy presence, to bring him to conviction, to show him that he was lost and guilty and ruined. This is the object of the Old Testament. The Law it is that gives the knowledge of sin, and brings the sinner under conviction.

The *first* commandment is, "Thou shalt love the LORD thy God with all thy heart," etc. The impossibility of obeying this commandment convicts the sinner of his *impotence,* and causes him thankfully to cast himself upon God's *omnipotence,* and cry out for a Saviour.

The *first* question of the New Testament therefore is, in Matt. ii. 2, "Where is HE that is born?" Where is this Saviour whom I need? He has sought me and brought me to conviction. Where is He that I might find Him, and know Him, and worship Him, and serve Him?

---

* Gen. iii. 1 is not a question, as the margin explains.

The First Fulfilment of Prophecy in the New Testament.

This opens a vast field of instruction, laying down for us the lines, and showing us the principles on which the Holy Spirit interprets His own prophecy. It is in the Gospel according to Matthew (i. 22, 23):

A | "Now all this was done that it might be fulfilled which was spoken of (ὑπό, *by*) the Lord by (διά, *through*) the prophet; saying,

B | Behold, a virgin shall be with child, and shall bring forth a son,

B | and they shall call His name Emmanuel,

A | which being interpreted is, God with us." *

Here notice, first, that the prophecy is quoted from Isa. vii. 14. In Matthew it is specially said to be "spoken by the Lord"; and in Isaiah it is written, "The Lord Himself shall give you a sign."

Thus the fact is emphasised that "the prophecy came not in old time by the will of man; but holy men of God spake as they were moved by the Holy Ghost" (2 Pet. i. 21).

As this is the first recorded fulfilment of Old Testament prophecy in the New Testament, we may expect to find in it the generic character of all prophecy, and the grand example of the Holy Spirit's own interpretation.

The prophecy here said to be fulfilled is thus written in Isa. vii. 14: "Behold a virgin † shall conceive and bear a son, and shall call His name Immanuel."

---

* Note that in this introversion we have, in A and *A*, the prophecy and the interpretation; while in B and *B* we have the prophecy fulfilled; in B His birth, and in *B* His name.

† The R.V. thus translates it like the A.V., but gives in the margin: "*the maiden is with child and beareth.*" The verbs occur twice besides, Gen. xvi. 11 and Judg. xiii. 5, 7; and *v.* 12 shows that birth was imminent. The noun virgin is הָעַלְמָה *Ha-almah*, and means the "maiden," or the "damsel." *Almah* occurs *seven* times, Gen. xxiv. 43; Exod. ii. 8; Ps. lxviii. 25; Prov. xxx. 19; Song i. 3; vi. 8; Isa. vii. 14, and means "a maid" or "unmarried woman." Here it is "the maid," *i.e.*, some particular maid well known to the prophet and to Ahaz, but not to us. The Hebrew for virgin in our technical sense is בְּתוּלָה, *Bethulah* (and occurs 50 (2×5^2) times; the first, Gen. xxiv. 16). The truth is that every *Bethulah* is indeed an *Almah*; but every

But there is another prophecy associated with this, which is recorded in the next chapter:

> "The king of Assyria . . . shall sweep onward into Judah;
> He shall overflow and pass through . . .
> And the stretching out of his wings shall fill the breadth of thy land, O Immanuel.
> Make an uproar, O ye peoples, and ye shall be broken in pieces; . . .
> Take counsel together, and it shall be brought to nought;
> Speak the word, and it shall not stand;
> For GOD IS WITH US (עִמָּנוּ אֵל, *Immanu-el*)."
>
> (Isa. viii. 7 10, R.V.)

Now in this first quotation of prophecy as fulfilled, we note the following facts for our instruction:—

1. Prophecy is, as we have seen, spoken by JEHOVAH, and the prophets, so-called, are only the instruments or agents. With this agrees 2 Pet. i. 20, 21, where it is said that they "spake as they were moved by the Holy Ghost."

Now the word Jehovah denotes Him who existed in eternity past, and will ever exist in eternity to come.

In the Old Testament we have the *word* (Jehovah) which implies the *interpretation*. While in the Apocalypse we have the *interpretation* which implies the word "which is, and which was, and which is to come" (i. 4, 8; iv. 8).

The *Name* of the "LORD," or Jehovah, therefore, is the key to the understanding of His *Word*, for He has magnified His Word above all His Name (Ps. cxxxviii. 2). His Word, therefore, in a still higher sense, will relate to what WAS, and IS, and is TO COME.

Notice, however, that in the New Testament (the Apocalypse) Jehovah Jesus, as the Son of Man, is about to fulfil all His holy promise, and carry out all His responsibility. Hence His name is—

In the O. T., He shall be	He is	He was	
In Apocalypse	He is	He was	He is to come.

Almah is not necessarily a *Bethulah*. The prophecy does not lose one fraction of its Messianic character and force by this admission of the truth, as we shall see below. When it was *filled* in the days of Ahaz it was merely *Almah*; but when it was fulfilled or *filled full*, the Holy Spirit interprets it by the Greek word παρθένος, and thus defines her as technically a virgin.

The future has become present, and what was present merges into the past.

The present is, in the Greek, expressed by the participle (not the indicative, which is only suitable to a definite beginning or ending), thus indicating the protracted fulfilment of prophecy between the past and the future, running from the announcement of the prophecy down to the period of the crisis.

In the Apocalypse the three-fold statement occurs twice more (xi. 17; xvi. 5). But these refer to the period *after* the Coming of Christ, and hence the *future* aspect of His name disappears. He is spoken of only as "which art, and wast." *

It will then be simply the one "who is and was." The coming is regarded as having taken place, and the Day of the Lord inaugurated; therefore nothing future in the name remains in relation to the prophetic word.

Thus the fact that the words were "spoken by Jehovah" gives us the first key to their prophetic unfolding.

2. The subject of the prophecy is Christ, for "the testimony of Jesus is the spirit of prophecy" (Rev. xix. 10).

3. This prophecy was originally uttered in connection with man's failure as man, in the person of Ahaz (Isa. vii. 10–14). Just as the prophecy of Gen. iii. 15 was given in connection with man's failure in Adam; and just as the prophets were first raised up as a special order of witnesses on Israel's failure. The Holy Spirit thus connects in this prophecy the *failure of man* and the *promise of the Messiah*, taking the different threads of His various utterances, and combining them in one. Thus establishing the principle that prophecy came in after man's failure.

4. On the other hand, He takes the words out of those combinations which were the direct cause of their original utterance. Thus prophecy is resolved into its elements by the Holy Spirit, and by Him the elements are re-combined in accordance with His plans.

---

* The words "and art to come" were put in by some later copyist from the earlier part (i. 4, 8), and have no manuscript authority. They are excluded by Griesbach, Lachmann, Tischendorf, Tregelles, Alford, Wordsworth, Westcott and Hort, and the R.V.

5. He takes up the threads of passages that follow the one actually quoted, which explain the reason why the original combinations in which the words were written did not allow of the *complete* fulfilment of the prophecy at the time they were spoken or written.

6. He connects meanings of names with prophetic truth; and, seizing the gist of the prophecy rather than the mere words, He views in Ahaz the idolatrous and unbelieving Jews making a covenant with their Gentile enemy.

7. He develops, defines, and adds to the original force of the Hebrew word *Almah*, because, in the ultimate fulfilment, the woman to bring forth the son would be a virgin. The use of *Almah* in Isaiah made it correct for the historic fulfilment, but did not thus preclude the *Futurist* fulfilment.

8. The whole prophecy, therefore, of Isa. vii. and viii. can receive its fulfilment only by separating that fulfilment into three parts, *Preteritist*, *Presentist*, and *Futurist*. Then, as the speaker is Jehovah, the LORD, as we have seen, it is interpreted according to the meaning of His name, which embodies past, present, and future, as that of the ever-existing and eternal God, "which is, and which was, and which is to come" (Rev. i. 4, 8).

It follows, therefore, from this that no interpretation of prophecy can be correct which confines itself to only one of these three parts, and denies the other two. This is not "rightly dividing the word of truth."

And also it follows that the power thus to divide the prophecy and re-combine the three divisions must be only that of the author of the prophecy, the LORD the Spirit.

Interpreters who take up *one* of these three principles are therefore divided into opposite and hostile camps against those who take up *another* of those principles. But not until we grasp the great principle laid down by the Holy Spirit here, and apply all of them, and all of them together, can we have a true understanding of prophecy.

Now let us prove these three principles.

First—The Preteritist.

Ahaz, being greatly moved at the confederacy of Ephraim with Syria, was tempted to make a counter-confederacy with the king of Assyria. A sign was given to him that he need not yield to the temptation, for it would be withdrawn. A child would be born to a certain maiden, who would be called Immanuel, and before that child would know how to distinguish between good and evil, the land that he abhorred (*i.e.*, Ephraim and Syria, regarded as one) would be forsaken of both her kings.

In the next chapter another sign was given to Ahaz. Again a child would be born, this time to the prophetess, and called *Maher-shalal-hash-baz,* and before he should be able to cry "father" or "mother," both Syria and Ephraim should be spoiled by the king of Assyria.

The words quoted in Matt. i. are taken partly from Isa. vii. 14; and they distinctly show that Ahaz had not to wait for the birth of Christ to see the promised "sign," but that it must have occurred in his own day. And it was so. Herein is the *Preteritist* interpretation fulfilled in the past.

Second—The Futurist.

But part of the quotation in Matt. i., "God with us," is taken from Isa. viii. 10, which clearly reaches forward to the same time as Ps. ii., when the kings of the earth take counsel against Messiah, and is, therefore, exclusively *futurist.*

"The king of Assyria . . . shall sweep onward into Judah : . . .
And the stretching out of his wings shall fill the breadth of
Thy land, O Immanuel.
Make an uproar, O ye peoples, and ye shall be broken
in pieces :
And give ear, all ye of far countries :
Gird yourselves, and ye shall be broken in pieces ;
Gird yourselves, and ye shall be broken in pieces.
Take counsel together, and it shall be brought to nought ;
Speak the word, and it shall not stand :
For GOD IS WITH US (Immanu El).
For the LORD spake thus to me with a strong hand,
And instructed me that I should not walk in the way of
this people." (Isa. viii. 8–12, R.V.)

This is continued in *v.* 21, and is evidently *futurist,* as it is the time of darkness, when the judgments of the Apocalypse are upon the earth. (See Isa. viii. 8—ix. 7.)

"She that was in anguish" in ix. 1 is clearly Zion, and it is Zion, or the nation, that will at the time of the end say: "Unto us a child is born." That is the time of Rev. xii. and Ps. lxxxvii., where Christ is seen as born of Zion. It is the time when He takes the kingdom and establishes His millennial reign (Luke i. 31–33).

Thus it is certain that a portion of these three chapters cannot be fully interpreted except on *Futurist* lines.

Third—The Presentist

lines, or those which run through the ages between the *past* (the prophet's own day) and the future (the day of the crisis), are also clearly discernible.

In vii. 17 we read the words, immediately following the prophecy of the birth of this mysterious child:—

> "The LORD shall bring upon thee,
> And upon thy people, and upon thy father's house,
> Days that have not come,
> From the day that Ephraim departed from Judah;
> Even the king of Assyria." (Isa. vii. 17.)

To understand this, it is necessary to know that Nebuchadnezzar stepped into the heritage of the kings of Assyria. Hence the Babylonians were called Assyrians, even so late as the times of Xenophon, who so speaks of them in his *Anabasis*. And even Darius, who we know was a Median, is still called "the king of Assyria" in the Word of God. (See Ezra vi. 22, and compare 2 Kings xxiii. 29 and 2 Chron. xxxvi. 23.)

Thus "the Assyrian" of Isaiah's prophecy, at the time of the end, is not necessarily a king of revived Assyria, and we are taught that these prophecies of the king of Assyria reach through to all the heads of the four Gentile empires spoken of in Daniel.

The prophecy of the king of Assyria spoken of in these chapters of Isaiah runs on in protracted *presentist* fulfilment, covering the whole period of "the times of the Gentiles."

Another proof of the necessity of this *presentist* fulfilment is given in Isa. viii. 13:—

> "The LORD of hosts, Him shall ye sanctify;
> And let Him be your fear, and let Him be your dread.
> And He shall be for a sanctuary;
> But for a stone of stumbling and for a rock of offence to both the houses of Israel,

For a gin and for a snare to the inhabitants of Jerusalem.
And many shall stumble thereon, and fall, and be broken,
And be snared and be taken.
Bind thou up the testimony,
Seal the law (or *teaching*) among my disciples.
And I will wait for the LORD,
That hideth His face from the house of Jacob,
And I will look for Him.
Behold! I and the children whom the LORD hath given me
Are for signs and wonders in Israel
From the LORD of hosts, which dwelleth in mount Zion."
(Isa. viii. 13–18, R.V.)

Here we have the present character of the dispensation as it is described in Rom. ix.—xi., the period of Israel's blindness. This is perfectly clear if we compare Isa. viii. 14 with Rom. ix. 32, 33.

Christ is the stumbling-stone and rock of offence to the masses; but He is believed on by a remnant of His disciples, "the remnant according to the election of grace." Christ and His disciples to day are the Lord's "signs and wonders" to Israel, for the disciples are counted as the Lord's "children":—

"A seed shall serve him;
It shall be accounted to the LORD for a generation."
(Ps. xxii. 30.) *

This is further set forth in the meanings of all the names employed. *The salvation of Jehovah* (for such is the meaning of the name ISAIAH) will be accomplished by Jehovah being *with His people* (IMMANUEL). That salvation is needed and brought about in consequence of the Assyrian *hasting to make a prey and spoil* of the nation (MAHER-SHALAL-HASH-BAZ). Then *the remnant shall return*, *i.e.* repent (SHEAR-JASHUB, Isa. vii. 3), and stay upon Jehovah and wait for Him.

Such is the purport and teaching of the whole Prophecy of Isaiah; for it is but *one* prophecy, a whole, complete in its parts, the "higher criticism," which would saw him asunder, notwithstanding.

Such, too, is the important lesson taught us by this *first recorded fulfilment of prophecy in the New Testament*, from which

* It is clear also from Heb. ii. 13, that Isa. viii. 18 had both a *preteritist* and then a *futurist* fulfilment.

we learn that prophecy is only comprehensible as an organic whole, when thus subdivided by (and by us under the guidance of) the Holy Spirit into its *Preteritist*, *Presentist*, and *Futurist* fulfilments according to the meaning of the name *Jehovah*—"which is, and which was, and which is to come."

Words that Occur only Once

are often instructive; they are called by the Greeks ἅπαξ λεγόμενα (*hapax legomena*). We give a few examples in detail.

(1) κριτικός (*kritikos*), "*critic*," *Heb.* iv. 12.

This is the origin of our word "critic." The Greek is *kritikos*, and "critic" is merely the English spelling of the Greek word, which is thus transliterated. It means *able to judge* or *skilled in judging;* and then, simply, *a judge*, but always with the idea of his ability to judge. It occurs only in Heb. iv. 12, where it is translated "a discerner."

The whole passage relates both to the *written* Word, which *is* a sword (Eph. vi. 17): and to the *living* Word (Christ), who *has* a sword.

The structure of the two verses distinguishes between God and His word:—

A | 12-. GOD it is whose Word is so wonderful.
 B | -12-. What His Word IS (living, powerful, and a sharp sword).
  C | -12-. What His Word DOES (piercing and dividing asunder, etc.).
 B | -12-. What His Word IS (a skilful judge).
A | 13. GOD it is who is omniscient.

Here we have in A and *A*, God the omniscient one; and in B, C, and *B* we have His Word. And we learn that the Word of God is a judge now, so wonderful that it distinguishes between the *thoughts* and *intentions* of the heart and judges them.

The Lord Himself bears witness that the same Word will be our judge hereafter—John xii. 48, "He that rejecteth Me, and receiveth not My words, hath one that judgeth him; the Word which I have spoken, the same shall judge him in the last day."

What a solemn truth. And how much more solemn, when man now dares to take this one word "*critic*" or "judge," which God has thus, by His only once using it, appropriated to His Word, and apply it to himself. And what is it that man is going to judge? Why, this very Word of God! thus making himself the judge of that Word which is to judge him! If the word *kritikos* were of frequent occurrence, and used of various things or persons, man might perhaps be led to look on himself as a judge of some one of them. But God has used it *only once*, and He has thus confined it to one thing—His Word. Therefore it is a daring presumption for man to transfer the word to himself. Not only does man do this, but he calls his work "higher criticism." Now there is a criticism which is lawful, because it judges not God's Word, but *man's work* as to the manuscripts; this is called Textual Criticism, which is quite a different thing. But this "higher criticism" is nothing but human *reasoning;* it is nothing more than the imagination of man's heart—those very *thoughts and intentions* which the Word itself judges!

What confusion! what perversion! and what folly! for the further man's criticism departs from the domain of *evidence* and enters on the sphere of *reason*, the "higher" he calls it! That is to say, the less like a skilled judge he acts, the higher he exalts his judgment! Poor man! Oh that you would submit yourself to this Word. For it must either judge you now, in this day of grace, and give you conviction of sin; or it will be your judge in the last day, when every mouth will be stopped, and you will be "speechless" and "without excuse."

(2) καπηλεύω (*kapeeleuō*), "*to corrupt*," 2 *Cor*. ii. 17.

This is another word which occurs only once, and it is, like all such words, full of instruction. It is derived from κάπη, *a crib* or *manger*, whence κάπτω, *to eat quickly* (Latin, *capio, to take*). Then comes κάπηλος, *one who sells provisions*, esp. *a victualler* or *vintner*, and the verb καπηλεύω, which means to be a κάπηλος, *to keep a tavern, to sell victuals and drink* (esp. wine). Then, like so many words which, in the course of their history, witness to the fallen nature of man,* and because all such retailers

* See page 92 and *note*.

were addicted to adulteration, the verb came to mean. simply, *to adulterate*. This cannot be more clearly shown than by referring to Isa. i. 22, where the Hebrew,

> "Thy silver is become dross,
> Thy wine mixed with water"

is rendered in the Septuagint,

> "Thy wine merchants (οἱ κάπηλοι) mix the wine with water."

That is exactly what is meant in 2 Cor. ii. 17, where the Apostle says "we are not as many which corrupt the Word of God," *i.e.* who adulterate and "water down" the Word.

The Holy Spirit, by confining the use of this verb solely to the ministration of the Word of God, places the greatest possible emphasis upon the practice of the "MANY!" He had just been most solemnly declaring that His ministry of that Word was to some the savour of death unto death (*i.e.* resulting in their endless death). The "many" do not so declare all the counsel of God, but they water it down, and adulterate all such discriminating truth, prophesying smooth things, and seeking to please the people instead of studying to show themselves approved unto God (2 Tim. ii. 15).

The margin of the A.V. reads "*deal deceitfully with.*" The R.V., while translating the word "corrupting" in the text, waters down the whole truth in the margin by giving the alternative rendering, "*making merchandise of,*" which, while it is far below the solemnity of the passage, exemplifies its truth.

(3) δολόω (*doloō*), "*to handle deceitfully,*" 2 *Cor.* iv. 2.

This is another word which is used only once, and here again it is in connection with the Word of God. Indeed, the three might well be compared—Heb. iv. 12; 2 Cor. ii. 17; and this word δολόω in 2 Cor. iv. 2. Like some other words which occur only once, its meaning is from that very cause not so clear or obvious as other words in more general use. We have therefore to search for its meaning. First, all verbs ending in όω are *causative*, carrying out the act which is proper to the noun. Hence δοῦλος (*doulos*) is *a slave*, therefore δουλόω (*doulo-ō*) means *to make a slave of another*, to enslave: πόλεμος (*polemos*) is *war*, therefore πολεμόω (*pole-mo-ō*) means *to make war*, or *to make hostile*.

Now with regard to this word, the noun δόλος (*dolos*) means any *cunning contrivance for catching by deceit.* Homer uses it * of the robe of *Penelopé*, which she used as a means of deceiving her many suitors, saying, she must finish the making of it before she could make up her mind. He uses it also † of the net with which Vulcan catches Mars, and of the Trojan horse; ‡ and of a mousetrap.§ Hence, δόλος means any *trick*, or *contrivance*, or *stratagem by which another is deceived.*

The verb δολόω therefore must mean the act of deceiving by a trick, or ensnaring by craft. The Greek writers use it of debasing gold, adulterating wine,|| of dyeing garments,¶ and of disguising oneself.**

In this passage, therefore, it means that the Apostle declares that he has not acted thus with the Word of God. He neither used it as a vintner did his wine, adulterating it or watering it down (2 Cor. ii. 17); nor did he use it as a juggler or trickster to catch them with it by wile, craft, cunning, or stratagem.††

An example may be given of the way in which ignorant rationalists thus deal with the Word of God. One ‡‡ quotes Jer. vii. 22 to prove that Jehovah "never gave any directions whatever about burnt offerings and sacrifices," omitting the words which define and limit the reference to "the day that I brought them out of the land of Egypt." This is a specimen of the jugglery which abounds on all hands either through ignorance or malice.

This "dealing deceitfully" with the Word of God is seen most frequently when words are quoted apart from their

---

* *Od.* 19. 137. † *Od.* 8. 276. ‡ *Od.* 8. 494.

§ Batr. 116. || Luc. Hermot. 59. ¶ Poll. ** *Soph. Phil.* 129.

†† It may be well to note the many words which have had to be used to meet man's fallen nature in his various forms of deception :

πλανάω (*planaō*) is "to lead astray," used of doctrinal error or religious deceit.

παραλογίζομαι (*paralogizomai*), "to deceive by false reasoning."

ἀπατάω (*apataō*), "to delude with false statements."

καπηλεύω (*kapeeleuō*), "to adulterate by admixture."

δολόω (*doloō*), "to deceive by stratagem."

ψεύδω (*pseudō*), "to deceive by lying."

βασκαίνω (*baskainō*), "to deceive by witchcraft."

‡‡ The author of "The Policy of the Pope," in the *Contemporary Review* for April 1894.

context, by which, of course, the Bible may be made to prove anything. This is a fruitful source of error even with those who love and are seeking after the Truth.

A glaring example of this wilful deceit is seen in a wall-text which reads, "Thou shalt not drink wine," thus giving as a Divine command that which is uttered as a threat of Divine judgment. See Micah vi. 15.

(4) ἄρτιος (*artios*), "*perfect*," 2 *Tim.* iii. 17.

This is another word which occurs only once, and again in reference to the Word of God. It is rendered "perfect," but it means *fitted*, and has reference to a special aptitude for any given use. The verb, in the same verse, is formed from this word, with the preposition ἐξ, *out*, prefixed, ἐξαρτίζω (*exartizō*), and it means *fitted out*, as a vessel for a voyage, *fully equipped*, *completely furnished*. The two words are, therefore, cognate, and should be similarly translated. They are, moreover, for the sake of emphasis, put out of their place, in order to attract our attention; one is put at the *beginning* of the sentence and the other at the *end*, thus:—"that *equipped* may be the man of God, for every good work *fully equipped*": or fitted . . . thoroughly fitted out; or furnished . . . completely furnished. That is to say, He who has "learned" and is "assured of" the Word of God, having been "made wise unto salvation," and has profited by the continued use of the holy Scripture as inspired by God, is "a man of God," *i.e.*, a *prophet*, and therefore knows from these Scriptures what he is to say as God's spokesman.* One who studies *man's* books will become *a man of men;* but he who studies God's book will become "a man of God." Moreover he will be *equipped* for every emergency, *fitted out* against every need, ready to meet every contingency; just as a vessel when fitted out for a long voyage has to be provided for calm and storm, ready to help a friend or defeat an enemy, prepared for fire and every accident, so the man of God, who truly profits by the study of the Scriptures, is equipped and furnished, prepared and ready for every emergency.

---

* See *The Man of God*, by the same author.

(5) ῥητῶς (*rheetōs*), "*expressly*," 1 *Tim.* iv. 1.

This word ῥητῶς (*rheetōs*) is from ῥητός, *spoken*, or *expressed in words*. The noun *rhetōr* (ῥήτωρ) was used of one who spoke to the people and advised them; then it is used of a hired orator; and *rhetoric* was used of the arts he employed. So that it may mean here that the Holy Spirit actually pronounced these solemn words of 1 Tim. iv. 1 audibly in the Apostle's ears * in order to emphasise their awful solemnity and the certainty of their truth. (See the context.)

(6) βασκαίνω (*baskainō*), "*to bewitch*," *Gal.* iii. 1.

"O foolish Galatians, who hath bewitched you, that ye should not obey the truth."

The word means *to fascinate*. Indeed the word fascinate is derived from it, the initial *f* in the Latin taking the place of the β in the Greek. Among the heathen this fascination was with the eye (Deut. xxviii. 54, 56; Ecclus. xiv. 8; Wisd. iv. 12). In Gal. iii. 1 it is used in a wider sense, and by using it only once, the Holy Spirit emphasises it and points to a danger common to the people of God through all time. When they profess that they are "*charmed*" by this teacher, or "*fascinated*" by that speaker, they prove themselves to be indeed "foolish" (ἀνόητος,† *without understanding*), because they are "fascinated" and deprived of the use of their faculties, and are in great danger of being deceived and turned away from the truth.

(7) ἐπιούσιος (*epiousios*), *Matt.* vi. 11.

This word *epi-ousios* was used only by the Lord, and in the Lord's prayer. (See Matt. vi. 11 and Luke xi. 3). It occurs nowhere else, not even in any other Greek writing, for it was coined by the Lord Jesus Himself. Hence there is no help to be obtained in understanding its meaning but from the Holy Spirit.

It is translated "daily": "Give us this day our daily bread," Matt. vi. 11.

---

* As on other occasions, Acts x. 19, 20; xiii. 2, etc.

† Luke xxiv. 25; Rom. i. 14; Gal. iii. 3; 1 Tim. vi. 9; Tit. iii. 3.

It has been variously understood and translated. The R.V., in the margin, treats it as an ellipsis, and supplies the word "day":—"Greek, *our bread for the coming day*." But this cannot be correct, for it is in direct opposition to verse 34, where we are expressly told to "take no thought for the morrow!" Besides, "Give us this day our bread for the coming day," is a denial of the great fact that our need is supplied day by day. The truth is that we have no stock of grace supplied for future use; that which we need on any particular day is not supplied by God either before or after, but on the very day, yea, at the very moment of our need. The R.V. is right in saying that the Greek means "*coming*," but it would be still more correct to say "*coming upon*," thus preserving the force of the preposition ἐπί (*epi*), *upon*.*

We must expect this peculiar word of the Lord Jesus to have such a fulness in it that no one English word is able to express it. It qualifies the word "bread." It is this bread which is *epiousios, i.e., coming upon us*. It is not the bread which perisheth, but the heavenly bread which *cometh down* from heaven (John vi. 32, 33), even Jesus the living Word of God. For "man doth not live by bread only, but by every word that proceedeth out of the mouth of the LORD doth man live." In other words, it is not the bread which *cometh up* from the earth which we ask our Father in this prayer; but it is the bread which *cometh down* from heaven, even Christ, the living Word, and the Scriptures, the written Word. By these alone, we truly live.

(8) σκόλοψ (*skolops*), "*a thorn*" (2 *Cor*. xii. 7),

is another word which occurs only once, in this place. "There was given to me *a thorn* in the flesh," or more literally, *for the flesh* (τῇ σαρκί). Commentators and expositors exhaust their ingenuity in trying to explain what this "thorn" was, while the true explanation is given by the Spirit in the words which follow. That we may make no mistake as to what the "thorn" was, it is immediately

* Ἐπιούσιος cannot be derived from ἐπί, *upon*, and εἰμί, *to be*, because the participle would then have been ἐποῦσα. It must be from ἐπί and εἶμι, *to go* or *come*, for the participle of this is, as here, ἐπιοῦσα, *going upon* or *coming upon*.

added ἄγγελος Σατανᾶ, "an angel of Satan."* That is to say, this "thorn for the flesh" was "an angel of Satan," allowed to come "in order that he might buffet me" (ἵνα με κολαφίζῃ). The word κολαφίζω means *to give a blow with the fist.*† No "thorn" could do this. But this evil angel, sent by Satan, could do so; and was permitted to do so, and to be to the Apostle what a thorn is to the flesh, in order that he might not be exalted above measure by the abundance of the revelations which he had received.

First, we have the word "thorn," then we have the explanation, "an angel of Satan." Why should we seek to go further and *explain the explanation* already given? Why not rest content with what is actually said, instead of seeking to introduce something which is not said? The word and the phrase occur only in this passage, to show us the importance of the great lesson which it teaches.

Thrice the Apostle prayed that "he might depart." Literally, "in order that he might withdraw or go away from me" (ἵνα ἀποστῇ ἀπ' ἐμοῦ). But his prayer was refused! Why? *Because he asked for what he did not need!* The grace of Christ was all-sufficient. It was needful for him to be humbled. To accomplish this the very buffeting of Satan was used to defeat his own designs. Satan's design is to lift up the servant of God with pride. Yet, here, the buffetings of the messenger of Satan were *over-ruled* to defeat his own ends, and Satan was taken in his own craftiness.

(9) ἀλλοτριοεπίσκοπος (*allotrio-episkopos*), 1 *Pet.* iv. 15.

Allotrio-episkopos is a word which occurs only here, not being used even by any of the Greek classical writers. It is composed of two words, ἀλλότριος (*allotrios*), "belonging to another," and ἐπίσκοπος (*episkopos*), "an overseer" (bishop). According to this, it would mean *one who takes the supervision of affairs which pertain to others and in no wise to himself.* Hence it is rendered in A.V. "a busybody (R.V. meddler) in other

---

* Not "the messenger of Satan." There is no article. But the nominative is placed in apposition, in order to explain the σκόλοψ (thorn). In the Received Text, the word "Satan" is also in the nominative, but this would in that case explain the angel—that the angel was Satan himself. L., T., Tr., A., and W. H. read Σατανᾶ, *of Satan.*

† It occurs elsewhere only in Matt. xxvi. 67; Mark xiv. 65; 1 Cor. iv. 11; 1 Pet. ii. 20.

men's matters." But this is evidently weak, and it is in fact far short of the facts referred to in the context. The Christians were being exhorted in this Epistle with regard to a great persecution, which was even then commencing, and in which they were charged with being "murderers," "thieves," "evil-doers," and "*allotrio-episkopoi*," whatever that may mean. Now it is clear that something more is meant here than a mere "busybody," or "meddler": these are not classed among criminals. The fact is, that these persecutions commenced with popular accusations. The "Christians" were regarded with general hatred, and the common charges brought against them were murders, incendiarism, etc., but chief of all they were charged with hatred of the world and *hostility to society*. The technical term for this latter crime was *odium humani generis*,* and it meant that the Christians were bent on relaxing the bonds which held society together, introducing divisions into families, setting children against parents, parents against children, and accomplishing all this by unlawful and magical arts. This charge was absolutely necessary to procure their death; for in the Roman Empire the right of inflicting capital punishment belonged only to a few high officials, and death was the punishment of magicians.

The Roman officials scorned a merely *religious* charge (see Acts xviii. 15–17; xix. 37; etc.).

It seems clear, therefore, that the word ἀλλοτριοεπίσκοπος was coined in order to express in Greek the Roman indictment of *odium humani generis*. So elastic an accusation could be easily proved in times of popular excitement. Christians were charged with breaking up the peace of family life, raising discontent and disobedience amongst slaves. True, they were hostile to the *vices* of Roman society, and doubtless denounced them. Society, then, must destroy these Christians in self-defence! This is the teaching involved in this word. It is no mere advice to disregard the taunts or jeers of others. It was a solemn exhortation, that when persecution came they were to suffer, not as murderers or thieves, or as being like our agitators—as the enemies of society—but as *Christians*. "Be ready always to

* Not *hatred of human kind;* but among the Romans *genus humanum* meant civilised society.

give an answer"* (1 Pet. iii. 15). "If ye suffer for righteousness' sake happy are ye, and be not afraid of their terror" (*ibid.* iii. 14). Do not suffer under those terrible accusations and false charges, but suffer "as a Christian." Be not ashamed of this, but glorify God on this behalf (*ibid.* iv. 12–16).†

Many Christians are to-day ignorant, and therefore unmindful, of what is meant by this solemn exhortation. As the leaders of the people they are taking the place of those whom we speak of as "agitators"; and, by preaching what is openly called "a social gospel" and "the gospel of the people," are helping forward the enemies of society, and are themselves disturbers of the peace, under the guise of what they call "Christian socialism." Such teachers would find it difficult to obey the exhortation to make a good defence against such charges, for in their case the accusation would be true and not false.

(10) δωδεκάφυλον (*dōdekaphulon*), "*twelve tribes*" (*Acts* xxvi. 7).

This word *dōdekaphulon* is used by St. Paul in Acts xxvi. 7, where, speaking of the hope of resurrection, he says, "Unto which promise our Twelve Tribes, instantly serving God, day and night, hope to come."

This shows that the idea of the Ten Tribes being "lost" is a popular fallacy.

It is true that in the Old Testament prophecies the term "Judah" may be used technically of the kingdom of Judah, and the term "Israel" of the Ten Tribes; but it does not follow that the current popular use of the words is marked by the same exactness. We speak to day of all the seed of Abraham as "Jews," but we do not by such a use of the word determine the fact that they are belonging only to the tribe of Judah! The popular belief is that at the time of the crucifixion only the tribe of *Judah* was in the land, and responsible for the death of the Lord Jesus.

But it is a fact that, at the time of the separation of the two kingdoms, there were "children of Israel that dwelt in the cities of Judah," 2 Chron. x. 17; and in 2 Chron. xi. 3 we

* ἀπολογία, *apologia*, is a strictly legal term for a *defence* against a formal indictment.

† See *The Spirits in Prison*, by the same author.

read of "all Israel in Judah." Long before the dispersion of the Ten Tribes and the captivity of Judah, *numbers from all the tribes* joined the kingdom of Judah on account of the idolatry introduced by the kings of Israel.

In 2 Chron. xi. 13, 16, 17, "the priests and the Levites that were in all Israel resorted to him (Rehoboam, king of Judah) out of all their coasts . . . . and after them *out of all the tribes of Israel* such as set their hearts to seek the LORD God of Israel came to Jerusalem, to sacrifice unto the LORD God of their fathers. So they strengthened the kingdom of Judah." *

In 2 Chron. xv. 9, Asa, king of Judah, moved by the prophet Azariah, made a reformation, "and he gathered all Judah and Benjamin and the strangers with them out of Ephraim and Manasseh, and out of Simeon: for *they fell to him out of Israel in abundance,*† when they saw that the LORD his God was with him."

Josephus says (*Ant.* xi. 5, 7) of the term "Jews," "that is the name they are called by from the day that they came up from Babylon, which is taken from the tribe of Judah, which came first to these places, and thence both they and the country gained that appellation." But the word soon obtained a wider application, and on the return from the captivity in Babylon, what we call "Judah" was not confined merely to the original *tribe*, but embraced the old kingdom of Judah and Benjamin, together with an "*abundance*" out of all the other tribes of Israel.

In the Gospels we read of "Anna, a prophetess, a daughter of Phanuel, of the tribe of *Asher*" (Luke ii. 36). So that here was one of the Ten Tribes who could trace her genealogy, and was yet living in the land.

In giving His instructions to the twelve Apostles, the Lord particularly enjoined them, "Go not into the way of the Gentiles, and into any city of the Samaritans enter ye not, but go rather to the lost sheep of *the house of Israel*" (Matt. x. 5, 6). And of Himself He said, "I am not sent but unto the lost sheep of *the house of Israel*" (Matt. xv. 24).

---

* But only for three years did this strength continue. Then they, too, fell into idolatry, and were no longer a strength, but a weakness.

† The Hebrew is רֹב, *rhōv*, and means "multitude." See Gen. xvi. 10; xxxii. 12; Deut. i. 10; xxviii. 62; Josh. xi. 4; Judges vi. 5; vii. 12; etc.

The fact is that the whole nation was spoken of by the Gentiles as "Jews," and the terms "Jews" and "Israelites" are not used in the New Testament with the distinction which modern usage has given to them.

It is clear from the Book of Esther that in Persia and elsewhere they were known as and spoken of as "Jews."

In Jer. xxxiv. 9, the term "Jew" is co-extensive with the term "Hebrew."

In Zech. viii., too, which carefully distinguishes between "the house of Judah" and "the house of Israel" (*v.* 13), the term "Jew" is clearly used of the whole nation (*v.* 23).

We see the same indiscriminate use of the words "Jew" and "Israelite" in the New Testament. Peter, on the day of Pentecost, addresses them as "men of Judea" (Acts ii. 14), and in *v.* 22, as "*men of Israel.*" And, again, in Acts iv. 8, "Peter, filled with the Holy Ghost, said unto them, Ye rulers of the people and *elders of Israel* . . . . Be it known unto you and to *all the people of Israel.*"

Further, in Acts iv. 27, we are expressly told that, so far from the Jews, as such, being guilty of the death of Jesus, it was "*all the people of Israel.*"

Peter and James addressed their Epistles to the *Diaspora,** the "Dispersion," *i.e.* "the Twelve Tribes scattered abroad."

And, finally, the Holy Spirit, by Paul, speaking of the promise of Resurrection made unto the fathers, says (Acts xxvi. 7), "Unto which promise *our Twelve Tribes,* instantly serving God, day and night, hope to come." We thus see that those whom we speak of as "Jews" are identical with the "Twelve Tribes."

Although neither we nor they may be able to separate and distinguish them now, we shall alike "marvel" when the true Joseph, who "is yet alive," shall show that He can do so, when He causes them to sit in order before Him (Gen. xliii. 33).

These must suffice as examples of the importance of *hapax legomena,* or words that occur only once. There are a large number of them, and we append a list (by no means exhaus-

* The word occurs only in John vii. 35; James i. 1; and 1 Pet. i. 1.

tive) for the further study of those who desire to follow up this interesting branch of Bible study.

דל (*dal*), Ps. cxli. 3, "the door."
זעה (*zēh-gah*), Gen. iii. 19, "In the sweat of."
זרזיף (*zar-zeeph*), Ps. lxxii. 6, "water."
חפף (*chah-phaph*), Deut. xxxiii. 12, "shall cover him."
חבב (*cha-vav*),* Deut. xxxiii. 3, "he loved."
בחן (*boh-chan*), Isa. xxviii. 16, "tried."
כנף (*kah-naph*), Isa. xxx. 20, "shall thy teachers."
כשלון (*kish-shāh-lōhn*), Prov. xvi. 18, "a fall."
לח (*lēh-ach*), Deut. xxxiv. 7, "natural force."
רן (*rōhn*), Ps. xxxii. 7, "songs of."
רהב (*rōh-hav*), Ps. xc. 10, "their strength."
טפש (*tah-phash*), Ps. cxix. 70, "is fat."
רגש (*rah-gash*), Ps. ii. 1, "do rage."
יונק (*yōh-nehk*), Isa. liii. 2, "as a tender plant."
רגע (*rah-gēh-ăg*), Ps. xxxv. 20, "them that are quiet."
ילל (*y'lehl*), Deut. xxxii. 10, "howling."
ימם (*yēh-meem*),† Gen. xxxvi. 24, "the mules."
קשט (*koh-shet*), Ps. lx. 4, "the truth."
יסודה (*y'soo-dah*), Ps. lxxxvii. 1, "foundation."
קפאון (*kip-pāh-ōhn*), Zech. xiv. 6, "dark."
בטחה (*bit-chah*), Isa. xxx. 15, "confidence."
קריאה (*k'reeah*), Jonah iii. 2, "preaching."
בלימה (*b'lee-mah*), Job xxvi. 7, "nothing."
בלם (*bah-lam*), Ps. xxxii. 9, "held in."
יעט (*yah-ghat*), Isa. lxi. 10, "he hath covered me."
צפין (*tzāh-pheen*), Ps. xvii. 14, "with thy hid treasure."
כמה (*kāh-mah*), Ps. lxiii. 1, "longeth."

---

* This is the word from which the name of the great modern Jewish Society (חובבי ציון), *Chovevei Zion*, is taken. It means *the Lovers of Zion*. The verb חָבַב means *to hide in the bosom, to love fervently with a tender protecting love*. The society is formed for the colonisation of Palestine, and has adopted a national flag for the restored nation of Israel.

† From יוּם, primarily חוּם, *to put in commotion, agitate*, hence *to be hot*. In Sanscrit, *Yamunah* is the river of that name; and in Syr. it means "*waters*." The A.V. followed the error of the Talmud. The R.V. has it correctly "hot-springs." The word for mules is פְּרָדִים.

צוק (*tzōhk*), Dan. ix. 25, "even in troublous times."

כרכרות (*kir-kāh-rohth*), Isa. lxvi. 20, "and upon swift beasts."

פלמוני (*pal-mōh-nee*), Dan. viii. 13, "unto that certain saint." (Marg., "Heb. Palmoni; or, *the numberer of secrets;* or, *the wonderful numberer*.")

מושעות (*mōh-shah-oth*), Ps. lxviii. 20, "of salvation."

מושכות (*mōh-sh'koth*), Job xxxviii. 31, "the bands of."

נשיה (*n'sheey-yāh*), Ps. lxxxviii. 12, "forgetfulness."

נבך (*neh-vech*), Job xxxviii. 16, "springs."

Or coming to the New Testament we may instance :—

ἀγρεύω (*agreuō*), Mark xii. 13, "to catch."

ἄγνωστος (*agnōstos*),* Acts xvii. 23, "unknown."

ἄδολος (*adolos*), 1 Pet. ii. 2, "sincere."

αἱματεκχυσία (*haimatekchusia*), Heb. ix. 22, "shedding of blood."

αἱρετίζω (*hairetizō*), Matt. xii. 18, "have chosen."

ἀπαράβατος (*aparabatos*), Heb. vii. 24, "unchangeable."

ἀπάτωρ (*apatōr*), Heb. vii. 3, "without father."

ἀμήτωρ (*ameetōr*), Heb. vii. 3, "without mother."

ἀπόβλητος (*apobleetos*), 1 Tim. iv. 4, "to be refused."

ἀπαύγασμα (*apaugasma*), Heb. i. 3, "brightness."

ἀποκλείω (*apokleiō*), Luke xiii. 25, "hath shut to."

ἄῤῥητος (*arrheetos*), 2 Cor. xii. 4, "unspeakable."

ἀρχιποίμην (*archipoimeen*), 1 Pet. v. 4, "chief shepherd."

ἄπειρος (*apeiros*), Heb. v. 13, "unskilful."

ἀποβλέπω (*apoblepō*), Heb. xi. 26, "have respect."

βοηθός (*boeethos*), Heb. xiii. 6, "helper."

βραβεύω (*brabeuō*), Col. iii. 15, "rule."

γυναικάριον (*gunaikarion*), 2 Tim. iii. 6, "silly women." (Neuter gender, to include silly women of both sexes!)

δακρύω (*dakruō*), John xi. 35, "Jesus wept."

δειλιάω (*deiliaō*), John xiv. 27, "let it be afraid."

δήπου (*deepou*), Heb. ii. 16, "verily."

διανυκτερεύω (*dianukterūō*), Luke vi. 12, "continued all night."

δικαιοκρισία (*dikaiokrisia*), Rom. ii. 5, "righteous judgment."

δότης (*dotees*), 2 Cor. ix. 7, "giver."

* Whence our word *Agnostic*, "ignoramus."

δυσνόητος (*dusnoeetos*), 2 Pet. iii. 16, "hard to be understood."

ἐγκατοικέω (*engkatoikeō*), 2 Pet. ii. 8, "dwelling among."

ἐγκρατής (*engkratees*), Tit. i. 8, "temperate."

εἰρηνοποιέω (*eireenopoieō*), Col. i. 20, "having made peace."

εἰσδέχομαι (*eisdechomai*), 2 Cor. vi. 17, "will receive."

ἐμέω (*emeō*), Rev. iii. 16, "spue."

ἐμπεριπατέω (*emperipateō*), 2 Cor. vi. 16, "walk in."

ἐμφυσάω (*emphusaō*), John xx. 22, "breathed on."

ἤπερ (*eeper*), John xii. 43, "than."

θαῦμα (*thauma*), Rev. xvii. 6, "admiration."

θεόπνευστος (*theopneustos*), 2 Tim. iii. 16, "inspiration of God" (*i.e.* God breathed).

θρόμβος (*thrombos*), Luke xxii. 44, "great drops."

ἱδρώς (*hidrōs*), Luke xxii. 44, "sweat."

ἱερουργέω (*hierourgeō*), Rom. xv. 16, "ministering."

ἱκανότης (*hikanotees*), 2 Cor. iii. 5, "sufficiency."

καρτερέω (*kartereō*), Heb. xi. 27, "endured."

κατανάθεμα (*katanathema*); Rev. xxii. 3, "curse."

καταμανθάνω (*katamanthanō*), Matt. vi. 28, "consider."

κατάλειμμα (*kataleimma*), Rom. ix. 27, "a remnant."

κατανύσσω (*katanussō*), Acts ii. 37, "were pricked." *

κατοπτρίζομαι (*katoptrizomai*), 2 Cor. iii. 18, "beholding as in a glass."

κέλευσμα (*keleusma*), 1 Thess. iv. 16, "a shout" (*i.e.* an assembling shout).

κνήθω (*kneethō*), 2 Tim. iv. 3, "itching."

λειτουργικός (*leitourgikos*), Heb. i. 14, "ministering" (*i.e.* worshipping).

μέγιστος (*megistos*), 2 Pet. i. 4, "exceeding great."

μετριοπαθέω (*metriopatheō*), Heb. v. 2, "have compassion."

μίασμα (*miasma*), 2 Pet. ii. 20, "pollutions."

μώλωψ (*mōlōps*), 1 Pet. ii. 24, "stripes."

νύττω (*nuttō*), John xix. 34, "pierced."

ὁλοτελής (*holotelees*), 1 Thess. v. 23, "wholly."

ὀρθοτομέω (*orthotomeō*), 2 Tim. ii. 15, "rightly dividing."

πάλη (*palee*), Eph. vi. 12, "wrestle" (*i.e.* the wrestling).

παραλλαγή (*parallagee*), James i. 17, "variableness."

---

* Note that these were pricked *in* their heart, while in Acts v. 33 and vii. 54, it is διαπρίομαι (*diapriomai*), they were cut *to* the heart—which makes all the difference.

πενιχρός (*penichros*), Luke xxi. 2, "poor."
περιούσιος (*periousios*), Tit. ii. 14, "peculiar."
πλατύς (*platus*), Matt. vii. 13, "wide."
πλάσμα (*plasma*), Rom. ix. 20, "thing formed."
πολυποίκιλος (*polupoikilos*), Eph. iii. 10, "manifold."
πολυμερῶς (*polumerōs*), Heb. i. 1, "at sundry times."
πολυτρόπως (*polutropōs*), Heb. i. 1, "in divers manners."
πρᾶος (*praos*), Matt. xi. 29, "meek."
προβλέπω (*problepō*), Heb. xi. 40, "having provided."
πρόδρομος (*prodromos*), Heb. vi. 20, "forerunner."
προελπίζω (*proelpizō*), Eph. i. 12, "who first trusted."
σάρκινος (*sarkinos*), 2 Cor. iii. 3, "fleshy," indicating the nature of the person (made of flesh): while σαρκικός (*fleshly*) indicates the bent of the mind.
σεβάζομαι (*sebazomai*), Rom. i. 25, "worshipped."
σινιάζω (*siniazō*), Luke xxii. 31, "sift."
στίγμα (*stigma*), Gal. vi. 17, "marks."
συναυξάνομαι (*sunauxanomai*), Matt. xiii. 30, "grow together."
συνωδίνω (*sunōdinō*), Rom. viii. 22, "travaileth in pain together."
συστενάζω (*sustenazō*), Rom. viii. 22, "groaneth together."
σωφρονῶς (*sōphronōs*), Tit. ii. 12, "soberly."
τάγμα (*tagma*), 1 Cor. xv. 23, "order" (rank).
ταρταρόω (*tartaroō*), 2 Pet. ii. 4, "cast down to hell."
τεκμήριον (*tekmeerion*), Acts i. 3, "infallible proofs."
τελειωτής (*teliōtees*), Heb. xii. 2, "finisher."
τροποφορέω (*tropophoreō*), Acts xiii. 18, "suffered he . . . . manners."
ὑδροποτέω (*hydropoteō*), 1 Tim. v. 23, "drink . . . . water."
ὑπερείδω (*hupereidō*), Acts xvii. 30, "winked at."
ὑπερνικάω (*hupernikaō*), Rom. viii. 37, "more than conquerors."
ὑπερυψόω (*huperupsoō*), Phil. ii. 9, "highly exalted."
ὑπέχω (*hupechō*), Jude 7, "suffering."
ὑπόδικος (*hupodikos*), Rom. iii. 19, "guilty."
φιλία (*philia*), James iv. 4, "friendship."
φιλοπρωτεύω (*philoprōteuō*), 3 John 9, "loveth to have the pre-eminence."
φιλοσοφία (*philosophia*), Col. ii. 8, "philosophy."
φιλόσοφος (*philosophos*), Acts xvii. 18, "philosophers."

φρυάσσω (*phruassō*), Acts iv. 25, "did . . . . rage."
φωσφόρος (*phōsphoros*), 2 Pet. i. 19, "day star."
χλιαρός (*chliaros*), Rev. iii. 16, "lukewarm."
χρώς (*chrōs*), Acts xix. 12, "body."
ψευδώνυμος (*psūdonumos*), 1 Tim. vi. 20, "falsely so called" (*pseudonym*).
ψύχομαι (*psuchomai*), Matt. xxiv. 12, "shall wax cold."
ὠρύομαι (*ōruomai*), 1 Pet. v. 8, "roaring."

What is true of *words* which occur only once is also true of

PHRASES WHICH OCCUR ONLY ONCE.

All these are of the greatest importance. We have noticed one above (pp. 76, 77), "Angel of Satan." There are many others; we give an example or two.

πνεῦμα Χριστοῦ (*pneuma Christou*), "*the Spirit of Christ*," *Rom.* viii. 9.*

"Now if any man have not the Spirit of Christ, he is none of His." Both the A.V. and R.V. print the word spirit with a capital "S," as though it meant the Person of the Holy Spirit; and most Commentators so interpret it.

But πνεῦμα Χριστοῦ is a remarkable expression. *First*, there is no article, "the," either before "Spirit" or "Christ"; and, *secondly*, this combination of the two words occurs no where else.* The expression is stamped therefore with special importance, and no help in understanding it can be gained from its use in other passages.

Πνεῦμα Χριστοῦ is, literally, *Christ-spirit*. It is the "new creature," or "new creation," which is created by the Holy Spirit in all those who are "in Christ" (2 Cor. v. 17). This new nature is called πνεῦμα (*pneuma*), or *spirit*, as opposed to that which is only σάρξ (*sarx*), *flesh*. It is said to be "of God." It is called, in same verse, πνεῦμα Θεοῦ (*pneuma Theou*), *Spirit of God*, or Divine Spirit. It is spoken of as "Christ in you" (Col. i. 27). It is "eternal life." It is Christ in us, indeed; for Christ risen and ascended is "our life," and this life, regarded in its abstract nature and origin, is called here (Rom. viii. 9) πνεῦμα Χριστοῦ (*pneuma Christou*). The context

* The apparently similar expression in 1 Pet. i. 11 has the article.

supports this exposition, for the very next verse contains a conclusion flowing from the statement: "If Christ be in you the body [μέν, indeed] is dead because of sin; but the spirit is life, because of righteousness" (Rom. viii. 10). There must be this πνεῦμα Χριστοῦ in us of the Holy Spirit's creation, before He can bear witness with our spirits! Hence this Christ-life in us is the subject of this wonderful chapter before the Person of the Holy Spirit is spoken of in the 16th verse.

Paul never speaks of being "born again," or being "converted." The πνεῦμα Χριστοῦ, the Christ-spirit in us, implies this, and more than this; for being "born again" or "converted" is necessary, even for the earthly portion of the kingdom, the τὰ ἐπίγεια (*ta epigeia*) or *earthly things* of John iii. 12.

When Christ was upon the earth He was, as He is, the life of men. But now that He has been raised from the dead and exalted to the right-hand of God, He has become our life in this especial manner—Resurrection life. And this life is πνεῦμα Χριστοῦ, or Christ formed in us by the creative act of the Holy Ghost, as the hope of glory. Christ is called "a quickening (or life giving) Spirit" (1 Cor. xv. 45), and he that is thus joined to Christ the Lord is one spirit (1 Cor. vi. 17).

So that we find in Scripture:

1. That God is Spirit (John iii. 24), πνεῦμα ὁ Θεός;
2. That Christ is Spirit, πνεῦμα (1 Cor. xv. 46);
3. That the Holy Ghost is Spirit, πνεῦμα; and
4. That our new nature is also πνεῦμα, for that which is born of Spirit is πνεῦμα (John iii. 6).

And thus we are told by our God and Father's wondrous grace that we are partakers of divine Nature (2 Peter i. 4). It is this Divine Nature which, in Rom. viii. 9, is called πνεῦμα Χριστοῦ.*

* The word πνεῦμα occurs nearly 400 times in the New Testament, 150 of which are in the Pauline Epistles. It is a question worthy of serious consideration as to what is the meaning of the various usages of πνεῦμα. With the article it is of course the Holy Spirit. But without the article and before Pentecost, what can πνεῦμα ἅγιον mean in Luke xi. 13, "How much rather shall My Father give holy or divine spirit to them that ask him?" What can it mean in John xx. 22? Certainly not the Person of the Holy Spirit, for He was not yet given, because Jesus was not yet glorified (John vii. 39).

The Church soon became corrupt, and before the Canon of Scripture was complete it had lost the true teaching concerning

1. The "Mystery" (or secret) concerning the Body of Christ, the Church of God;
2. Justification on the principle of faith alone; and
3. The work of the Holy Spirit.

At the Reformation, the *second* of these was partially recovered. Some sixty years ago the *first* was recovered, but was speedily perverted; while the *third* has never been fully or properly recovered. Where is the Commentary on the Romans in which "the spirit of life in Christ Jesus" and the "spirit of adoption" (*i.e.* Sonship spirit) is not confounded with the indwelling of and with the Person of the Holy Ghost?

All modern sects and all modern spiritual movements have in each case *added* some new and distinct form of false teaching concerning the Holy Spirit's work to their special and peculiar errors.

Yet the truth of God remains, and the Word is still the Spirit's sword.

ἔννομος Χριστοῦ * (*ennomos Christou*), "*under the Law to Christ,*" 1 *Cor.* ix. 21.

This is another difficult expression. One thing is certain, viz., that there is no article with either of the two words "Law" or "Christ," and that there is nothing about "the" Law. The R.V. omits the article, and renders "under law to Christ." Another thing is certain, viz., that there is no "to." The word Χριστοῦ is in the genitive case, and not the dative (according to all the critical texts).

Gentile Christians are very anxious to put themselves under "the Law." But God has never put them there. The Law was given by God to Israel by the hand of Moses. Gentile Christians have never thus been *put* under that Law. Indeed, as a Jew, Paul declares distinctly of himself and his Jewish brethren in Christ, Rom. vii. 6 (following the A.V. margin), "Now we are delivered from the

* The word ἔννομος occurs twice (here and Acts xix. 39, *lawful*), but this phrase only once.

Law, being dead to that wherein we were held;" or, as in R.V., "having died to that wherein we were held," *i.e.* as Jews they had, in Christ, died to the Law, and on resurrection ground their old husband had no more claim upon them.

Then in 1 Cor. ix. 20, 21, he says, "Unto the Jews I became as a Jew, that I might gain the Jews; to them that are under the Law as under the Law." Here there is an important sentence dropped out by a later scribe, but it is found in all the ancient versions and critical texts, and it is restored in the R.V.—"NOT BEING MYSELF UNDER THE LAW!" Then he goes on to continue his argument: "to them that are without Law as without Law" (being not ἄνομος Θεοῦ, but ἔννομος Χριστοῦ); or, being not an outlaw of God, but a subject-of-the-Law of Christ; or, being not destitute of Divine Law, but under Christ's Law; *i.e.* though I am not under the Law of Moses, I am under a law of God. How? I am *under obedience to the commandments of Christ!* As much as to say, If I keep Christ's commandments what law shall I break? None! For if I walk in the love of Christ I shall fulfil the Law of Moses (Rom. xiii. 10). If I walk in love I shall "fulfil the Law of Christ" (Gal. vi. 2).

The conclusion therefore is, that Gentiles who never were under the "Law," and Israelites who were, if they are both "in Christ," are not under the Law of Moses, but are under obedience to the commandments of Christ, which are far higher and far holier. The passage therefore does not prove that Gentiles or Christians are under the Law, but are "freed from the Law."

Another phase of this great subject is where

Only One Word

is employed to denote a certain thing, though that word may be used and occur many times.

The Hebrew noun for *Truth* is a remarkable illustration of this. Many are the words used for *deceit* and *lies*,* but there is *only one word for truth*. God's truth is one! Man's lies are almost infinite! The word אֱמֶת (*Emeth*) means *firmness* and *stability*, *perpetuity*, *security*. This is what God is. This is exactly what man is not! Man is altogether vanity. "All men are liars" (Ps. cxvi. 11). "His mouth is full of

* See page 73.

cursing, deceit (Heb. pl., *deceits*), and fraud: under his tongue is ungodliness and vanity" (Ps. x. 7). "They speak vanity every one with his neighbour: with flattering lips and a double heart do they speak" (Ps. xii. 2).

Truth is found only in the Word of God, in Christ, who says of Himself, the living Word, "I am the truth" (John xiv. 6); and of the *written* Word, the Scriptures, "Thy word is truth" (John xvii. 17; 1 John v. 6).

Truth is heard only in the Word of God. It is taught only by Jesus. Hence it is written (Eph. iv. 20, 21), "Ye have not so learned Christ, if so be that ye have heard HIM, and have been taught by HIM, as the truth is in Jesus." These last words are generally misquoted, as though they said, "the truth as it is in Jesus." But this is quite a different thing! This implies that there is some truth to be found apart from Jesus! No, it says, "even as the truth is in Jesus" (R.V.), *i.e.*, in Him, and no where else. By nature all men are like Jacob. He was a *deceiver*, and in attempting to gain his blessings by deceit, he brought sorrows and troubles upon himself. Those blessings which God designed for him were, and will be, wrought by the "God of truth," as it is written, "Thou wilt perform the truth to Jacob" (Micah vii. 20).

The Rabbins have pointed out that man being pure falsehood, God appointed him to death, that with the fear of death before his eyes he might be pious and learn the truth. Hence out of the word אמת (*Emeth*) they made (by the rule of *Notricon* or *Acrostic*) three words:

א standing for ארון (*Aron*), "a coffin."
מ " " מטה (*Mittah*), "a bier."
ת " " תכריכים (*Tachreechcem*), "shrouds."

Hence they taught that the death of God's saints was "precious in the sight of the LORD" (Ps. cxvi. 15), for only in resurrection can he know what he has lost, viz., the image of God, and thus "Truth shall spring out of the earth" (Ps. lxxxv. 11).

But a more simple fact concerning this remarkable word is this, that the first letter, *Aleph* (א), is the first letter of the alphabet; the middle letter, *Mem* (מ), is in the middle of the alphabet; while the last letter, *Tau* (ת), is the last letter of the alphabet. As much as to say to us, that the Word of the Lord is altogether truth. From beginning to end every letter and every word expresses, and contains, and is the Truth of God. While Jesus is Himself the Alpha and the Omega,* the first and the last, the beginning and the ending of the ways, and works, and words of God (Rev. i. 8, 17).

We must distinguish between *Emeth, truth,* and *Emunah,* which means "faithfulness"; † and also *Aman,* אָמַן (*Ahman*), which is from a different root, and as an adverb means *truly, certainly,* and as an adjective *firm* or *faithful.* It is from this that the Latins derived their word *omen* and *ominous,* because they firmly believed in their *omens.* How much more should we believe that to which we put our *Amen,* when we use this selfsame word.

---

* These are the *first* and *last* letters of the Greek alphabet.

† Hab. ii. 4. The righteous man believes God, and lives in the firm expectation that what God has said He will perform. Hence his faith is the proof and evidence that God has justified him, and it is thus counted to him for righteousness. Hab. ii. 4 is quoted three times in the New Testament, viz., Rom. i. 17; Gal. iii. 11; and Heb. x. 38.

TWO.

We now come to the spiritual significance of the number Two. We have seen that *One* excludes all difference, and denotes that which is sovereign. But Two affirms that there is a difference—there is *another;* while ONE affirms that there is not another!

This *difference* may be for good or for evil. A thing may differ from evil, and be good; or it may differ from good, and be evil. Hence, the number Two takes a two-fold colouring, according to the context.

It is the first number by which we can *divide* another, and therefore in all its uses we may trace this fundamental idea of *division* or *difference.*

The *two* may be, though different in character, yet one as to testimony and friendship. The Second that comes in may be for help and deliverance. But, alas! where man is concerned, this number testifies of his fall, for it more often denotes that difference which implies *opposition, enmity,* and *oppression.**

When the earth lay in the chaos which had overwhelmed it (Gen. i. 2), its condition was universal ruin and darkness. The *second* thing recorded in connection with the Creation was the introduction of a *second* thing—Light; and immediately there was difference and division, for God DIVIDED the light from the darkness.

So the *second* day had *division* for its great characteristic (Gen. i. 6). "Let there be a firmament in the midst of the waters, and let it DIVIDE the waters from the waters." Here we have *Division* connected with the *second* day.

* Like many other words; *e.g.*, the verb "*prevent*" meant originally for one to get before another. But because whenever one man got before another it was always to the hindrance and hurt of that other, the word gradually took on the meaning *to hinder,* and thus testifies of man's fall. So with the word *simple:* it meant originally sincere, open, honest. But in man's judgment, any one who so acts is a *fool.* Hence, man soon came to use the word *simple* as denoting a very foolish person! So in the French with the word *chef,* which means "chief." But as man makes "a god of his belly" he who can best gratify its lusts has a unique claim to this word.

This great spiritual significance is maintained throughout the Word of God. Of course we cannot recognise any human arrangements or divisions of books, chapters, or verses, etc. We can take only that division, order, and arrangement which is Divine.

The *second* of any number of things always bears upon it the stamp of *difference*, and generally of *enmity*.

Take the *second* statement in the Bible. The first is—

Gen. i. 1: "In the beginning God created the heaven and the earth."

The *second* is, "And the earth was (or rather *became*) without form and void."

Here the first speaks of perfection and of order. The *second* of ruin and desolation, which came to pass at some time, and in some way, and for some reason which are not revealed.*

THE DIVISIONS OF THE BIBLE.

Then we have seen (pp. 34, 35) that the Book of Genesis is Divinely divided into twelve parts (consisting of an Introduction and eleven *Tol'doth*). The first of these twelve divisions records the perfection of God's sovereign work. The *second* (Gen. ii. 4—iv. 26) contains the account of the Fall; the entrance of a *second* being—the Enemy—that old Serpent the Devil, introducing discord, and sin, and death. "Enmity" is seen first in this *second* division. "I will put enmity" (Gen. iii. 15). We see a *second*, an enemy in the Serpent; a *second* creature in the woman, who was deceived and "in the transgression"; a *second* man, in the Seed of the woman, the subject of the great primeval promise and prophecy. Hence the number *two* becomes associated with Incarnation, with the *second* Person of the ever-blessed Trinity, "the second Man," "the last Adam."

The *second* "Tol'doth" (Gen. v. 1—vi. 8) begins with the words, "The book of the generations of Adam." While of "the second Man" it is written (Matt. i. 1) "the book of the generation of Jesus Christ."

If we look at the Pentateuch as a whole, we see, in the First book, Divine sovereignty (see p. 53), but the *Second*

* See *The New Creation and the Old*, by the same author.

book (Exodus) opens with "the oppression of the enemy." Here, again, there is "another," even the Deliverer and the Redeemer, who says, "I am come down to deliver" (Exod. iii. 8). To Him the praise is offered in the Song of Moses: "Thou in Thy mercy hast led forth the people which Thou hast redeemed" (Exod. xv. 13). And thus Redemption is introduced into the Bible, and mentioned for the first time in this *second* book, and in connection with the enemy (just as was the first promise of the Redeemer in Gen. iii. 15).

The *second* of the three great divisions of the Old Testament, called *Nebiim*, or the Prophets (Joshua, Judges, Ruth, 1 and 2 Samuel, 1 and 2 Kings, Isaiah, Jeremiah, and Ezekiel) contains the record of Israel's enmity to God, and of God's controversy with Israel. In the first book (Joshua) we have God's sovereignty in giving the conquest of the land; while in the *second* (Judges) we see the rebellion and enmity in the land, leading to departure from God and the oppression of the enemy. Here, again, we have side by side with the enemy the "saviours" whom God raised up to deliver His people.

In the third great division of the Old Testament, called "the Psalms," because it commences with the Book of Psalms, we have in the Hebrew Canon,* as the *second* Book, the Book of Job. Here, again, we see the enemy in all his power and malignity opposing and oppressing a child of God; and we are taken within the veil to behold the living God as the shield of His people, a very present help in the needful time of trouble.

Besides Genesis, the Book of Psalms is the only book which is marked by any similar Divine divisions.

It consists of Five Books:

The first	... ...	Pss. i.—xli.
The second	... ...	Pss. xlii.—lxxii.
The third	... ...	Pss. lxxiii.—lxxxix.
The fourth	... ...	Pss. xc.—cvi.
The fifth	... ...	Pss. cvii.—cl.

The *Second* Book of the Psalms commences (as does Exodus) with "the oppression of the enemy" (Ps. xlii. 9).

---

* See *The Names and Order of the Books of the Old Testament*, by the same author and publisher.

This is the burden of the whole of this Psalm, and indeed of the whole of this *second* Book!

Not only is this true of this *Second* Book, but it is true also of the *second* Psalm of each of the other books! *e.g.*:—

The *second* Psalm of *First* Book (Ps. ii.):—

"Why do the heathen rage,
And [*why*] do the people imagine a vain thing?
[*Why do*] the kings of the earth set themselves,
And [*why do*] the rulers take counsel together
Against the LORD and against His anointed?"

But here, again, we have the Deliverer, in verse 6.

"Yet have I set My King."

The *second* Psalm of the *Second* Book (Ps. xliii.) opens with "the oppression of the enemy," repeated in *v.* 2, together with the prophecy of praise for the promised Deliverer.

The *second* Psalm of the *Third* Book (Ps. lxxiv.):—

"Lift up Thy feet unto the perpetual desolations:
Even all *that* the ENEMY hath done wickedly in the sanctuary,
Thine ENEMIES roar in the midst of Thy congregations . . .
O God, how long shall the ADVERSARY reproach?
Shall the ENEMY blaspheme Thy name for ever? . . .
Remember this, that the ENEMY hath reproached, O LORD . . .
O let not the oppressed return ashamed . . .
Arise, O God, plead Thine own cause . . .
Forget not the voice of Thine ENEMIES."

The *second* Psalm of the *Fourth* Book (Ps. xci.) would have to be quoted as a whole. It describes how the enemy shall be finally trodden down by the coming Deliverer.

The *second* Psalm of the *Fifth* Book (Ps. cviii.):—

"That Thy beloved may be delivered:
Save *with* Thy right hand, and answer me . . .
Give us help from trouble,
For vain is the help of man.
Through God we shall do valiantly:
For He *it is that* shall tread down our ENEMIES."

The same significance of the number Two is seen in the New Testament. Wherever there are two Epistles, the second has some special reference to the enemy.

In 2 Cor. there is a marked emphasis on the power of the enemy, and the working of Satan (ii. 11; xi. 14; xii. 7. See pp. 76, 77).

In 2 Thess. we have a special account of the working of Satan in the revelation of "the man of sin" and "the lawless one."

In 2 Tim. we see the church in its *ruin*, as in the first epistle we see it in its *rule*.

In 2 Peter we have the coming apostasy foretold and described. While

In 2 John we have the "antichrist" mentioned by this name, and are forbidden to receive into our house any who come with his doctrine.*

It is impossible even to name the vast number of things which are introduced to us in pairs, so that the one may teach concerning the other by way of contrast or *difference*.

The two foundations of Matt. vii. 24–27: the one which "fell not, for it was founded upon a rock"; the other which "fell, and great was the fall of it." The two goats (Lev. xvi. 7); the two birds (Lev. xiv. 4–7); the two opinions (1 Kings xviii. 21); the two masters (Matt. vi. 24); the two commandments (Matt. xxii. 40); the two debtors (Luke vii. 41); the two covenants (Gal. iv. 24); the two men (Luke xviii. 10); the two sons (Matt. xxi. 28, and Luke xv. 11, and Gal. iv. 22), etc., etc.

THE LIFE TYPES OF GENESIS.

The *second* of the *seven* life-types of Genesis † has the same character.

The first Adam sets forth our first parents in their innocence, fall, and expulsion, driven out from the presence of God (Gen. iii. 24). How could they again walk with God? This is the great problem which is to be solved in the words which immediately follow, written on the fore-

* Brand (*Pop. Ant.* iii. 145) quotes *Numerus Infaustus*, in the preface to which the author says, "Such of the kings of England as were the second of any name proved very unfortunate persons, William II., Henry II., Edward II., Richard II., Charles II., James II."

† See *The New Creation and the Old*, by the same author.

front of revelation to set before us the answer to the all-important question, "How can TWO walk together except they be agreed?" (Amos iii. 3).

The solution is given in Gen. iv., in the *second* life-type, which is two-fold in the persons of Cain and Abel. Here are presented and described *the Two ways*—"The way of God" (Acts xviii. 26) and "The way of Cain" (Jude 11), the only *two Religions* which the world has ever seen. One, the true; the other, the false.

True religion is one and unchangeable. Its language is—

"NOTHING in my hand I bring,
Simply to Thy cross I cling."

False religion is one and unchangeable. It has many varieties; its one language is—

"SOMETHING in my hand I bring."

Men quarrel bitterly as to what that something is to be. They persecute, and burn, and destroy one another in the heat of their controversies about it. But however this "something" may vary, it is *one*, in that it is not "the way of God," not the way which God has appointed, but it is "the way of Cain," man's way. The one is "faith," the other is "works." The one is "grace," the other is human "merit." The one is "the path of life," the other ends in "the second death."

Not only have we this contrast or eternal difference in Cain and Abel, but others are presented in this manner, in order to bring out truths of the deepest significance and solemnity.

Abraham and Lot

are so presented. These two were related as uncle and nephew; both descended from Shem through Terah. Both started together from Ur of the Chaldees to Haran in Mesopotamia (Gen. xi.); they both started together from Haran to go into the land of Canaan (Gen. xii. 4); and afterwards they both go up together out of Egypt (Gen. xiii. 1). But soon the *difference* between the two was manifested, and "there was a strife" between them. The *difference* was manifested.

Lot, the *second* of this pair, lifted up his own eyes and chose his own portion (xiii. 11); while Abram's portion was chosen for him by God (xiii. 14). Thus they were "separated" (xiii. 11, 14).

First, Lot looked and "*beheld*" the plain of Jordan with its cities of Sodom and Gomorrah, and it seemed to him "as the garden of the LORD" (Gen. xiii. 10); then he "*chose*" this for his portion (xiii. 11); then he "pitched his tent towards Sodom" (xiii. 12); then he "dwelt in Sodom," and shared in Sodom's troubles and wars, and lost all the treasure which he had laid up there (xiv. 12). He afterwards "sat in the gate of Sodom" (xix. 1) and held office there as a judge in spite of his being daily "vexed" with their ungodly words and deeds (2 Pet. ii. 6-9); and finally he escaped from its overthrow, only with his life.

Abram, on the other hand, had his portion with God. He walked by faith; he pitched his tent only where he could build his altar (xii. 8; xiii. 3, 4); he held communion with God who was his "shield and exceeding great reward" (xv. 1). Though he was a stranger on earth, he was "the friend of God," and received the secrets of God's purposes (Ps. xxv. 14; Amos iii. 7; John xv. 15). Truly there was a *difference*. And this difference was greater in their two wives. Sarah was a type of the Heavenly Jerusalem (Gal. iv. 21-31); while "Lot's wife" became a pillar of salt, and remains a beacon of warning to be for ever remembered (Luke xvii. 32).

ISAAC AND ISHMAEL

are presented together. Here the relationship was nearer, for they were step-brothers. Both were the sons of Abram, Sarah being the mother of Isaac, and Hagar the mother of Ishmael. Though the relationship according to the flesh was nearer than that between Abram and Lot, the *difference* was morally and spiritually greater. For it is written, "neither because they are the seed of Abraham are they all children: for in Isaac shall thy seed be called" (Rom. ix. 7). Oh! how great was the difference! Isaac, "born after the spirit"; Ishmael, "born after the flesh" (Gal. iv. 29, 30), and therefore a *persecutor*. We read of no "just" Ishmael, no "righteous" Ishmael, as we do of Lot. Lot's descendants were the Moabites and Ammonites, and Ruth the Moabitess was an ancestress of Jesus. But Ishmael's posterity were "cast out," and continue to this day wild and unsubdued.

JACOB AND ESAU

are presented together. Here the relationship is still closer. Not only were they the children of the same father (Isaac), but of the same mother (Rebekah). But the spiritual *difference* is still greater. The enmity was manifested when the babes "struggled together," being yet unborn (Gen. xxv. 22). And it is written in the Scriptures of truth, "Jacob have I loved, but Esau have I hated" (Mal. i. 2, 3; Rom. ix. 13). Esau was "a fornicator and a profane person," despising his birthright (Heb. xii. 16, 17); while Jacob so loved and prized it that he sinned grievously in grasping it. As the *difference* is seen in the posterity of Abraham and Lot, Isaac and Ishmael, so here it is still more marked. Israel is Jehovah's glory, the "everlasting nation" (Isa. xliii. 12, 13; xliv. 7); while the Edomites were accursed. And of the Amalekites Jehovah declared that He would "have war with Amalek from generation to generation" (Exod. xvii. 16).

We see the same significance in the

WORDS WHICH OCCUR TWICE.

A long list of these might be made. We give a few from the Hebrew and from the Greek. In all such words we can see important instruction. In ἀποπλέω (*apopleō*) we see the work of the enemy *seducing* the very elect, were it possible (Matt. xiii. 22), and causing them to *err* from the faith (1 Tim. vi. 10).

In ἀποπνίγω (*apopnigō*) we see the enemy *choking* the seed (Matt. xiii. 7), and himself *choked* in the sea (Luke viii. 33).

In ἀπόλαυσις (*apolausis*) we have the things which God has given us for *enjoyment* (1 Tim. vi. 17), and the *enjoyment* of the pleasures of sin (Heb. xi. 25).

In ἀποκυέω (*apokueō*) we have sin *bringing forth* death (James i. 15), and God *begetting* us by the word of truth (James i. 18).

In ἀτμίς (*atmis*) we see the *difference* between earthly life, which is but a *vapour*, compared with life which is eternal (James iv. 14; Acts ii. 19).

In πανοπλία (*panoplia*) (panoply) we see a *difference* indeed. It is not that the word occurs twice (merely as a word), but it is used in two senses and two places, namely, of the armour of Satan (Luke xi. 22), and the armour of God (Eph. vi. 11, 17).

The armour of the "strong man" is taken from him by the "stronger than he," and the soul is delivered, never more to be under the dominion of Satan. All the armour in which Satan trusted is then taken away from him (Luke xi. 21, 22), and the poor sinner who was before in his power is now endued with the "whole armour of God." *

Similar studies may be made with other words. And even where a word may occur often, it may occur only twice in connection with another word making a phrase. This may be significant. For example, ὁ υἱὸς τῆς ἀπωλειάς, *the son of perdition*. Both of these words, "son" and "perdition," occur many times, but *only twice together* (John xvii. 12 and 2 Thess. ii. 3, pointing to Ps. cix.). Some have questioned from this whether Judas Iscariot will be revealed again as the man of sin.

The following are a few other words which occur only twice :—

אבד (*ōhvehd*), perish, Num. xxiv. 20, 24.
אבק (*āhvak*), to wrestle, Gen. xxxii. 24, 25.
אגרוף (*egrŏph*), with the fist, Exod. xxi. 18; Isa. lviii. 4.
אול (*ool*), strength or might, 2 Kings xxiv. 15; Ps. lxxiii. 4.
אכזב (*ach-zahv*), liar, Jer. xv. 18; Micah i. 14.
אסמים (*asah-meem*), storehouses, Deut. xxviii. 8; Prov. iii. 10.
ארב (*eh-rev*), lie in wait, Job xxxvii. 8; xxxviii. 40.
אצעדה (*etz-āh-dah*), chains, Num. xxxi. 50; 2 Sam. i. 10.
ארה (*ah-rah*), to pluck, Ps. lxxx. 12; Song v. 1.
בדא (*bāh-dah*), feign, 1 Kings xii. 33; Neh. vi. 8.
בזר (*bah-zar*), scatter, Dan. xi. 24; Ps. lxviii. 30.
בלק (*bah-lak*), waste, Isa. xxiv. 1; Nah. ii. 10.
בעט (*bah-gat*), to kick, Deut. xxxii. 15; 1 Sam. ii. 29.
בתר (*bah-thar*), to divide, Gen. xv. 10.

* Not so when Satan "*goes out*" of a man of his own accord. For this parable is given in immediate connection with the other. Satan is not despoiled of his armour in this case. He is not "cast out." Hence the man sweeps his house and garnishes it. He takes pledges, and wears badges, but the house is "empty." Satan returns with all his power, and the last state of that man is worse than the first (Luke xi. 24–26; Matt. xii. 43–45).

גבהות (*gav-hooth*), lofty, Isa. ii. 11, 17.
דחי (*d'ghee*), from falling, Pss. lvi. 13; cxvi. 8.
דחק (*dah-chak*), thrust or vex, Judg. ii. 18; Joel ii. 8.
דמע (*dah-mag*), weep, Jer. xiii. 17, 17.
חנק (*chah-nak*), hanged, 2 Sam. xvii. 23; Nah. ii. 12.
חסם (*chah-sam*), muzzle, Deut. xxv. 4; Ezek. xxxix. 11.
חסר (*cheh-ser*), want, poverty, Job xxx. 3; Prov. xxviii. 22.
חשבנות (*chish-sh'voh-nôhth*), engines, 2 Chron. xxvi. 15; inventions, Eccles. vii. 29.
חשש (*chashash*), chaff, Isa. v. 24; xxxiii. 11.
טין (*teen*), miry, Dan. ii. 41, 43.
יון (*yah-vehn*), miry, Ps. xl. 2; mire, Ps. lxix. 2.
ירט (*yah-rat*), perverse, Num. xxii. 32; Job xvi. 11.
כבל (*keh-vel*), fetters, Ps. cv. 18; cxlix. 8.
כלוא (*k'loo*), prison, Jer. xxxvii. 4; lii. 31.
כסח (*kah-sagh*), cut down, Ps. lxxx. 16; Isa. xxxiii. 12
לעג (*lah-ehg*), mockers, Ps. xxxv. 16; Isa. xxviii. 11.
מחתרת (*magh-teh-reth*), breaking up, Exod. xxii. 2 secret search (marg. *digging*), Jer. ii. 34.
מלק (*mah-lak*), wring off, Lev. i. 15; v. 8.
משטמה (*mas-teh-māh*), hatred, Hos. ix. 7, 8.
משרה (*mis-rah*), government, Isa. ix. 6, 7.
נגח (*nag-gahgh*), push, Exod. xxi. 29, 36.
נדה (*nah-dah*), cast out, Isa. lvi. 5; put away, Amos vi. 3.
נחש (*nah-chash*), enchantment, Num. xxiii. 23; xxiv. 1.
ניר (*neer*), to break up, Jer. iv. 3; Hos. x. 12.
נכת (*n'ckoth*), precious things, 2 Kings xx. 13; Isa xxxix. 2.
נקע (*nah-kag*), alienated, Ezek. xxiii. 18; xxiii. 28.
נשף (*nah-shaph*), to blow, Exod. xv. 10; Isa. xl. 24.
סחף (*sah-chaph*), to sweep away, Prov. xxviii. 3; Jer xlvi. 15.
פרשה (*pah-rah-shah*), sum, Est. iv. 7; declaration, *ib.* x. 2
צנינים (*tz'nee-neem*), thorns, Num. xxxiii. 55; Josh. xxiii. 13.
קמוש (*kim-mosh*), nettles, Isa. xxxiv. 13; Hos. ix. 6.
קמל (*kah-mal*), wither, Isa. xix. 6; xxxiii. 9 (marg.)
ראש (*rehsh*), poverty, Prov. vi. 11; xxx. 8.
רפס (*r'phas*), stamp, Dan. vii. 7, 19.
שובב (*shoh-vehv*), backsliding, Jer. xxxi. 22; xlix. 4.

ἀγγεῖον (*angeion*), vessels, Matt. xiii. 48; xxv. 4.

ἄγε (*age*), go to, James iv. 13; v. 1.

ἄγναφος (*agnaphos*), new, Matt. ix. 16; Mark ii. 21.

ἀγνωσία (*agnōsia*), not the knowledge, 1 Cor. xv. 34; ignorance, 1 Pet. ii. 15.

ἀγοραῖος (*agoraios*), the public place, Acts xvii. 5; baser sort, xix. 38; law (ἀγοραῖοι, public or court days).

ἄδηλος (*adeelos*), appear not, Luke xi. 44; uncertain, 1 Cor. xiv. 8.

ἄθεσμος (*athesmos*), wicked, 2 Pet. ii. 7; iii. 17.

ἀθλέω (*athleō*), strive, 2 Tim. ii. 5, 5.

αἰφνίδιος (*aiphnidios*), unawares, Luke xxi. 34; sudden, 1 Thess. v. 3.

ἀκάνθινος (*akanthinos*), thorns, Mark xv. 17; John xix. 5.

ἀκρασία (*akrasia*), excess, Matt. xxiii. 25; 1 Cor. vii. 5, incontinency.

ἀλαζών (*alazōn*), boasters, Rom. i. 30; 2 Tim. iii. 2.

ἀλαλάζω (*alalazō*), wailed, Mark v. 38; tinkling, 1 Cor. xiii. 1.

ἀνακαινόω (*anakainoō*), renew, 2 Cor. iv. 16; Col. iii. 10.

ἀνακαίνωσις (*anakainōsis*), renewing, Rom. xii. 2; Titus iii. 5.

ἀνάπηρος (*anapeeros*), maimed, Luke xiv. 13, 21.

ἀναπολόγητος (*anapologeetos*), without excuse, Rom. i. 20; ii. 1.

ἀνατρέπω (*anatrepō*), overthrow, 2 Tim. ii. 18; subvert, Titus i. 11.

ἀνεξιχνίαστος (*anexichniastos*), past finding out, Rom. xi. 33; unsearchable, Eph. iii. 8. (The word means that which cannot be tracked or traced.*)

ἀνθρακιά (*anthrakia*), the enemy's fire, John xviii. 18; and the friend's fire, John xxi. 9.

ἄνοια (*anoia*), madness, Luke vi. 11; folly, 2 Tim. iii. 9.

ἀνόμως (*anomōs*), without law, Rom. ii. 12 (twice).

ἀνόσιος (*anosios*), unholy, 1 Tim. i. 9; 2 Tim. iii. 2.

ἀντάλλαγμα (*antallagma*), exchange, Matt. xvi. 26; Mark viii. 37.

ἀνταπόδομα (*antapodoma*), recompence, Luke xiv. 12; Rom. xi. 9.

ἀντιμισθία (*antimisthia*), recompence, Rom. i. 27; 2 Cor. vi. 13.

---

* Differing from ἀνεξερεύνητος, (*anexereūneetos*), *that which cannot be understood*, occurring only once (Rom. xi. 33).

ἀνωφελής (*anōphelees*), unprofitable, Titus iii. 9; Heb. vii. 18.

ἀξίνη (*axinee*), axe, Matt. iii. 10; Luke iii. 9.

ἀπειλέω (*apeileō*), threaten, Acts iv. 17; 1 Pet. ii. 23.

ἀπεκδύομαι (*apekduomai*), put off, Col. iii. 9; spoil, Col. ii. 15.

ἀποβολή (*apobolee*), loss, Acts xxvii. 22; casting away, Rom. xi. 15.

ἀποκαραδοκία (*apokaradokia*), earnest expectation, Rom. viii. 19; Phil. i. 20.

ἀποκυέω (*apokueō*), bring forth, James i. 15; beget, *ib.* 18.

ἀπόλαυσις (*apolausis*), enjoy, 1 Tim. vi. 17; Heb. xi. 25.

ἀποχωρίζομαι (*apochōrizomai*), depart asunder, Acts xv. 39; Rev. vi. 14.

ἀρσενοκοίτης (*arsenokoitees*), sodomites, 1 Cor. vi. 9; 1 Tim. i. 10.

ἀσεβέω (*asebeō*), live ungodly, 2 Pet. ii. 6; Jude 15.

ἄσπονδος (*aspondos*), implacable, Rom. i. 31; truce-breakers, 2 Tim. iii. 3.

ἀστεῖος (*asteios*), exceeding fair, Acts vii. 20; proper, Heb. xi. 23.

ἀστήρικτος (*asteeriktos*), unstable, 2 Pet. ii. 14; iii. 16.

ἄστοργος (*astorgos*), without natural affection, Rom. i. 31; 2 Tim. iii. 3.

ἀσχημονέω (*ascheemoneō*), behave unseemly, 1 Cor. vii. 36; xiii. 5.

ἀσχημοσύνη (*aschemosunee*), unseemly, Rom. i. 27; Rev. xvi. 15.

ἀτάκτως (*ataktōs*), disorderly, 2 Thess. iii. 6, 11.

ἀτμίς (*atmis*), vapour, Acts ii. 19; James iv. 14.

ἀχρεῖος (*achreios*), unprofitable, Matt. xxv. 30; Luke xvii. 10.

ἄχυρον (*achuron*), chaff, Matt. iii. 12; Luke iii. 17.

Not only do we trace this significance where we have the number "two," but where two things are named, though they are not numbered.

For example:—

THE POTTER'S TWO VESSELS OF JER. XVIII. 1–4.

The *first* vessel which he made was marred; the *second* was "another" vessel, as it pleased the potter to make it.

This is interpreted in the context, of Israel ruined, but to be restored; broken off, but to be grafted in again; self-destroyed, but finding Divine help.

The same great *difference* may be seen in the Two COVENANTS. The first marred, not faultless, waxen old, and taken away (Heb. viii. 7, 8, 13; x. 9); the second "a better Covenant," "new," and "established" (Heb. viii. 6, 8; x. 9, 16, 17).

The ORDINANCES of the Law, "weak" and "unprofitable" (Heb. vii. 18; x. 6, 9). The ordinances of grace, the "good things to come."

"The FIRST MAN," marred (Gen. ii. 7; iii. 19), and of the earth, earthy. "The second man," the Lord from Heaven (1 Cor. xv. 47). The first Adam condemned to death, the last Adam living again for evermore.

The BODY, marred in the Fall, and made subject to death and corruption, but in Resurrection to be made like Christ's own body of glory (1 John iii. 1-3; Phil. iii. 21; Rom. viii. 23; 1 Cor. xv. 42-49).*

The OLD CREATION under the curse marred and ruined (Gen. iii.); "The New Heavens and the New Earth" established in righteousness (Rev. xxi., xxii.);—a mighty *difference* indeed. "No night there," "no need of the sun," "no more sorrow," "no more curse," no more sin, or suffering, or death. Oh, wondrous *difference!* and this for ever and for ever. "He taketh away the first that He may ESTABLISH the second." "Praise the LORD!" Rebellious ISRAEL'S heart taken away, and a new heart given. ORDINANCES which "perish with the using" replaced by the Christ of God. MAN ruined and lost, but saved with an everlasting salvation. The BODY of humiliation sown in corruption, but raised in incorruption. The HEAVENS AND EARTH passed away, and the new heavens and the new earth established for ever in glory.

But we have seen that where there are two, though there is still *difference*, this difference may be in a good sense. It may be for oppression or hindrance, or it may be for association and mutual help. See Ruth iv. 11, where of Leah

* See *The Resurrection of the Body*, by the same author.

and Rachel it is written: "Which two did build up the house of Israel." It may be the proverbial "Two and two" of apostleship and service. Or it may be our association with Christ in death and resurrection, of which Baptism and the Lord's Supper are the great sign and token.

Especially does it mark that "other," the Saviour and mighty deliverer, spoken of in Ps. lxxxix. 19: "I have laid help on one that is mighty." The *second* person of the Trinity partook of *two* natures—perfect God and perfect man. Perfect man indeed, but oh, how *different!* "Two are better than one, because they have a good reward for their labour. For if they fall, the one will lift up his fellow; but woe to him that is alone when he falleth, for he hath not another to help him up."

It is still "another," but there is "help" instead of *enmity*. No longer the two differing, but the two agreed; for "How can two walk together except they be agreed?" (Amos iii. 3).

Two *testimonies* may be *different*, but yet one may support, strengthen, and corroborate the other. Jesus said: "The testimony of two men is true. I am one that bear witness of myself, and the Father that sent me beareth witness of me" (John viii. 17, 18). And it is written in the Law: "At the mouth of two witnesses, or three witnesses," shall the matter be established (Num. xxxv. 30; Deut. xvii. 6; xix. 15; Matt. xviii. 16; 2 Cor. xiii. 1; 1 Tim. v. 19; Heb. x. 28). The whole Law itself hung on "two commandments" (Matt. xxii. 40).

God's own revelation is two-fold. The Old Covenant and the New are God's sufficient testimony to man. And yet how different. The Law and Grace; Faith and Works!

We may notice also that it is the *second* Person of the Trinity who is specially called "the Faithful Witness" (Rev. i. 5). And we have other examples of the number Two in connection with faithful testimony. Caleb and Joshua were two faithful witnesses of the truth of God's Word. Faithlessness said: "We be not able to go up against the people. For they are stronger than we." But Faith could say "Let us go up at once, and possess it; for we are well able to overcome it" (Num. xiii. 30, 31). And these were the two who alone out of 600,000 men did possess their inheritance in the land. To-day, also, it is not numbers. The testimony of numbers may be as false to-day as was that of the Spies. It is the testimony of the two based on God's Word which alone was true. May this encourage us to stand firm in these days of apostasy, with ears deaf to the words of man, but attentive to the words of Jehovah. Firm, even though the whole congregation be against us, and we be only the few who are waiting to be caught up to meet the Lord in the air.

Let us have for our seal the faithfulness of Jehovah, and say always and ever, "Let God be true, and every man a liar."

It is remarkable that words having special reference to Testimony, should occur twice; for example:—

ἀληθεύω (*aleetheuō*), to tell the truth, Gal. iv. 16; to speak the truth, Eph. iv. 15.

ἀμετάθετος (*ametathetos*), immutable, Heb. vi. 18; immutability, Heb. vi. 17.

ἀνακεφαλαιόομαι (*anakephalaioomai*), comprehend, Rom. xiii. 9; gather together in one, Eph. i. 10.

βεβαίωσις (*bebaiōsis*), confirmation, Phil. i. 7; Heb. vi. 16.

κεραία (*keraia*), tittle, Matt. v. 18; Luke xvi. 17.

νομοθετέω (*nomotheteō*), received the law, Heb. vii. 11; was established, Heb. viii. 6.

ἀμεταμέλητος (*ametameleetos*), without repentance, Rom. xi. 29; not to be repented of, 2 Cor. vii. 10.

ἐγγράφω (*engraphō*), written in, 2 Cor. iii. 2, 3.

δικαίωσις * (*dikaiōsis*), justification, Rom. iv. 25; v. 18.

* See under the number *Nine*.

THREE.

In this number we have quite a new set of phenomena. We come to the first geometrical figure. Two straight lines cannot possibly enclose any space, or form a plane figure; neither can two plane surfaces form a solid. *Three* lines are necessary to form a plane figure; and three dimensions of length, breadth, and height, are necessary to form a solid. Hence *three* is the symbol of the *cube*—the simplest form of solid figure. As two is the symbol of the square, or plane contents (x^2), so three is the symbol of the cube, or solid contents (x^3).

Three, therefore, stands for that which is *solid*, *real*, *substantial*, *complete*, and *entire*.

All things that are specially *complete* are stamped with this number three.

God's attributes are *three:* omniscience, omnipresence, and omnipotence.

There are three great divisions completing time—*past*, *present*, and *future*.

Three persons, in grammar, express and include all the relationships of mankind.

Thought, word, and deed, complete the sum of human capability.

Three degrees of comparison complete our knowledge of qualities.

The simplest proposition requires three things to complete it; viz., the *subject*, the *predicate*, and the *copula*.

Three propositions are necessary to complete the simplest form of argument—the *major premiss*, the *minor*, and the *conclusion*.

Three kingdoms embrace our ideas of matter—*mineral*, *vegetable*, and *animal*.

When we turn to the Scriptures, this completion becomes *Divine*, and marks Divine completeness or perfection.

Three is the first of four perfect numbers. (See p. 23.)

Three denotes *divine* perfection;
Seven denotes *spiritual* perfection;
Ten denotes *ordinal* perfection; and
Twelve denotes *governmental* perfection.

Hence the number *three* points us to what is real, essential, perfect, substantial, complete, and Divine. There is nothing real in man or of man. Everything "under the sun" and apart from God is "vanity." "Every man at his best estate is altogether vanity" (Ps. xxxix. 5, 11; lxii. 9; cxliv. 4; Eccles. i. 2, 14; ii. 11, 17, 26; iii. 19; iv. 4; xi. 8; xii. 8; Rom. viii. 20).

Three is the number associated with the Godhead, for there are "three persons in one God." Three times the Seraphim cry, "Holy, Holy, Holy"—one for each of the three persons in the Trinity (Isa. vi. 3): the living creatures also in Rev. iv. 8.

Three times is the blessing given in Num. vi. 23, 24:—

> "The LORD bless thee and keep thee (the Father);
> The LORD make His face shine upon thee; and be gracious unto thee (the Son);
> The LORD lift up His countenance upon thee, and give thee peace" (the Holy Spirit).

Each of these three blessings is two-fold, so that there are two members in each, while the name Jehovah occurs *three* times. This marks the blessing as Divine in its source. No merit drew it forth; grace was its origin and peace was its result.

In Gen. xviii. 2, the same three persons appear to Abraham. Abraham "looked, and, lo, THREE men stood by him." But verse 1 declares that it was "Jehovah appeared unto him." It is remarkable that Abraham addresses them both as one and as three. We read first that "they said," then "he said," and finally, in verses 13 and 17, 20, etc., "And the LORD said." The whole narrative, which begins with the appearance of the LORD, ends (verse 33), "And the LORD went His way."

As we have in the number *one* the sovereignty of the one God; and in *two* the second person, the Son, the great Deliverer; so in "three" we have the third person, the Holy Spirit, marking and completing "the fulness of the Godhead." This word "fulness" is remarkable, occurring only three times, and in connection with the Three Persons of the Trinity:

Eph. iii. 19, "The fulness of God."
Eph. iv. 13, "The fulness of Christ."
Col. ii. 9, "The fulness of the Godhead."

The "fulness" was manifested visibly in Christ, and is communicated by the Holy Spirit, for it is a fulness of which we receive by His mighty power (John i. 16).

This is why Abraham brought "three measures of meal" for his heavenly guest. This is why "three measures of meal" formed the great meal offering; because it set forth the perfection of Christ's perfect and Divine nature. In Leviticus no particular quantity of meal was prescribed, but in Num. xv. 9, we read, "Then shall he bring with the bullock a meal offering of THREE tenth deals of flour." This was the measure for the whole burnt offering, and also for great special occasions such as the New Moon and the New Year, etc. It was also the special measure for the cleansing of the leper (Lev. xiv. 10). The poor leper had several gracious blessings beyond others. He alone was favoured with the anointing which was given only to the Prophet, Priest, and King! albeit it was not the holy oil (10-18). It is sinners who are *now* singled out from the mass of those who are lost, and dead in trespasses and sins, to be anointed with the Spirit, and made, in Christ, kings and priests unto God.

But there is more in these "three measures of meal." We have them in the parable (Matt. xiii. 33), pointing to Christ in all the perfection of His person and His work, when He said, "Lo, I come to do Thy will, O God." There are different opinions about the "leaven," but what is the "meal." This is the point on which the interpretation turns. According to the popular interpretation, this pure "meal" is the corrupt mass of mankind, and the defiling "leaven" is the pure Gospel of Christ! Was there ever such an exhibition of man's perversity in calling sweet bitter, and bitter sweet? Was there ever such a proof that man's thoughts are contrary to God's? No! the "three measures of meal" point us to the perfections of Christ and the purity of His Gospel. And the hidden "leaven" points us to man's corruption of the Truth. A corruption for which we have to look, not after the third century, but in the *first!*

No leaven could be put into any sacrifice or offering made by fire to the LORD, because in Christ was no sin; therefore, there was to be no leaven. He was, in Himself, "a sweet savour to Jehovah."

True, in *one* offering there was leaven. But mark the difference and the lesson. In Lev. xxiii. we have a list of the Feasts:—

1st. The Passover (verse 5), on the 14th day.

2nd. The wave-sheaf of first-fruits on the morrow after the Sabbath (verse 11), which might be burnt on the altar as a sweet savour (Lev. ii. 14-16), because unleavened.

3rd. Then (50 days after) the oblation of the first-fruits at Pentecost (verses 15-17). This might not be burnt on the altar (Lev. ii. 12), because it was mixed with *leaven!*

In the antitype of this we see Christ:—

1st. Christ our Passover sacrificed for us.

2nd. As the wave-sheaf of first-fruits, He was raised from the dead and became the first-fruits of them that slept (1 Cor. xv. 20), for in Him there was no sin (and hence no leaven).

3rd. Then, after fifty days, on the Feast of Pentecost came the oblation of the first-fruits in the descent of the Holy Ghost; for "we are a kind of first-fruits of His creatures" (James i. 18). But His people are not without sin, therefore *this* oblation had *leaven* mixed with it. It could not be offered to the LORD as a "sweet savour" (Lev. ii. 12). It was accepted only because a *sin-offering was offered with it* (Lev. xxiii. 18, 19), and the Priest waved all together for a wave-offering before the LORD.

This proves that the "leaven" is a type of error, evil, and sin. While the "three measures of meal" with which it was mixed and hidden typified the truth and purity of Christ and His Truth, and not the corrupt mass of mankind amongst whom it was introduced. The popular interpretation reverses the types of the meal and the leaven, and makes the leaven that which is good, and the meal that which is evil. But the great Teacher made no such mistake. "Church doctrine" is not "Bible truth," but it is leavened meal.

The number *three*, therefore, must be taken as the number of *Divine fulness*. It signifies and represents the Holy Spirit as taking of the things of Christ and making them *real* and *solid* in our experience. It is only by the Spirit that we realise spiritual things. Without Him and His gracious operation, all is surface work: all is what a *plane* figure is to a *solid* (John iii. 6). He it is who has wrought all our works in us, and by whom alone we can serve or worship (John iv. 24).

Hence it is that the Holy of Holies, which was the central and highest place of worship, was a *cube.*

Hence it is that the *third* Book in the Bible is Leviticus, the book in which we learn what true worship is. Here we see Jehovah calling His people near unto Himself, prescribing every detail of their worship, leaving nothing to their imagination or their taste, crowning all with the "MUST" of the great rubric of John iv. 24. In true worship we see the FATHER seeking these true worshippers (John iv. 23); the SON, the one object of all worship; and the Spirit qualifying and enduing the worshippers with the only power in which they can worship. Thus in *Genesis* we have sovereignty in giving life—the Father, the beginning of all things; in *Exodus* we have the oppressor and the Deliverer—the Son redeeming His people; while in *Leviticus* we have the Spirit prescribing, and ordering, and empowering them for Divine worship.

THE FIRST OCCURRENCE

of the number is in Gen. i. 13. "The *third* day" was the day on which the earth was caused to rise up out of the water, symbolical of that resurrection life which we have in Christ, and in which alone we can worship, or serve, or do any "good works."

Hence *three* is a number of RESURRECTION, for it was on the *third* day that Jesus rose again from the dead. This was Divine in operation, and Divine in its prophetic foreshowing in the person of Jonah (Matt. xii. 39, 40; Luke xi. 29; Jonah i. 17). It was the *third* day on which Jesus was "perfected" (Luke xiii. 32). It was at the *third* hour He was crucified; and it was for *three* hours (from the 6th to the 9th) that darkness shrouded the Divine Sufferer and Redeemer. The "loud voice" at the end of those twice three hours, when, "about the ninth hour," He cried, "My God, My God, why hast Thou forsaken Me" (Matt. xxvii. 46), shows completely that nothing of nature, nothing of the light or intelligence of this world, could give help in that hour of darkness. Does not this show us *our* impotence in the matter? Does it not prove our incapacity to aid in delivering ourselves from our natural condition?

With the light at the ninth hour came the Divine declaration, "It is finished." So divinely finished, completed, and perfected, that now there is no such darkness for those who have died with Christ. Light, uninterrupted light, shines upon all who are risen with Him; uninterrupted sunshine—even "the glory of God in the face of Jesus Christ." That three hours' darkness, therefore, testifies to our complete ruin, and our complete salvation, and shows that His people are "complete in Him."

While we are speaking of the Divine perfections of Christ, let us note the many marks and seals of this completeness.

"The Spirit, the water, and the blood," are the divinely perfect witness to the grace of God on earth (1 John v. 7).

The three years of His seeking fruit testifies to the completeness of Israel's failure (Luke xiii. 7).

His three-fold "it is written" shows that the Word of God is the perfection of all ministry (Matt. iv.).

The Divine testimony concerning Him was complete in the threefold voice from Heaven (Matt. iii. 17; xvii. 5; John xii. 28).

He raised *three* persons from the dead.

The inscriptions on the Cross in three languages show the completeness of His rejection by Man.

The perfection of His offices are shown in His being Prophet, Priest, and King, raised up from among His brethren (Deut. xvii. 15; xviii. 3-5, and xviii. 15).

The Divine completeness of the Shepherd's care (John vi. 39), is seen in His revelation as—

The "Good Shepherd" in *death*, John x. 14.

The "Great Shepherd" in *resurrection*, Heb. xiii. 20.

The "Chief Shepherd" in *glory*, 1 Pet. iv. 5.

His three appearings in Heb. ix. show that His work will not be divinely perfect and complete until He appears again.

1. He "hath appeared" in the end of the age to "put away sin," and to "bear the sins of many" (Heb. ix. 26, 28).

2. "Now to appear in the presence of God for us," He has ascended into Heaven (verse 24).

3. He "shall appear" again apart from all question of sin for those who look for Him (verse 28).

Abraham's Covenant.

To go back to the Old Testament history we have God's Covenant with Abraham stamped with this number of Divine perfection (Gen. xv.). It was (like David's, 2 Sam. vii.) Divinely "ordered in all things, and sure." God was ONE, *i.e.*, the one party to it; for Abraham, who would willingly have been the other party, was put to sleep, that the Covenant might be *unconditional,* and "sure to all his seed." The Divine seal is seen in the choice of *three* animals, each of *three* years old (the heifer, the she-goat, and the ram). These, together with the two birds (the dove and the pigeon), made *five* in all, marking it all as a perfect act of free-grace on the part of a sovereign God.

The Complete Separation of Israel

is shown in "*the three days' journey* into the wilderness" (Exod. v. 3), marking the complete separation with which God would separate His people from Egypt then, and from the world now. We can understand Pharaoh's objection in first wishing them to hold their feast "in the land" (Exod. viii. 25), and when that could not be, at last consenting to their going, but adding, "only ye shall not go very far away." So Satan now, is well content that we should worship "in the land;" and if we must go into the wilderness, that we should be within easy reach of the world and its influences. Not so Jehovah. He will have no such borderland service; He will have a "scientific frontier," a divinely perfect "three days' journey into the wilderness," completely separating them from all their old associations. The difficulty of "drawing the line," which so many Christians experience, arises from the fact that it is a crooked line, and that it is an attempt to include that which cannot be included. Drawn at a proper distance it can be ruled straight, and be divinely perfect and effectual.

THE SPIES

brought *three* things which testified to the divinely perfect goodness of the land; and the substantial realities proved the truth of Jehovah's word: "Grapes, figs, and pomegranates" (Num. xiii. 23).

AT THE GIVING OF THE LAW

three times Israel said, "All that the LORD hath spoken we will do" (Exod. xix. 8; xxiv. 3, 7), marking the completeness of the Covenant-making on the part of Israel; but from that very reason foreshadowing its perfect breach, for man has never yet kept any Covenant which he made with God.

AHIMAN, SHESHAI, AND TALMAI,

were the three children of Anak, marking the completeness of the giant power of the enemy (Num. xiii. 22).

JORDAN

was three times divided, the perfection of the Divine miracle (Josh. iv.; 2 Kings ii. 8, 14).

THE THREE DAYS' SEARCH

for Elijah was conclusive testimony that he could not be found (2 Kings ii. 17).

THE TEMPLE

is marked by *three*, as the Tabernacle is by *five*. The Holy of Holies in each was a cube; in the Tabernacle a cube of ten cubits; in the Temple a cube of twenty cubits. Each consisted of *three* parts:—The Court, the Holy Place, and the Sanctuary. The Temple had *three* chambers round about. The Brazen Sea or Laver held *three* thousand baths; and was compassed by a line of thirty cubits on which were 300 knops (1 Kings vii. 24). It was supported by twelve oxen (3×4); three looking north, three looking west, three looking south, and three looking east. This order in naming the points of the compass occurs nowhere else. It is the same in both accounts of Kings and Chronicles (see 1 Kings vii. 25; 2 Chron. iv. 4, 5). Why is this? Is it because this was the order in which the Gospel was to be afterwards preached throughout the world? Whether this was the reason or not, the fact remains that the Gospel was preached first in the north (Samaria, Damascus, Antioch); then in the west (Cæsarea, Joppa, Cyprus, Corinth, Rome); then in the south (Alexandria and Egypt); then in the east (Mesopotamia, Babylon, Persia, India).

The Great Feasts

were three; Unleavened Bread, Weeks, Tabernacles (Deut. xvi. 16).

The Sheet

let down *three* times to Peter was the fulness of the testimony as to the admission of the Gentiles into the Church (Acts x. 16).

The Old Testament

Testimony was complete and perfect in its *three*-fold division—Law, Prophets, and Psalms (Luke xxiv. 44).* The same three divisions mark its character to the present day.

"Two or Three."

As *three* marks completeness and perfection of testimony, so it marks the number of spiritual worshippers; and intimates that true spiritual worshippers would always be few.

Completeness of People.

Shem, Ham, and Japheth.
Abraham, Isaac, and Jacob.
Gershom, Kohath, and Merari.
Saul, David, and Solomon.
Noah, Daniel, and Job.
Shadrach, Meshach, and Abednego.
Peter, James, and John, etc.

Completeness of Apostasy (*Jude* 11).

"The way of Cain."
"The error of Balaam."
"The gainsaying of Korah."

---

* See *The Names and Order of the Books of the Old Testament*, by the same author and publisher.

COMPLETENESS OF DIVINE JUDGMENT (*Dan.* vi. 25–28).

MENE. God hath NUMBERED thy kingdom and finished it.

TEKEL. Thou art WEIGHED in the balances and found wanting.

PERES. Thy kingdom is DIVIDED and given to the Medes and Persians.

THE THREE GIFTS OF GRACE:

Faith, Hope, and Love, five times repeated.

THE THREE-FOLD NATURE OF MAN:

Spirit, and Soul, and Body, the man consisting of neither separately, but of the whole three together.

THE THREE-FOLD NATURE OF TEMPTATION (1 John ii. 16).

"The lust of the flesh."
"The lust of the eyes."
"The pride of life."

These seen in our first parents when Eve saw (Gen. iii. 6) that the Tree of Knowledge of Good and Evil was—

"Good for food,"
"Pleasant to the eyes,"
"To be desired to make one wise."

THE THREE-FOLD CORRUPTION OF GOD'S WORD

By taking from,
adding to, and
altering.

This led up to the *first sin.*

(1) God had said, "of every tree in the garden thou mayest FREELY eat" (Gen. ii. 16). In repeating this, Eve *omitted* the word "freely" (iii. 2), making God less bountiful than He was.

(2) God had said, "But of the Tree of the Knowledge of Good and Evil, thou shalt not eat of it" (Gen. ii. 17).

In repeating this Eve *added* the words, "NEITHER SHALL YE TOUCH IT" (iii. 3), making God more severe than He was.

(3) God had said, "Thou shalt SURELY die" (Gen. iii. 17, מוֹת תָּמוּת). In repeating this Eve *altered* it to פֶּן־תְּמֻתוּן, "LEST ye die" (iii. 3), thus weakening the certainty of the Divine threat into a contingency.

No wonder that dealing thus with the Word of God she listened to the words of the Devil, and became an easy prey to his guile with which he deceived her.

No wonder also that "the second man," "the last Adam," when He was tempted by the same tempter, *three* times repeated the words "It is written"! as though to call attention to the occasion of the Fall in the three-fold perversion of God's words. "It is written," and I will not *omit* anything from it; "It is written," and I will not *add* anything to it; "It is written," and I will not *alter* it. It is worthy of note that both the temptations began in precisely the same way, by the Tempter questioning the truth of Jehovah's Word. In the former saying, "Hath God said?" In the latter saying, "If Thou be the Son of God" (Matt. iv. 3), when the voice from Heaven had only just declared, "This IS My beloved Son" (Matt. iii. 17).

Man's Three Great Enemies

are "the World, the Flesh, and the Devil":

The World is set over against the Father (1 John ii. 15, 16).
The Flesh is set over against the Spirit (Gal. v. 17).
The Devil is set over against the Son (the Living Word, Matt. iv. 1, etc., and 1 John iii. 8; and the Written Word, John viii. 44).

"Ask of Me."

To three people did God give this command:

To Solomon (1 Kings iii. 5).
To Ahaz (Isa. vii. 11).
And to the Messiah (Ps. ii. 9).

THE THREE PRAYERS OF MARK V.

form a divinely perfect lesson as to prayer and its answer.

(1.) Prayer was made by the Legion of *Devils*, who "BESOUGHT Him, saying, Send us into the herd of swine . . . and forthwith Jesus gave them leave" (*vv.* 12, 13).

(2.) Prayer was made by the *Gadarenes*, who "began to PRAY Him to depart out of their coasts" (*v.* 17). Jesus granted their request, and departed at once (*v.* 18).

(3.) Prayer was made by the man who had just been the recipient of marvellous grace and healing, who "PRAYED Him that he might be with Him. Howbeit Jesus suffered him not" (*vv.* 18, 19).

From this we learn the perfect lesson with regard to prayer, that "*No*" is an *answer* as well as "*Yes:*" and "No" is answered always with the same omnipotent grace, infinite wisdom, and perfect love as "Yes." We hear much about "definiteness in prayer." Surely the knowledge of one's intense ignorance as to what is best and wise for us, will make us say more definitely than ever, in the words of Him through whose merits alone prayer is heard at all, "Thy will be done."

THREE THINGS PREDICATED OF GOD
(in John's Gospel and Epistles).

"God is love" (1 John iv. 8, 16). We are therefore to "Walk in love" (Eph. v. 2).

"God is spirit" (John iv. 24, R.V., margin). We are exhorted to "Walk in the spirit" (Gal. v. 16).

"God is light"* (1 John i. 5). We are to "Walk in the light" (Eph. v. 8).

---

* Light, like God, is three-fold. It has three great rays :—

The *Heat* ray (red), which is *felt*, not seen, witnesses of the Father, "whom no man hath seen at any time" (John i. 18 ; 1 John iv. 12).

The *Light* ray (yellow), which is *seen*, not felt, witnesses of Jesus, who hath "declared the Father" (John i. 18 ; xii. 45 ; xiv. 9 ; Col. i. 15; Heb. i. 3).

The *Actinic* or chemical ray (blue), which is neither seen nor felt, but whose presence is revealed by its effects in a chemical *action*, which produces changes, as in Photography. This witnesses of the Holy Spirit, who is known by His wondrous operations (John iii. 8).

There are a multitude of *Threes* or Triads, and they all bespeak the same Divine perfection and completeness wherever they are found.

REVELATION I.

The first or introductory section of the Apocalypse of Jesus Christ is specially marked by this great Divine seal stamped upon it in chapter i.

v. 1. This Revelation is—
Divinely *given*,
Divinely *sent*,
Divinely *signified*.

v. 2. John bare record of—
The Divine "Word of God."
The Divine witness ("the Testimony of Jesus Christ").
The Divine vision ("all things that he saw").

v. 3. The Divine blessing on—
The reader,
The hearer, and
The keeper of this record.

vv. 4 and 8. The Divine Being—
Which was,
And which is,
And which is to come.

v. 5. The Coming Lord is presented as—
The Divine Prophet ("the faithful witness").
The Divine Priest ("the first-begotten from the dead").
The Divine King ("the Prince of the kings of the earth").

vv. 5, 6. His people are Divinely—
Loved,
Cleansed, and
Crowned.

vv. 17, 18. Christ is presented as—
"The first and the last" (Divinely eternal).
The dead and living One (Divinely living).
The omnipotent One (Divinely powerful).

v. 19. The Divine Revelation—
The things which thou hast seen,
Which are, and
Which shall be after these things.

Words that Occur Three Times

refer also in various ways to some Divinely perfect matter. We append a few examples, which may be studied in order to search out the lessons:—

אדר (*ah-dar*), glorious, Exod. xv. 6, 11; Isa. xlii. 21.

אפסי (*aph-see*), beside me, Isa. xlvii. 8, 10; Zeph. ii. 15.

גמולה (*g'moo-lāh*), recompense, 2 Sam. xix. 36; Isa. lix. 18; Jer. li. 56.

נכה (*nah-cheh*), lame, 2 Sam. iv. 4; ix. 3; contrite, Isa. lvi. 2.

עתיק (*at-teek*), ancient, Dan. vii. 9, 13, 22.

רפאות (*r'phoo-oth*), medicines, Jer. xxx. 13; xlvi. 11; Ezek. xxx. 21.

ἀββᾶ (*abba*), Father, Mark xiv. 36; Rom. viii. 15; Gal. iv. 6.

αἱρέομαι (*haireomai*), to choose, Phil. i. 22; 2 Thess. ii. 13; Heb. xi. 25.

ἀπόκρυφος (*apokruphos*), hid, Luke viii. 17; Col. ii. 3; kept secret, Mark iv. 22.

ἀποφθέγγομαι (*apophthengomai*), speak forth, Acts xxvi. 25; utterance, Acts ii. 4; say, Acts ii. 14.

ἀχειροποίητος (*acheiropoietos*), made without hands, Mark xiv. 58; 2 Cor. v. 1; Col. ii. 11.

εὐωδία (*eūōdia*), sweet savour, 2 Cor. ii. 15; Eph. v. 2; Phil. iv. 18.

κατευθύνω (*kateuthuno*), guide or direct, Luke i. 70; 1 Thess. iii. 11.; 2 Thess. iii. 5.

μορφή (*morphee*), form, Mark xvi. 12; Phil. ii. 6, 7.

Phrases that Occur Three Times

are also similarly significant.

"*Before the foundation of the world*" (πρὸ καταβολῆς κόσμου).

John xvii. 24. "Thou lovedst Me before," etc.

Eph. i. 4. "Chosen us in Him before," etc.

1 Pet. i. 20. "The blood of Christ foreordained before," etc. (when it speaks of this blood as "shed" it is ἀπό, *from* the foundation, etc.).

The phrase occurs three times, because it is the act of Deity, and flows from uninfluenced grace.

When, however, such acts relate to His work *in* us rather than *for* us, the words, even in a similar connection, occur *seven* times, because *seven* is the number of *spiritual* perfection. Hence the phrase, "From (ἀπό) the foundation of the world" occurs *seven* times. See under "*seven.*"

"*Walk worthy*" (περιπατεῖν ἀξίως, *peripatein axiōs*), walk worthily.

This occurs three times, as the Divine and perfect claim on our walk.

"Walk worthily"

Of our vocation (Eph. iv. 1),
Of the Lord (Col. i. 10),
Of God (1 Thess. ii. 12).

THE THREE-FOLD COMBINATIONS OF A NUMBER

denotes the essence of such number, the concentration of the significance of the number thus expressed.

444 is the gematria or number of the word "DAMASCUS," which is the oldest city in the world; *four* being the world number. (See under *Four.*)

666 is the number of *man*, and it symbolises fitly, therefore, the essence of human wisdom, and also of imperfection. (See further under *Six* and "666.")

888 is the number or gematria of the name "JESUS." (See under *Eight.*)

999 is the number connected with *judgment*, hence the numerical value of the phrase τῇ ὀργῇ μου (*tee orgee mou*), *my wrath*, is 999. The same number is very prominent in the judgment on Sodom. (See further under *Nine.*)

THE TALMUD

has many references, among other numbers, to the number *three*. The Rabbis say that there were

Three things Moses asked of God.

(1.) That the Schechinah might rest on Israel.
(2.) That it might rest on none but Israel.
(3.) That God's ways might be known to him.
(*Beracheth*, fol. 7, col. 1).

Three precious gifts were given to Israel.

(1.) The Law.
(2.) The Land.
(3.) The World to come (*i.e.*, the Heavenly Calling).

Three men

handed down the ancient wisdom and Divine secrets, viz., Adam, Seth, and Enoch.

Whatever may be thought of these, there can be no doubt that in the invariable employment of the number *three* in the Word of God, we have that which signifies Divine perfection.

FOUR.

We have seen that *three* signifies Divine perfection, with special reference to the Trinity: The Father, *one* in sovereignty; the Son, the *second* person, in incarnation and salvation, delivering from every enemy; the Holy Spirit, the *third* person, realising in us and to us Divine things.

Now the number *four* is made up of three and one (3 + 1 = 4), and it denotes, therefore, and marks that which follows the revelation of God in the Trinity, namely, *His creative works.* He is known by the things that are seen. Hence the written revelation commences with the words, "In-the-beginning God CREATED." Creation is therefore the next thing—the *fourth* thing, and the number *four* always has reference to all that is *created.* It is emphatically the *number of Creation;* of man in his relation to the world as created; while *six* is the number of man in his opposition to and independence of God. It is the number of things that have a beginning, of things that are made, of material things, and matter itself. It is the number of *material completeness.* Hence it is the *world number,* and especially the "city" number.

The *fourth* day saw the *material creation* finished (for on the *fifth* and *sixth* days it was only the *furnishing* and *peopling* of the earth with living creatures). The sun, moon, and stars completed the work, and they were to give light upon the earth which had been created, and to rule over the day and over the night (Gen. i. 14–19).

Four is the number of the great elements—earth, air, fire, and water.

Four are the regions of the earth—north, south, east, and west.

Four are the divisions of the day—morning, noon, evening, and midnight. Or in our Lord's words, when He speaks of His coming at evening, midnight, cock-crowing, or in the morning (Mark xiii. 35). We are never to put off His coming in our minds beyond to-morrow morning.

Four are the seasons of the year—spring, summer, autumn, and winter.

Four are the great variations of the lunar phases.

In Gen. ii. 10, 11, the one river of Paradise was parted, and became into *four* heads, and "the fourth river is Euphrates." Here, as so often elsewhere, the four is made up of 3 + 1. For three of these rivers are now unnamed, while *one* is still known by its original name "Euphrates."

Four marks *division* also. For the river was "*parted*." It is the first number which is not a "prime," the first which can be *divided*. It is the first *square* number also, and therefore it marks a kind of *completeness* as well, which we have called *material completeness*.

In the next chapter (Gen. iii. 22-24) the cherubim are first mentioned. These are *four*, and they have to do with *creation* always. They are first seen here, keeping, *i.e.*, guarding (Gen. ii. 15), the Tree of Life, and thus preserving the blessed hope of immortality for creation. They are next seen in connection with atonement, showing the only ground on which creation could hope for the end of its groaning. They are seen on the veil and on the mercy-seat, binding up the hope of creation with Him who is called "the Hope of Israel." So that there is no hope for a groaning creation apart from atonement, apart from Christ, or apart from Israel. In the Apocalypse the same four cherubim are called *Ζῶα*, "the living creatures" (Rev. iv.). These announce the Coming One; these sing of *creation* and of Him who created all things, and for whose pleasure they were created (Rev. iv. 11). Whenever they speak it is in connection with the earth. These call forth and announce the judgments or plagues (Rev. vi.) which issue in the ejection of the Usurper from the earth, and the destruction of them which destroy the earth, and in the exaltation and enthronement of Him when all the kingdoms of the world become the kingdom of our Lord and His anointed, and when the LORD God omnipotent reigneth.

Hence it was that these four cherubic forms were placed in the Signs of the Zodiac, and so placed that they divide it into *four* equal parts, thus uniting in one the twelve signs which set forth the blessed hope of a groaning creation, which waits for the Promised Seed of the woman to come and crush the serpent's head and bring in universal blessing.*

* See *The Witness of the Stars*, by the same author.

They are the *four* heads of animal creation: the lion, of wild beasts; the ox, of tame beasts; the eagle, of birds; and man the head of all. Again we have the *four* divided into 3 + 1: three animal, and one human.

They mark the purpose of God from the moment the curse was pronounced, and are the pledge that it will one day be removed.

Other characteristics mark the cherubim off from all else. They are not Divine, for they are never worshipped, and all likeness of God was forbidden; moreover the God-head is presented at the same time with them, for they are connected with His throne. They are distinguished from angels, and they are never dismissed on errands. They are distinguished from the Church in Rev. v. 9, 10, a passage which is supposed to prove their identity with it; for in verse 9, the word "us" should be omitted, with Lachmann, Tischendorf, Alford, Westcott and Hort, and the R.V.; and the words "us" and "we" in verse 10, should be "them" and "they" (with *all* the textual and ancient authorities), the verses reading as in R.V.:—"Thou wast slain, and didst purchase unto God with Thy blood, *men* of every tribe, and tongue, and people, and nation,* and madest them to be unto our God a kingdom and priests; and they reign upon the earth."

The fact, therefore, of the living creatures being *four* (and no other number) marks them as connected with *Creation*, and as a symbolical representation that its hope of deliverance from the curse is bound up with the blood-shedding of the coming Redeemer.

The Four-fold Division of Mankind.

In Gen. x., "the generations of the sons of Noah" are comprised in a four-fold description. However the order may be varied, the number is preserved:

Verse 5.	lands,	tongues,	families,	nations.
,, 20.	families,	tongues,	countries,	nations.
,, 31.	families,	tongues,	lands,	nations.

In Revelation there are seven similar descriptions, and though no two are alike, yet the number four is pre-

* Note the *four*-fold description.

served. See Rev. v. 9; vii. 9; x. 11; xi. 9; xiii. 7*; xiv. 6; xvii. 15.

The *three* in Genesis, and *seven* in Revelation make *ten* such descriptions in all, which is the number of ordinal perfection.

The Great Prophetic World-powers

are four, and these are divided into 3 + 1, where the one stands out in great and marked contrast to the other three. The first three wild beasts are *named* (lion, bear, leopard); while the *fourth* is only described, not named (Dan. vii. 7, 23).

So in the image of Nebuchadnezzar's dream, *three* are metals; *one* is a mixture of metal and mire!

In Dan. vii. 2, 3 we read, "The FOUR winds of the heaven STROVE upon the great sea, and FOUR beasts came up from the sea DIVERSE one from another." Such is the history of man's power in the world—*strife* and *division!*

No sooner are mankind *divided* in Gen. x., than Abraham is called out from them to walk with God (Gen. xi., xii.). But he soon finds it to be a world of strife and enmity, for Gen. xiv. opens with the names of *four* kings, and "these made war" with *five* others which are named afterwards.

The Fourth Book

of the Bible is Numbers. In Hebrew it is called *B'Midbar*, i.e., *the Wilderness*. The gematria of *B'Midbar* is 248 (4 × 62).

It relates to the earth, which is a wilderness compared with Heaven; and to our pilgrimage through it. It tells of Meribah and *striving* (xx. 13), and records the history of the murmurings, rebellions, and wanderings.

The Fourth Book of the Psalms

is the Book of the Wilderness.† The first Psalm is the "Prayer of Moses, the man of God,"—the man of the wilderness. All the illustrations and metaphors, etc., are drawn from the *earth*, and this fourth book sets forth

---

* In Rev. xiii. 7, the A.V. gives only *three;* but the R.V., with G., L., T., Tr., A., W. & H., give καὶ λαόν (*kai laon*), *people*, thus making *four*.

† See *A Key to the Psalms*, Appendix, by the same author.

Jehovah's counsels and purposes in relation to the *earth.* (See Psalms xc.—cvi).

In the *First Book of the Psalms* (i.—xli.), the *fourth* Psalm has to do with earth.* It tells how there is nothing satisfying in it; that apart from God there can be no real prosperity in the earth.

> "Many there be that say, Who will show us any good?
> LORD, lift Thou up the light of Thy countenance upon us.
> Thou hast put gladness in my heart
> More than they have when their corn and their wine are increased."—(Ps. iv. 6, 7, R.V.)

We may note also the *fourth* Psalms of the other Books of the Psalms, viz.:—Ps. xlv. (the *fourth* of the second book), Ps. lxxvi. (the *fourth* of the third book), Ps. xciii. (the *fourth* of the fourth book), and Ps. cx. (the *fourth* of the fifth book). All these tell of Dominion in the earth, and they speak of the coming reign of earth's rightful King and Lord.

The *Fourth* Commandment is the first that refers to the earth.

The *fourth* clause of the Lord's Prayer is the first that mentions the earth.

FOUR IN CONTRAST WITH SEVEN.

Seven stamps everything with *spiritual* perfection, for it is the number of heaven, and stands therefore in contrast to the earth. Hence, when in Rev. v. 12 the heavenly multitudes praise, they praise with a *seven*-fold blessing, and say:

"Worthy is the Lamb that was slain to receive (1) power, and (2) riches, and (3) wisdom, and (4) strength, and (5) honour, and (6) glory, and (7) blessing."

Whereas in *v.* 13, when the created earthly beings praise,—the creatures that are "on the earth, and under the earth, and such as are in the sea, and all that are in them"—when these join in *their* ascription, it is only *four-fold*:—(1) "Blessing, and (2) honour, and (3) glory, and (4) power, be unto Him that sitteth upon the throne, and unto the Lamb for ever and ever."

---

* The *first* Psalm speaks of Genesis and the counsels of God for man. The *second* tells of Exodus and deliverance from the hand of the enemy. The *third* tells of Leviticus—of Salvation being of the Lord, and how His blessing can be upon His people.

THE DEATH AND LIFE OF CHRIST

are set forth by a *four*-fold type and record.

His death. The four great offerings (Ps. xl. 6).*

a | "Sacrifice (peace offering), and offering (meal offering), Thou wouldest not:

b | Mine ears hast Thou opened.

a | Burnt offering and sin offering hast Thou not required.

b | Then said I, Lo, I come," etc.

Four great offerings were necessary to set forth the four aspects of the Lord's death. No one offering alone could do this. Hence we have (1) the Burnt offering, (2) the Meal offering, (3) the Peace offering, and (4) the Sin and Trespass offerings.

Of the four great offerings, three were connected with blood and life; while *one* was meal.

The meal offering (Lev. ii.) was either baked in *three* ways (oven, flat-plate, or frying-pan); or not at all.

The sin offering (Lev. iv.) was offered for three classes of individuals—

The Priest that is anointed (*v.* 3),
The Ruler (*v.* 22),
The Common person (*v.* 27)—

or for the whole congregation as *one* (*v.* 13).

For the same reason that Four offerings were required to set forth the great aspects of the Lord's *death*, Four Gospels are required to set forth the different aspects of the Lord's *life* on earth.

These are, in like manner, seen to be divided into three and one, and this, not from any of the alleged reasons of the Modern Critics which give rise to their Terminology concerning "the Synoptic Gospels" and "the Fourth Gospel," but because this division into *three* and *one*, is necessitated by the facts of the case.

In the Four Gospels the Lord Jesus is presented in four different aspects, *three* of which are on the side of His Humanity, and *one* on the side of His Deity.

---

* Here the alternate structure shows that "b" and "*b*" relate to the obedience of Christ as the fifth great offering to which the *four* pointed.

These *three* are united by one fact, common to each of them, viz., the perfect humanity of the Lord; while the three are one, united by the word "Branch" which is used of each. In the one (JOHN) the Lord is presented as GOD, and He, too, is called the Branch" (Isa. iv. 2).

The materials of the Tabernacle were *four*, *three* being metals (gold, silver, brass); and *one* non-metal (wood).

The coverings of the Tabernacle were *four*,—*three* animal (goats' hair, rams' skins, and badger skins*); and *one* vegetable (fine linen).

The ornamentations of the curtains were *four*, *three* being *colours* (blue, purple and scarlet); while *one* was a pattern (the cherubim.)

The Priests and Levites were of *four* orders or persons: *one* was Aaron and his sons (Aaronites); the *three* were the sons of Gershon, Kohath, and Merari (Levites).

The Manna (Exod. xvi. 14, 31) has a *four*-fold description, *three* referring to sight or appearance (small, white, round); and *one* to taste (sweet).

Of the four prohibited or unclean animals, *three* chewed the cud, but did not divide the hoof (camel, hare, and coney); while *one* divided the hoof, but did not chew the cud (the swine); and thus the swine stands out in marked contrast to the other three.

Of the four Houses of God (*i.e.*, erected by Divine plan) in the earth, *three* were, or will be, material, *viz.*, the Tabernacle, the Temple (Solomon's), and Ezekiel's; whilst the *one* is a Spiritual house (1 Pet. ii. 5).

Four houses were built by Solomon; three were for himself,—his own house (1 Kings vii. 1), the house of the forest of Lebanon (*v.* 2), the house for Pharaoh's daughter (*v.* 8); while *one* was the House of the LORD (1 Kings vi. 37).

---

* No badgers were ever found so far south as Palestine. The word תַּחַשׁ (*Tachash*) is a word of uncertain meaning, but it refers to an animal the skins of which were used (Exod. xxv. 5; xxvi. 14; Num. iv. 6, 8, etc.). The ancient versions understand it as a *colour* (the LXX., Chald., and Syr., as *red*, Arabic, *black*). It was probably the red or dark skins of the larger sacrificial animals; the two smaller animals are named as being goats and rams.

God's four sore judgments in the earth (Ezek. xiv. 21): *three* are inanimate (the sword, famine, and pestilence); while *one* is animate (the noisome beast).

In Jer. xv. 3, they are still *four*, but *three* are animate (dogs, fowls, and beasts), and *one* is inanimate (the sword).

Of the four kinds of flesh in 1 Cor. xv. 39, *three* are animals (beasts, birds, and fishes); while *one* is human (man).

The four glories of 1 Cor. xv. 40, 41: *three* are celestial and are detailed (the sun, moon, and stars); while *one* is not detailed and is terrestrial.

The body is sown and raised (1 Cor. xv. 42–44) in *three* ways that relate to corruptibility:

sown "in corruption, raised in incorruption";
sown "in dishonour, raised in glory";
sown "in weakness, raised in power";

while in the *one*, "it is sown a natural body; it is raised a spiritual body."

In the parable of the sower (Matt. xiii.) the kinds of soil are four; but *three* are characterised as being all alike in contrast to the one (viz., the wayside, the stony ground, and the thorns). These are all *unprepared!* while the *one* is good because it is *prepared!* The essence of the parable lies in this. It reduces the four soils to two, and confirms what is said of the *two religions* on pp. 96, 97.

In the Lost Son's welcome (Luke xv.), *three* things were material (the robe, the ring, and the shoes); while *one* was moral (the kiss).

"*The Seventy*" went forth with a four-fold prohibition (Luke x. 4), of which *three* related to matters (carry no purse, no scrip, no shoes); while *one* related to action ("salute no man by the way").

God's four-fold witness in the earth (Heb. ii. 4): *three* are impersonal (signs, wonders, and miracles), and *one* personal (the gifts of the Holy Ghost).

Fours of Persons.

The *four* of the Book of Job:—

Eliphaz, Bildad, Zophar (friends); and Elihu (mediator).

The children of Lamech:—

Jubal, Jabal, Tubal-Cain (sons); and Naamah (daughter).

The *four* bound with brass:—

Samson (Judg. xvi. 21) ... ... } not liberated.
Jehoiachim (2 Chron. xxxvi. 6) ... ... }
Zedekiah (2 Kings xxv. 7; Jer. lii. 11 and xxxix. 7) ... ... }
Manasseh (2 Chron. xxxiii. 11) ... ... liberated.

The *four* whose names were changed:—

Abram (Gen. xxvii. 5) ... } in blessing.
Sarai (Gen. xxvii. 15) ... }
Jacob (xxxv. 10; xxxii. 28) }
Pashur (Jer. xx. 3) ... in judgment.

Four Prophetesses of the Old Testament:—

Miriam (Exod. xv. 20) ... } good.
Deborah (Judg. iv. 4) ... }
Huldah (2 Kings xxii. 14) }
Noadiah (Neh. vi. 14) ... bad.

The *four* "children" of the Book of Daniel:—

Daniel ... alone.
Shadrach } together.
Meshach }
Abednego }

The *four* in the furnace:—

Shadrach } human.
Meshach }
Abednego }
The son of God, Spiritual.*

The *four* kings named in Daniel:—

Nebuchadnezzar (i.–iv.) } the first and last of Babylon.
Belshazzar (v.) ... }
Darius (vi.) "the Median" (v. 31).
Cyrus (vi. 28; x. 1) "the Persian."

The *four* women in the Lord's genealogy (Matt. i.):—

Thamar (Gen. xxxviii. 27, &c.; Matt. i. 3).
Rahab (Ruth iv. 20; Matt. i. 5).
Ruth (Ruth iv. 13, 14; Matt. i. 5).
Wife of Uriah (2 Sam. xii. 24; Matt. i. 6).

---

* There is no article. It is literally "a son of God," *i.e.* an angel.

Four names of Satan in Rev. xx. 2 :—
The Dragon (rebellious and apostate).
The Old Serpent (seductive).
The Devil (accusing).
Satan (personal).

The *four*-fold witness to show Nature's inability to find wisdom (Job xxviii. 7, 8) :—
The fowl.
The vulture's eye.
The lion's whelps.
The fierce lion.

Four things "little and wise" * (Prov. xxx. 24–28) :—
The ant.
The coney.
The locust.
The spider.

The brazen altar which displayed the Divine judgment is *four* sided, and had four horns. So with the golden altar.

The camp was *four*-square.

The rainbow, which has special reference to the earth and its judgment, is mentioned *four* times,—twice in the Old Testament (Gen. ix. and Ezek. i. 28) and twice in the New Testament (Rev. iv. 3; x. 1).

The fulness of material blessing in the earth is described in Isa. lx. 17 :—
For brass I will bring gold.
For iron I will bring silver.
For wood I will bring brass.
For stones I will bring iron.

The sphere of suffering is *four*-fold in 2 Cor. iv. 8, 9:—
Troubled, but not distressed.
Perplexed, but not in despair.
Persecuted, but not forsaken.
Cast down, but not destroyed.

---

* See *Sunday School Lessons*, First series, pp. 37–40, by the same author.

The prophecy of Zechariah which has special reference to the earth:—

In ch. i. we have the *four* horns or Gentile powers, and the *four* carpenters to fray them.

In ch. vi. we have the *four* chariots with horses of *four* colours, signifying the spirits of the heavens acting for God in the midst of the *four* Gentile powers.

Gematria.

This is too large a subject to enter on here, but it is most significant that we get the number *four* in its concentrated form in connection with דַּמֶּשֶׂק, Damascus, which is the oldest city in the world. The number of its name is 444: thus—

ד = 4
מ = 40
שׂ = 300
ק = 100
} 444.

The name occurs 39 times, *i.e.*, 3 × 13, for the significance of which see under the number 13.

Words that Occur Four Times

partake also the same significance. We give a few from the commencement of the alphabet, and a careful study of them and others will bring out much interesting and instructive information:

אבדה (*ăvēh-dāh*), "lost thing," Exod. xxii. 9; Lev. vi. 3, 4; Deut. xxii. 3.

גבה (*gah-vah*), "high-look or proud," Ps. ci. 5; Prov. xvi. 5; Eccles. vii. 8; Ezek. xxxi. 3.

גנה (*gin-nah*), "garden," Est. i. 5; vii. 7, 8; Song vi. 11.

דגל (*dah-gal*), "banners," Ps. xx. 6; Song v. 10; vi. 4, 10.

דך (*dack*), "oppressed or afflicted," Ps. ix. 9; x. 18; lxxiv. 21; Prov. xxvi. 28.

חרבה (*chah-rah-vah*), "dry land," 8 times (2 × 4).

חרש (*cheh-resh*), "craftsmen," Jos. ii. 1 ("secretly," *i.e.* as craftsmen), 1 Chron. iv. 14, *marg.*; Neh. xi. 35; Isa. iii. 3 ("cunning").

משכרת (*mas-koh-reth*), "wages," Gen. xxix. 15; xxxi. 7, 41; "reward," Ruth ii. 12.*

נסח (*nah-sach*), "plucked," Deut. xxviii. 63; "pluck," Ps. lii. 7; "rooted out," Prov. ii. 22; "destroy," xv. 25.

נצר (*neh-tzer*), "branch," Isa. xi. 1; xiv. 19; lx. 21; Dan. xi. 7.

נשא (*nah-shah*), "to be in debt," 1 Sam. xxii. 2; Neh. v. 7; Ps. lxxxix. 22; Isa. xxiv. 2.

ἄγνοια (*agnoia*), "ignorance," Acts iii. 17; xvii. 30; Eph. iv. 18; 1 Pet. i. 14.

ἀγρυπνέω (*agrupneō*), "watch," Mark xiii. 33; Luke xxi. 36; Eph. vi. 18; Heb. xiii. 17.

αἴτιον (*aition*), "fault," Luke xxiii. 4, 14, 22; Acts xix. 40.

ἀμνός (*amnos*), "Lamb," John i. 29, 36; Acts viii. 32; 1 Pet. i. 19.

ἄνθος (*anthos*), "flower," James i. 10, 11; 1 Pet. i. 24 (twice).

ἀστήρ (*asteer*), "star," 24 times (4 × 6).†

ἄστρον (*astron*), "star," Luke xxi. 25; Acts vii. 43; xxvii. 20; Heb. xi. 12.†

ἀποστολή (*apostolee*), "apostleship," Acts i. 25; Rom. i. 5; 1 Cor. ix. 2; Gal. ii. 8.

---

* But "gift" occurs five times.

† The two words together 28 times (4 × 7).

FIVE.

Five is four *plus* one (4 + 1). We have had hitherto the three persons of the Godhead, and their manifestation in creation. Now we have a further revelation of a People called out from mankind, redeemed and saved, to walk with God from earth to heaven. Hence, Redemption follows creation. Inasmuch as in consequence of the fall of man creation came under the curse and was "made subject to vanity," therefore man and creation must be redeemed. Thus we have:

1. Father.
2. Son.
3. Spirit.
4. Creation.
5. Redemption.

These are the five great mysteries, and *five* is therefore the number of GRACE.

If *four* is the number of the world, then it represents man's weakness, and helplessness, and vanity, as we have seen.

But four *plus* one (4 + 1 = 5) is significant of Divine strength added to and made perfect in that weakness; of omnipotence combined with the impotence of earth; of Divine *favour* uninfluenced and invincible.

The word "the earth" is הארץ (*Ha-Eretz*).

The gematria of this word is 296, a multiple of *four*; while the word for "the heavens" is השמים (*Ha-shemayeem*), the gematria of which is 395, a multiple of *five*.

The gematria of ἡ χάρις (*grace*) is 725, a multiple of the square of five ($5^2 \times 29$).

The numerical value of the words "My grace is sufficient for thee" (Ἀρκεῖ σοι ἡ χάρις μου) is 1845, of which the factors are $5 \times 3^2 \times 41$. (See pp. 76, 77.)

Grace means *favour*. But what kind of favour? for favour is of many kinds. Favour shown to the *miserable* we call mercy; favour shown to the *poor* we call pity; favour shown to the *suffering* we call compassion; favour shown to the *obstinate* we call patience: but favour shown to the *unworthy* we call GRACE! This is favour indeed; favour which is truly Divine in its source and in its character. Light is thrown upon it in Rom. iii. 24, "being justified freely by His grace." The word here translated "freely" occurs again in John xv. 25, and is translated "without a cause" ("they hated me without a cause"). Was there any real cause why they hated the Lord Jesus? No! Nor is there any cause in us why God should ever justify us. So we might read Rom. iii. 24 thus: "Being justified without a cause by His grace." Yes, this is grace indeed,—favour to the unworthy.

It was so with Abram. There was no cause in him why God should have called him and chosen him! There was no cause why God should have made an unconditional covenant with him and his seed for ever. Therefore the number *five* shall be stamped upon this covenant by causing it to be made with *five* sacrifices—a heifer, a goat, a ram, a dove, and a pigeon (Gen. xv. 9). See pp. 54, 113.

It is remarkable, also, that afterwards, when God changed Abram's name to Abraham (Gen. xvii. 5), the change was made very simply, but very significantly (for there is no chance with God), by inserting in the middle of it the *fifth* letter of the alphabet, ה (*Hey*), the symbol of the number *five*, and אברם, Abram, became אברהם AbraHam (Gen. xvii. 5). All this was of *grace*, and it is stamped with this significance. It is worthy of note that this change was made at a particular moment. It was when Abraham was called to "walk before" God in a very special manner. He was to look for the promised "seed" from no earthly source, and thus he was to "walk by faith and not by sight." It was at this moment that God revealed Himself *for the first time* by His name of EL SHADDAI, *i.e.* the *all bountiful One!* able to supply all Abraham's need; able to meet all his necessities; able to do for him all that he required. How gracious! How suitable! How perfect! It is the same in 2 Cor. vi. 17, 18, when we are called, as Abraham was, to "come out," to "be separate," and walk by faith with God. He reveals himself (for the first time in the New Testament) by the same wonderful name, "Ye shall be My sons and daughters, saith the Lord ALMIGHTY!"—able to support and to sustain you; able to supply all your need. This is grace.

THE FIFTH BOOK OF THE BIBLE (DEUTERONOMY) magnifies the grace of God, and in it special pains, so to speak, are taken to emphasise the great fact that not for the sake of the people, but for God's own Name's sake had He called, and chosen, and blessed them. Read Deut. iv. 7, 20, 32, 37; viii. 11, 17, etc.

THE FIFTH BOOK OF PSALMS sets forth the same great fact. Its first Psalm (Ps. cvii.) magnifies this, and shows how "He sent His word and healed them" (*v.* 20), and again and again delivered them out of all their trouble.

THE FIFTH PSALM OF THE FIRST BOOK has also special reference to God's "FAVOUR," or grace, with which He encompasses His people. Ps. v. 12, "For thou LORD wilt bless the righteous; with FAVOUR wilt Thou compass him (Heb. *crown him*) as with a shield."

THE "STONE" KINGDOM will be the *fifth* kingdom, succeeding and comprehending the four great world-powers, absorbing all earthly dominion, when the kingdoms of this world shall become the kingdom of our Lord and of His Anointed, and He shall reign in glory and in grace.

ISRAEL CAME OUT OF EGYPT five in a rank. In Exod. xiii. 18 it says, "The children of Israel went up harnessed out of the land of Egypt." In the margin it says they went up *by five in a rank,* חמשים from חמש, *five.* It may be *in ranks, i.e. fifties,* as in 2 Kings i. 9 and Isa. iii. 5.* The point is that they went up in perfect weakness; help-

* In Joshua i. 14, "Ye shall pass over before your brethren armed." Margin: "Heb., *marshalled by five.*" This may have some reference to the fact that the number *five* was specially hateful to the Egyptians, if indeed it were not the cause of such hatred. Sir Gardner Wilkinson tells us that even down to the present day the number *five* is regarded as an *evil* number in modern Egypt. On their watches the *fifth* hour, "V," is marked by a small circle, "o."

less, and defenceless; *but* they were invincible through the presence of Jehovah in their midst.

"Five Smooth Stones"

were chosen by David when he went to meet the giant enemy of Israel (1 Sam. xvii. 40). They were significant of his own perfect weakness supplemented by Divine strength. And he was stronger in this weakness than in all the armour of Saul. It is worthy of note that after all he used only the *one*, not any of the *four*. That one was sufficient to conquer the mightiest foe.

It was the Fifth Book

that David's son and David's Lord used in His conflict with that great enemy of whom Goliath was the faintest type. It was only the Book of Deuteronomy which formed the *one stone* with which he defeated the Devil himself (compare Matt. iv. 1–11 and Deut. viii. 3; vi. 13, 16). No wonder that this Book of Deuteronomy is the object of Satan's hatred. "No marvel" that to-day his ministers, "transformed as the ministers of righteousness" (2 Cor. xi. 14, 15), are engaged in the attempt to demolish this Book of Deuteronomy with their destructive criticism. But their labour is all in vain, for it is stamped with the number which marks the omnipotence of Jehovah's power and grace.

The Promise.

"Five of you shall chase a thousand, and a hundred of you shall put ten thousand to flight" (Lev. xxvi. 8), conveys the truth elsewhere revealed;—"If God be for us who can be against us?" (Rom. viii. 31). But note, it does not say "five shall chase a thousand"; but "five OF YOU,"—five of those whom God has redeemed and delivered, and whom He will strengthen with His own might.

The Preference.

"I had rather speak *five* words with the understanding, than ten thousand words in an unknown tongue" (1 Cor. xiv. 19). That is to say, a few words spoken in the fear of God, in human weakness, depending on Divine strength and blessing, will be able to accomplish that which God has purposed; while words without end will be spoken in vain. Man may applaud the latter and bestow his admiration on their eloquence. But God will own only the former, and follow them with this blessing, making them to work effectually in them that believe (1 Thess. i. 6; ii. 13).

JEHOVAH'S DEMAND TO PHARAOH

was *five*-fold in its nature, because it was the expression of His grace in the deliverance of His people. It brought out, therefore, five distinct objections from Pharaoh. Jehovah's demand sprang purely from His own spontaneous grace. Nothing necessitated it; neither Israel's misery nor Israel's merit called it forth. "God heard their groaning, and God remembered HIS covenant with Abraham, with Isaac, and with Jacob. And God looked upon the children of Israel, and God had respect unto them" (Exod. ii. 24, 25). It was not their covenant with God, as with Israel afterwards at Sinai; but it was God's covenant which HE had made with their fathers. All was of grace. Hence, Jehovah's demand to Pharaoh (in Exod. v. 1) was stamped by the *five* great facts which it embraced:

(1.) **Jehovah and His Word.**—"Thus saith Jehovah, God of Israel." To this was opposed the objection of Pharaoh (*v.* 2), "Who is Jehovah that I should obey His voice?"

(2.) **Jehovah's People.**—"Let my people go." To this Pharaoh objected (x. 9-11), "Who are they that shall go?" Moses said, "We will go with our young and with our old, with our sons and with our daughters, etc." "Not so; go now, ye that are men" (x. 11), was Pharaoh's reply. In other words, God's people consist of His *redeemed;* and the enemy will be quite content for parents to go and serve God in the wilderness, provided they will leave their little ones behind in Egypt!

(3.) **Jehovah's Demand.**—"Let my people go." No, said Pharaoh; "Go ye, sacrifice to your God in the land" (viii. 25). And many think to-day that they can worship in Egypt, but "Moses said, It is not meet so to do" (viii. 26).

(4.) **Jehovah's Feast.**—"That they may hold a feast unto me." Pharaoh's objection was (x. 24), "Go ye, serve the LORD; only let your flocks and your herds be stayed." How subtle was the opposition! But how perfect was Moses's reply (x. 26), "We know not with what we must serve the LORD until we come thither." We cannot know God's will for us until we are on God's ground. Light for the second step will not be given until we have used the light given for the first.

(5.) **Jehovah's Separation.**—"In the wilderness." When Pharaoh objected to their going at all, and wished them to serve God "in the land," Moses insisted on a separation of "three days' journey into the wilderness" (viii. 27). There must be a divinely perfect separation of the redeemed from Egypt and all its belongings. See p. 113.

But now Pharaoh's objection is more subtle. He said (viii. 28), "I will let you go, that ye may sacrifice to the LORD your God in the wilderness; only ye shall not go very far away!" Oh! how many yield to this temptation, and are always within easy reach of the world. Living within the borderland, they are always open to the enemy's enticements, and always in danger of his snares.

Behold, here, then, the perfection of grace, manifested in the demand of Jehovah for those "whom He hath redeemed from the hand of the enemy" (Ps. cvii. 2). Each of its five-fold parts was stoutly resisted by the enemy, but the grace of Jehovah is invincible.

THE TABERNACLE

had *five* for its all-pervading number; nearly every measurement was a multiple of *five.* Before mentioning these measurements we ought to notice that worship itself is all of grace! No one can worship except those who are sought and called of the Father (John iv. 23). "Blessed is the man whom Thou choosest and causest to approach unto Thee, that he may dwell in Thy courts; we shall be satisfied with the goodness of Thy house, even of Thy holy temple" (Ps. lxv. 4).

The Divine title of the book we call Leviticus is in the Hebrew Canon "He CALLED." It is the book of worship, showing how those who are to worship must be called by God, and showing how He wills to be approached. The book opens with the direction that if any man will bring an offering to the Lord he shall bring such and such an offering. The offerers and the priests are told minutely all that is to be done. Nothing is left to their imagination.

We have seen that Leviticus is the *third* book of the Bible. It comes to us stamped with the number of Divine perfection. The opening words are, "And Jehovah spake," an expression which occurs in the book 36 times ($3^2 \times 2^2$).*

Indeed, this third book is unique, consisting, as it does, almost wholly of the words of Jehovah. No other book of the Bible is so full of Divine utterances. It is fitting, therefore, that the number three should be stamped upon it.

> "I AM JEHOVAH" occurs 21 times (3 × 7).†
> "I AM THE JEHOVAH YOUR GOD" occurs 21 times (3 × 7).‡
> "I JEHOVAH AM" occurs *three* times (xix. 1; xx. 26; xxi. 8); and "I JEHOVAH DO" twice (xxi. 15; xxii. 9), or *five* times together.

Here then we have Divine communication, and the number of Deity stamped upon it. This might have been brought out under the number *three*, but it is well to have it here in connection with worship as springing from the will of God, and being founded in grace.

The Tabernacle has this number of grace (*five*) stamped upon it.

---

* Lev. iv. 1; v. 14; vi. 1, 8, 19, 24; vii. 22, 28; viii. 1; x. 8; xi. 1; xii. 1; xiii. 1; xiv. 1, 33; xv. 1; xvi. 1, 2; xvii. 1; xviii. 1; xix. 1; xx. 1; xxi. 1, 16; xxii. 1, 17, 26; xxiii. 1, 9, 23, 26, 33; xxiv. 1, 13; xxv. 1; xxvii. 1.

† Lev. xi. 45; xviii. 5, 6, 22; xix. 12, 14, 16, 18, 28, 30, 32, 37; xx. 8; xxi. 12; xxii. 2, 8, 31, 32, 33; xxvi. 2, 45.

‡ Lev. xi. 44; xviii. 4, 30; xix. 3, 4, 10, 25, 31, 34, 36; xx. 7, 24; xxiii. 22, 43; xxiv. 22; xxv. 17, 38, 55; xxvi. 1, 13, 44.

The outer court was 100 cubits long and 50 cubits wide. On either side were 20 pillars, and along each end were 10 pillars, or 60 in all; that is 5 × 12, or grace in governmental display before the world, 12 being the number of the Tribes.

The pillars that held up the curtains were 5 cubits apart and 5 cubits high, and the whole of the outer curtain was divided into squares of 25 cubits (5 × 5). Each pair of pillars thus supported an area of 5^2 cubits of fine white linen, thus witnessing to the perfect grace by which alone God's people can witness for Him before the world. Their own righteousness (the fine linen) is "filthy rags" (Isa. lxiv. 6), and we can only say "by the grace of God I am what I am" (1 Cor. xv.)—a sinner saved by grace. This righteousness is based on *atonement*, for 5 × 5 was also the measure of the brazen altar of burnt offering. This was the perfect answer of Christ to God's righteous requirements, and to what was required of man.

True, this brazen altar was only 3 cubits high, but this tells us that the provision was Divine in its origin, that atonement emanates solely from God.

The *building* itself was 10 cubits high, 10 cubits wide, and 30 cubits long. Its length was divided into two unequal parts, the Holy place being 20 cubits long; and the Holy of Holies 10 cubits, being therefore a perfect cube of 10 cubits. It was formed of forty-eight boards, twenty on either side, and eight at the end, the front being formed of a curtain hung on five pillars. These forty-eight boards (3 × 4^2) are significant of the nation as before God in the fulness of privilege on the earth (4 × 12). The twenty boards on each side were held together by *five* bars passing through rings which were attached to them.

The *curtains* which covered the Tabernacle structure were four in number. The first was made of ten curtains of byssus in various colours adorned with embroidered cherubim. Each curtain was 28 (4 × 7) cubits long and four wide. They were hung *five* on each side, probably sewn together to form one large sheet (20 × 28); the two sheets coupled together by loops, and fifty (5 × 10) taches of gold. The second covering was formed of eleven curtains of goats' hair, each 30 cubits long and four wide, joined together in two sheets fastened by loops and taches of brass. The *third* was of rams' skins dyed red, and the fourth was of *tachash* (or coloured) skins,* of which the dimensions are not given.

The *Entrance Vails* were three in number. The *first* was "the gate of the court," 20 cubits wide and 5 high, hung on 5 pillars. The *second* was "the door of the Tabernacle," 10 cubits wide and 10 high, hung like the gate of the court on 5 pillars. The *third* was the "beautiful vail," also 10 cubits square, which divided the Holy place from the Holy of Holies. One feature of these three vails is remarkable. The dimensions of the vail of the court and those of the Tabernacle were different, but yet the *area* was the same. The former was 20 cubits by 5 = 100 cubits; the latter were 10 cubits by 10, equalling 100 cubits also. Thus while there was only one gate, one door, one vail, they each typified Christ as the only door of entrance for all the blessings connected with salvation. But note that the "gate" which admitted to the benefits of *atonement* was wider and lower (20 cubits wide, and 5 cubits high); while the door which admitted to *worship* was both higher and narrower, being only 10 cubits wide, half the width, and twice the height (10 cubits high); thus saying to us, that not all who experience the blessings of atonement understand or appreciate the true nature of spiritual worship. The highest worship—admittance to the mercy-seat—was impossible for the Israelites except in the person of their substitute—the high priest; for the beautiful vail barred their access. Yet this vail was rent in twain the moment the true grace which came by Jesus Christ was perfectly manifested. And it was rent by the act of God in grace, for it was rent "from the top to the bottom."

It is worthy of note, and it is a subject which might well be further investigated by those who have leisure, that the *Gematria* of Heb. ix., which gives an account of the Tabernacle, yields the number *five* as a factor. Taking each letter as standing for its corresponding figure, the value of Heb. ix. 2–10, describing the Tabernacle and its furniture, is 103,480. The factors of this number are all full of significance, viz., 5 × 8 × 13 × 199; where we have *five* the number of grace, *four* the number of the world, the sphere in which it is

* Probably of a sacrificial animal. See p. 129.

manifested, while in *thirteen* we have the number of sin and atonement. (See under *Thirteen.*)

In like manner the second section of the chapter (Heb. ix. 11–28), which relates to the application of the type to Christ and His atoning work, is a simple multiple of thirteen, viz., 204,451 (13 × 15,727).

While the important digression in verses 16, 17, and 18, amounts to 11,830, which is $13^2 \times 14 \times 5$, where we have the same great important factors.

The Prepositions Connected with Substitution

used in connection with atonement, expressing Christ's death *on behalf of* His people, occur also in multiples of five:—

ὑπέρ (*huper*), which means *on behalf of, in the interests of*, occurs 585 times, the factors of this being 5 × 13 × 9, *i.e. grace, atonement*, and *judgment.*

περί (*peri*), a word of similar sense and usage, meaning *about* or *concerning*, occurs 195 times, of which the factors are 5 × 13 × 3, or *grace, atonement*, and *divinity.*

The Holy Anointing Oil (Exod. xxx. 23–25)

was composed of *five* parts, for it was a revelation of pure grace. This *five* is marked by the numbers *four* and *one.* For four parts were spices, and one was oil.

The four principal *spices*:—

1. Myrrh, 500 shekels (5 × 100),
2. Sweet cinnamon, 250 shekels (5 × 50),
3. Sweet calamus, 250 shekels (5 × 50),
4. Cassia, 500 shekels(5 × 100),

And olive oil, *one* hin.

This anointing oil was holy, for it separated to God; nothing else could separate. It was of God, and therefore of grace; and therefore the number of its ingredients was *five*, and their quantities were all multiples of five.

Seven classes of persons or things were consecrated with this holy oil:—

1. Aaron and his sons.
2. The Tabernacle itself.
3. The table and its vessels.
4. The candlestick and its furniture.

5. The altar of burnt offering and its vessels.
6. The altar of incense.
7. The laver and its foot.

The word for "consecration" and the act are so misunderstood that it may be well to make a passing note upon it. The Hebrew is מלא (*Mah-leh*). It means, *to fill, fill up, complete.* Its first occurrence is Gen. i. 22, "multiply and *fill* the waters in the seas." So xxi. 19, "she *filled* the bottle with water"; xxix. 21, "My days are fulfilled"; Exod. xv. 9, "My soul shall have its fill of them"; xxviii. 41, "Thou shalt fill their hand." This has been translated *consecrate,* which is a comment rather than a translation.

When this word is used with the word יד (*yad*), *hand,* it means to fill the hand, especially with that which is the sign and symbol of office, *i.e., to fill the hand with a sceptre* was to set apart or consecrate to the office of king. To fill the hand with certain parts of sacrifices, was to set apart for the office of priest and to confirm their right to offer both gifts and sacrifices to God, Exod. xxix. 22-25; xxviii. 41; xxix. 9; xxxii. 29. (See also Heb. v. 1; viii. 3, 4.) A "ram of consecration" (or of filling) was a ram with parts of which the hands of the priests were filled when they were set apart to their office.

Whenever the word refers to official appointment, or separation to a work or dignity, it is the sovereign act of God, and the accompanying symbolical act was the filling of the hand of the person so appointed with the sign which marked his office. Hence the verb means in this usage *to invest with an office, to communicate a dignity.* It is needless to say that no man can do this for himself. It must be the act of God.

When the word is used of *what man can do* it is followed by the preposition ל, which means "*to*" or "*for,*" as in 2 Chron. xxix. 31, *to fill the hand for* one, *i.e., to bring offerings* (to Jehovah), which is quite a different thing altogether. There is no idea here of what is called to-day, "*consecration.*" It is a simple offering of gifts, which the offerer brings in his hands.

Only Jehovah Himself can invest a man with the privilege of any office in His service. "No man taketh this honour unto himself but he that is called of God" (Heb. v. 4). Hence the Lord Jesus is specially called "*the Anointed*," which is in Hebrew *Messiah*, and in Greek Χριστός, *Christos*, and in English *Christ*. Those who vainly talk about "consecrating themselves" should read 2 Chron. xiii. 9.

At the consecration of the priest under the Old Covenant in Exod. xxix. 20, the numbers *three* and *five* accompany the act of Divine grace. *Three* acts, each associated with *five*. The blood, and afterwards the holy oil upon it, was put—

(1) On the tip of the right ear, signifying that the Holy Spirit would cause him to hear the Word of God, and separating his *five* senses for God;

(2) On the thumb of his right hand (one of the *five* digits), signifying that he was to do and act for God;

(3) On the great toe of his right foot (again *five*), signifying that his personal walk was to be conformed to God's Word.

Thus it is now that the Holy Spirit consecrates all who are priests unto God. It is a Divine act, an act of sovereign grace. A grand reality when done for the sinner by God the Holy Ghost, but a worthless vanity when presumptuously done by a mortal man.

The Incense (Exod. xxx. 34)

also was composed of *five* parts. Four were "sweet spices," סמים (*Sa-meem*), and one was *salt*. מלח, *to salt*, being rendered "tempered together." See *v.* 35, margin.

The *four* "sweet spices" were:—

1. "Stacte," נטף (*Nataph*), "to drop"; hence a drop of aromatic gum. The LXX. is στακτή from σταζεῖν, "to drop." The Rabbins call it *opobalsamum*, as the R.V. margin.

2. "On'ycha," שחלת (*Sh'cheyleth*), "a shell"; Greek ὄνυξ, the shell of a species of mussel which burnt with an odour of musk.

3. "Gal'banum," חלבנה (*Chel-b'nah*), "a fragrant gum."

4. "Frankincense," לבונה (*L'bonah*), "a bright burning gum."

5. The *one*, salt. The verb מלח (*Mah-lach*), "to salt," occurs only here and Lev. ii. 13 and Ezek. xvi. 4, from which its meaning may be seen.

This incense was called by various names,—"pure," "perpetual," "sweet," "holy." No imitation of it was allowed. It indicates those precious merits of Christ through which alone our prayers can go up with acceptance before God. The incense was to symbolise "the prayers of the saints" offered by Christ Himself (Rev. v. 3). Our prayers are real prayers only when they ascend through His merits. The smoke of the incense was always associated with the smoke of the burnt offering! It was the fire from the brazen altar which kindled the incense on the golden altar! It was fire of *no earthly origin.* It came down originally from heaven (Lev. ix. 24; Judg. vi. 21; 1 Kings xviii. 38; 1 Chron. xxi. 26; 2 Chron. vii. 1). Incense kindled with "strange fire" was visited with immediate death (Lev. x. 1; Num. iii. 4; xxvi. 61). And incense not made of the prescribed *five* ingredients was forbidden to be offered (Exod. xxx. 9). Solemn provisions these, when we apply them to our prayers. They show us that our own words are nothing, and that Christ's merits are everything. David said, "Let my prayer be set forth before Thee as incense; and the lifting up of my hands as the evening sacrifice" (Ps. cxli. 2), *i.e.*, as incense goes up (Heb. *directed*) to Thee, and the smoke of the burnt offering (the evening sacrifice), so let my prayers be accepted through the merits of that sacrifice.

"There was given unto him much incense that he should offer it WITH the prayers of all saints . . . and the smoke of the incense which came WITH the prayers of the saints, ascended up before God out of the angel's hand" (Rev. viii. 3, 4). Rome has of course perverted this in her Vulgate Version, and in her various translations of it. She reads (Rev. viii.), *ut daret de orationibus sanctorum omnium*, i.e., "that he might offer the prayers of all the saints." And verse 4, *et ascendit fumus incensorum de orationibus sanctorum*, i.e., "and the smoke of the incense of the prayers of the saints ascended." The incense and the prayers are perfectly distinct; the one represents the merits of Christ, the other our imperfect prayers. But Rome confuses them, and her reason for doing so is shown by the notes which she puts in her various versions. The teaching of Scripture is clear, that apart from Christ's merits all our prayers are absolutely worthless. Hence the exhortation in Heb. xiii. 15, "BY HIM therefore let us offer the sacrifice of praise to God continually; that is, the fruit of our lips giving thanks to His name" (See Lev. vii. 12; Ps. li. 12; Hos. xiv. 3, LXX.).

WORDS THAT OCCUR FIVE TIMES.

Among many words stamped with this significance are:—

מתן (*Mat-tahn*), "gift" (Gen. xxxiv. 12; Num. xviii. 11; Prov. xviii. 16; xix. 6; xxi. 14). It is suitable that this word should occur *five* times, for gifts are of *grace*. It is noteworthy that משכרת (*mas-koh-reth*), "wages," occurs *four* times, for wages are of the earth, earthy.

נקיון (*nik-kah-yohn*), "innocency" (Gen. xx. 5; Pss. xxvi. 6; lxxiii. 13; Hos. viii. 5; Amos iv. 6).

παράκλητος (*parakleetos*), translated *Comforter* four times in the Gospel of John, viz., xiv., 16, 26; xv. 26; and xvi. 7; and *Advocate* once in the Epistle, 1 John ii. 1.

What a gracious provision! one Advocate within us (the Holy Spirit) that we may not sin (spoken of four times); and another with the Father for us if we do sin—even "Jesus Christ the righteous." The word means *one called to one's side* to give any help and to meet any need. *Two* advocates speaking of the enemy which causes our need, and of the Helper who supplies it.

Other words are:—

ἀγαλλίασις (*agalliasis*), "gladness" (Luke i. 14; Acts ii. 46; Heb. i. 9), "joy" (Luke i. 44), "exceeding joy" (Jude 24).

ᾄδω (*adō*), "to sing" (Eph. v. 19; Col. iii. 16; Rev. v. 9; xiv. 3; xv. 3).

ἀνάπαυσις (*anapausis*), "rest" (Matt. xi. 29; xii. 43; Luke xi. 24; Rev. iv. 8; xiv. 11).

ἀσφαλής (*asphalees*), "certainty" (Acts xxi. 34; xxii. 30; xxv. 26; Phil. iii. 1; Heb. vi. 19).

Phrases which occur Five Times.

"Bless the Lord, O my soul."—All in Psalms ciii. and civ., viz., ciii. 1, 2, 23 and civ. 1, 35. The Talmud calls attention to this and says, "As God fills the earth and nourishes it, so He nourishes and blesses the soul."

"Whosoever hath, to him shall be given" (Matt. xiii. 12; xxv. 29; Mark iv. 25; Luke viii. 18; xix. 26).—*Five* times, telling of the *grace* which gives.

"The kingdom of God."—*Five* times in the Gospel (Matthew) which alone speaks of "the kingdom of heaven." The latter refers to earth, and the kingdom to be established here. While the former relates to the larger kingdom of *grace*, which includes it and the Church and all beside * (Matt. vi. 33; xii. 28; xix. 24; xxi. 31 and 43).

The Talmud † asks (under Hag. i. 8), "How is it that the word ואכבר, 'And I will be glorified,' is written without the final ה (which stands for *five*) and is yet read as if it had it (ואכבדה)? Because it indicates that the second Temple lacked *five* things that were found in the *first* Temple, viz. :—

The Ark that is the mercy-seat of the Cherubim,
The Fire from heaven on the altar,
The Shechinah,
The Spirit of prophecy, and
The Urim and Thummim."

This answer is correct as far as it goes, but it is written nevertheless, in Hag. ii. 9, "The glory of this latter house shall be greater than the former." True, it lacked the Law that was contained in the Ark, but it had the presence of Him who was full of grace and truth, and who had that Law within His heart.

---

* See *Christ's Prophetic Teaching*, by the same author.

† *Yoma*, fol. 21, col 2.

SIX.

Six is either 4 *plus* 2, *i.e.*, man's world (4) with man's enmity to God (2) brought in: or it is 5 *plus* 1, the grace of God made of none effect by man's addition to it, or perversion, or corruption of it: or it is 7 *minus* 1, *i.e.*, man's coming short of spiritual perfection. In any case, therefore, it has to do with *man;* it is the number of imperfection; the human number; the number of MAN as destitute of God, without God, without Christ.

The Hebrew שֵׁשׁ (*shaish*) is supposed to be derived from the root שָׁדַשׁ (*shah-dash*), but nothing is known about its origin or signification.

At any rate it is certain that *man* was created on the *sixth* day, and thus he has the number *six* impressed upon him. Moreover, *six* days were appointed to him for his labour; while *one* day is associated in sovereignty with the Lord God, as His rest.

Six, therefore, is the number of *labour* also, of man's labour as apart and distinct from God's rest. True, it marks the completion of Creation as God's work, and therefore the number is significant of *secular completeness.*

The serpent also was created on the *sixth* day.

The Sixth Commandment relates to the worst sin,—murder.

The *sixth* clause of the Lord's prayer treats of sin.

Six is the number stamped on all that is connected with *human labour*. We see it stamped upon his *measures* which he uses in his labour, and on the *time* during which he labours. And we see this from the very beginning.

The number *six* is stamped upon the measurements of the Great Pyramid, the unit of which was the inch and its sexagesimal multiples. The first multiple is the foot, 12 inches (2 × 6); and after this the rises are 18 (3 × 6), 24 (4 × 6), 30 (5 × 6), and 36 (6 × 6 or 6^2 = the yard).*

* On the other hand, the *sacred* cubit, though not a round number, was a multiple, indeed the square of 5, being 25·3 inches.

Corresponding to these measures we have the first division of the natural time-spaces which measure man's *labour* and rest,—the day, consisting of 24 hours (4×6), divided into the day and night of 12 hours. The multiples and sub-divisions are also stamped by the number *six*. The months being 12; while the hours consist of 60 minutes (6 × 10), and the minutes of 60 seconds (6 × 10).

The base of the Great Pyramid shows that the unit-inch * was obtained by a division of the original *circuit*, 36,000 inches or 1,000 yards.

On account of the curse (Gen. iii.), the number *six* tells not only of labour, but of "labour and sorrow," and it specially marks all that is "under the sun," all that is "not of God." The true "sabbath-keeping," now, is in reserve; for there is no rest apart from "peace with God"; the rest which God gives and which we find (Matt. xi. 28).

But now to turn to the Scripture examples and illustrations, we note first that

CAIN'S DESCENDANTS

are given only as far as the *sixth* generation.

IMPERFECTION.

When *twelve* (the number of governmental perfection) is divided, it indicates imperfection in rule and administration. Solomon's throne had *six* steps (1 Kings x. 19), and his kingdom was soon divided. The 12 loaves of the Shew Bread were divided into two *sixes* (Lev. xxiv. 6), and the Twelve Tribes were divided tribes.

Abraham's *six* intercessions for Sodom (Gen. xviii.) marked man's imperfection in prayer, which falls short of that of the Divine Intercessor.

THE BURNT OFFERING IN GENESIS XXII.

is mentioned *six* times (*vv.* 2, 3, 6, 7, 8, 13) because the seventh was that of the Divine Substitute which God Himself would provide (*v.* 8).

"THE MAN OF THE EARTH."

In Psalms ix. and x., through which there is a running alphabetical acrostic, uniting the two Psalms, *six* letters of

* Differing from the Pyramid inch by only 1 in 40,000.

the alphabet are wanting (מ to צ). It is the Scripture which describes "the Man of the Earth" (Ps. x. 18), the coming Anti-Christ, and the Apostasy which marks his presence, called the "times of trouble" (Ps. ix. 9; x. 1).

Six Earthquakes

are mentioned: Exod. xix. 18; 1 Kings xix. 11; Amos i. 1 (Zech. xiv. 5); Matt. xxvii. 54; xxviii. 2; Acts xvi. 26.

The Six Years of Athaliah's Reign

were *six* years of usurpation of the throne of David (2 Kings xi.; 2 Chron. xxiii.). Athaliah slew all the seed-royal, as she thought; but God in His providence over-ruled events so that one son, Joash, was "rescued from among the king's sons that were slain." He was hid in the house of God during the *six* years with Jehosheba, who was shut up with him, her affections being centred upon him, while Jehoiada her husband was occupied for the king, going about and securing loyal adherents by his simple repetition of Jehovah's promise, "Behold, the king's son shall reign, as the Lord hath said of the sons of David" (2 Chron. xxiii. 3). This promise was the support of the hearts of the faithful during those *six* years of usurpation, until the *seventh* year came, and Joash was manifested upon his throne and all his enemies destroyed. Which things are a type of the King's son, even Jesus, who was rescued, by resurrection, from among the dead, and is now hid in the house of God on high. While He is seated and expecting, (Heb. x. 12, 13), all who are "in Christ" are hid with Him (Col. iii. 3); and while, in this aspect, their hearts (like Jehosheba's) are occupied with the person of the King, their activities (like Jehoiada's) are going out for Him, witnessing and testifying to the blessed truth that the King is coming again and will surely reign, and the *seventh* year of blessing will come at last. Until that moment arrives, the promise of Jehovah will be their support, that the Seed of the woman shall in due time crush the serpent's head (Gen. iii. 15).

Six Times Jesus Charged with Having a Devil.

1. Mark iii. 22, and Matt. xii. 24, "He hath Beelzebub."
2. John vii. 20, "Thou hast a devil."

3. John viii. 48, "Say we not well that . . . Thou hast a devil?"

4. John viii. 52, "Now we know that Thou hast a devil."

5. John x. 20, "He hath a devil, and is mad."

6. Luke xi. 15, "He casteth out devils by Beelzebub."

This is most significant. Man's emnity to the Person of the Lord Jesus is thus branded with *man's* number. It will repay careful study to note the chronological order of these occasions and speakers. The very order and structure is important.

A | 1. Beelzebub, and casting out devils.
  B | 2. A simple charge, "Thou hast,"
    C | 3. Introduced by "Say we not well," } Both in
    C | 4. Introduced by "Now we know." } John viii.
  B | 5. A simple charge, "He hath."
A | 6. Beelzebub, and casting out devils.

THE SIX-FOLD OPPOSITION TO THE WORK OF GOD

on the part of *man* is seen in the opposition to Nehemiah. It forms a lesson for all time, being enacted every day where any, like Nehemiah, begin a work for God.

There was—

1. *Grief*, ii. 10.
2. *Laughter*, ii. 19.
3. *Wrath, indignation*, and *mocking*, iv. 1–4.
4. *Fighting* and *open opposition*, iv. 7, 8.
5. *Conference*, vi. 1, 2.—"Come and let us meet together." "Let us take counsel together" (*v.* 7). This attempt was to "weaken them from the work" (*v.* 9). But Nehemiah refused to parley with the enemies, or meet them in conference.
6. *False friends*, vi. 10–14.—Here was the greatest danger of all. Satan, "as an angel of light," seeking to mar, and hinder, and stop the work.

The careful study of these *six* steps in *man's* opposition to the work of God will yield great spiritual profit, and arm us against the wiles of the Devil.

WORDS.

Now let us pass to the number, as it concerns words, and first note that there are

Six Words Used for Man

in the Bible. Four in the Old Testament, and two in the New.

1. אדם (*ah-dahm*). Man as a human being (Lat. *homo*), having regard to his being created, and to his earthly origin. This is the word used of Messiah as the "Son of Man." See a few examples:—

   Gen. i. 26, "Let us make *man*."

   Gen. ii. 7, "God formed *man* of the dust of the ground."

   Gen. iii. 24, "So He drove out the *man*."

   Isa. ii. 11, "The lofty looks of *man* shall be humbled."

   Isa. ii. 17, "The loftiness of *man* shall be bowed down."

   Isa. ii. 9, "The mean *man* boweth down."

   Isa. ii. 9, "The great man (*Ish*, see next word) humbleth himself."

   Isa. v. 15, "The mean *man* shall be brought down."

   Isa. v. 15, "The mighty man (*Ish*) shall be humbled."

   2 Sam. vii. 19, "Is this the manner of *man*, O Lord God?"

   Ps. viii. 4, "What is man (*Enōsh*, see the third word) that Thou art mindful of him? and the son of *man*, that Thou visitest him?"

2. איש (*Ish*). Man, as strong and vigorous of mind and body. Man with some degree of pre-eminence of strength and endowment.

   Zech. vi. 12, "Behold the *man* whose name is the Branch."

   Ps. xxii. 6, "I am a worm, and no *man*; a reproach of men (*Adam*, see No. 1), and despised of the people."

Ps. xxv. 12, "What *man* is he that feareth the LORD?"

Ps. xxxix. 11, "When Thou with rebukes dost correct *man* for iniquity: surely every *man* is vanity."

Ps. xc. Title, "The *man* of God."

3. אנוש (*Enōsh*). Weak man, as mortal and subject to suffering and death; the heir of corruption.

Ps. viii. 4, "What is *man* that Thou art mindful of him? or the son of man" (*Adam*, see No. 1).

Ps. lxxiii. 5, "They are not in trouble as other *men*."

Ps. ciii. 15, "As for *man*, his days are as grass."

4. גבר (*Gehver*), a strong man, a man of might and valour. Man as distinct from God (Job xxii. 2), and from a woman or wife (Prov. vi. 34).

Zech. xiii. 7, "Awake, O sword, against . . . the *man* that is My fellow, saith the LORD of Hosts."

Exod. x. 11, "Go now, ye that are *men*."

Exod. xii. 37, "Six hundred thousand on foot that were men."

Ps. lii. 7, "Lo, this is the *man* that made not God his strength."

Jer. xvii. 5, "Cursed be the *man* that trusteth in man" (*Adam*, see No. 1).

Jer. xvii. 7, "Blessed is the *man* that trusteth in the LORD."

Then in the New Testament we have the two words:

5. ἄνθρωπος, which answers to *Adam* (No. 1), and

6. ἀνηρ, which answers to *Ish* (No. 2).

It is worthy of note that these four Hebrew words are each used of the Messiah, and that the Holy Spirit has revealed a blessing for each in and through the man Christ Jesus.

1. אדם (*Adam*), Ps. xxxii. 2, "Blessed is the man unto whom the LORD imputeth not iniquity."

2. איש (*Ish*), Ps. i. 1, "Blessed is the man that walketh not in the counsel of the ungodly, nor standeth in the way of sinners, nor sitteth in the seat of the scornful."
3. אנוש (*Enōsh*), Job v. 17, "Happy* is the man whom God correcteth, therefore despise not thou the chastening of the Almighty."
4. גבר (*Gehver*), Ps. xciv. 12, "Blessed is the man whom Thou chastenest, O Lord, and teachest him out of Thy law."

THE SERPENT HAS SIX NAMES.

The Talmud calls attention to this fact, and gives the following:—

1. נחש (*nachash*), *a shining one* (Gen. iii. 1; Job xxvi. 13. See also No. 6 below).
2. עכשוב (*ak-shoov*), from עכש, "to bend back," "lie in wait." Translated *adder*, Ps. cxl. 3.
3. אפעה (*ephah*), any *poisonous* serpent. Translated *adder;* also *viper* (Job xx. 16; Isa. xxx. 6; lix. 5).
4. צפעני (*tsiph-ohnee*), a small *hissing* serpent (Isa. xi. 8; lix. 5; Prov. xxiii. 32), from צפע, *to hiss.* Translated *viper.*
5. תנין (*Tanneen*), *a great serpent*, or dragon (from the root "to stretch out" or "extend"), on account of its length (Exod. vii. 9, 10, 12).
6. שרף (*Saraph*), from root "to burn"; a venomous, deadly serpent, from the heat and inflammation caused by its bite. Translated *serpents*, Num. xxi. 8; Isa. xiv. 29; xxx. 6.

THE LION HAS SIX NAMES IN THE OLD TESTAMENT,

and all are found in the Book of Job (Job iv. 10, 11; and xxviii. 8).

1. ארי (*Aree*), the *roaring lion* (Gen. xlix. 9; Num. xxiii. 24; xxiv. 9, etc.).

---

* The same word as in the other passages, viz., אשר (*Ashrai*), blessed. Lit. *Oh, the blessednesses of.*

2. שחל (*Shachal*), the *fierce lion*, with special reference to his voice (Job iv. 10; x. 16; xxviii. 8; Ps. xci. 13; Hos. xiii. 7).

3. כפיר (*K'pheer*), the *young lion*—not a whelp as in Ezek. xix. 2—(Judg. xiv. 5; Job iv. 10; xxxviii. 39; Ps. xvii. 12; xxxiv. 10).

4. ליש (*Lah-yish*), the *old lion*—not from age, but brave and strong—(Job iv. 11; Prov. xxx. 30; Isa. xxx. 6).

5. לביא (*Lahvee*), the old *lioness* (from root *to roar*) (Gen. xlix. 9; Num. xxiii. 24; Deut. xxxiii. 20, etc.).

6. שחץ (*Shachatz*), the lion's whelps (Job xxviii. 8; xli. 34 (translated "*of pride*").

Some Words that Occur Six Times.

אבדון (*avad-dōhn*), destruction.

מוט (*moht*), bar, staff, or yoke.

מכתם (*mich-tahm*), Michtam (Pss. xvi., lvi., lvii., lviii., lix., and lx.). This word is connected with *death*, and at the same time with resurrection also (3 × 2). It is from כתם, *to cut in, engrave* (LXX., στηλογραφία, *a sculptured writing; στήλη* was the word for *grave-stone*). Hence "Michtam," like our "*Resurgam*," indicates that these *six* Psalms, though connected with death, point to the hope of resurrection. This is notably true of Ps. xvi., and may be traced in the others also.

αἰσχύνη (*aischunee*), shame.
ἀλλάττω (*allattō*), to change.
ἀσέβεια (*asebeia*), ungodliness.
ἀτιμάζω (*atimazō*), entreat shamefully.
βδέλυγμα (*bdelugma*), abomination. Three in Gospels: Matt. xxiv. 15; Mark xiii. 14; Luke xvi. 15. Three in Revelation: Rev. xvii. 4, 5; xxi. 27.

For the combinations of 6, 66, and 666, see further under the number *Six hundred and sixty six*.

SEVEN.

We come now to the great number of *spiritual perfection.* A number which, therefore, occupies so large a place in the works, and especially in the Word of God as being inspired by the Holy Spirit.

In the *first* part of this book we have enlarged somewhat on the importance of this number in Nature and in Grace, so that we need not here repeat many of the interesting facts already given.

As a number the actual word and number "SEVEN" is used as *no other number* is. *Seven* and its compounds occur in multiples of seven in the Old Testament.

Seven occurs 287 times, or 7 × 41.

"*Seventh,*" the fractional part, occurs 98 times, or 7 × 14.

"*Seven-fold,*" occurs 7 times.

The above three numbers together are of course a multiple of *seven*, but a very remarkable one, 287 + 98 + 7 = 392, and 392 is $7^2 + 7^3$, or 8 times the square of *seven* ($7^2 \times 8$).

Then again *seven,* in combination with other numbers, is remarkable, such as fifty *and seven,* a hundred *and seven,* etc. There are 112 of these combinations, or 7 × 16.

"*Seventy*" occurs 56 times, or 7 × 8.

"*Seventy,*" in combination with other numbers, occurs 35 times, or 7 × 5.

It is, however, when we come to consider its *significance* that the true glories of its *spiritual perfection* are revealed.

We have just seen that *six* is the number which is stamped upon all things *human,* as being emphatically the number of *man.* Let us first observe the use of the two numbers

SIX AND SEVEN TOGETHER

as combining and contrasting what is *human* and what is *spiritual.*

A remarkable illustration of this is seen in

THE TWO GENEALOGIES OF JESUS CHRIST.

Note, first, in which two of the four Gospels they are found, for this is also significant.

In Matt. God says to us, "Behold thy King" (Zech. ix. 9).
In Mark He says, "Behold My Servant" (Isa. xl. 1).
In Luke He says, "Behold the Man" (Zech. vi. 12).
In John He says, "Behold your God" (Isa. xl. 9).

Now a *servant* need not produce his genealogy; neither can *God* have one. It is a *King* who *must* have one, and a *Man* who should have one. Therefore it is that we have two genealogies, and not more than two. And that is why we have one in Matthew giving the *Royal* genealogy of Jesus as King; and one in Luke giving the *Human* genealogy of Jesus as Man. Hence also it is that Matthew's is a *descending* genealogy, while Luke's is an *ascending* one. For *kings* must trace their *descent*, all power in the world being derived from God, who says, "By Me kings reign": and *man* must trace his *ascent* to some particular ancestor. Matthew's, therefore, begins with Abraham, and comes down to Joseph, the son of Heli; while Luke's starts from Joseph, and goes up to Adam and God.

As far as David both the lists agree. But here an impor-tant divergence takes place. In Matthew, after David, we have his son *Solomon;* while in Luke we have another son, Solomon's younger brother, *Nathan.*

From this point, therefore, we have two lines. One (Matthew) gives the regal legal line through *Solomon;* the other (Luke) gives the *natural* line through *Nathan.*

Both lines meet, unite, and are exhausted in JESUS CHRIST, who, as the son of Mary (Heli's daughter), was "David's Son" by natural descent ("Who was made of David's seed, according to (the) flesh"; Rom. i. 3); and was entitled to "the Throne of His father David" (Luke i. 31, 32) as being "according to LAW" * the son of Joseph, Mary's *husband.*

* This is supported by the true reading of Luke iii. 23, which, according to Lachmann, Tischendorf, Tregelles, Alford, Westcott and Hort, and the R.V., should read "Jesus when He began to teach was about thirty years of age, being (the) son—as was supposed (ὢν υἱὸς, ὡς ἐνομίζετο, *i.e.* being son *according to Law*) of Joseph the son of Heli." The verb νομίζω (*nomizō*) means *to lay down a thing as law, to hold by custom or usage, to own as a custom, to take for granted.* Here it refers not to any *supposition* as to the Lord being Joseph's son, but to the legal sanction and customary practice, which reckoned Joseph as Heli's son through marriage with his daughter Mary—strictly "according to law." See Ruth i. 11-13, where Ruth by marriage with Naomi's son was called her daughter; Neh. vii. 63, where Hakkoz by marriage with Barzillai's daughter was "called after their name"; and

Both lines being extinguished by His *death*—He became, consequently, by His *Resurrection* from the dead—KING—according to "the Decree" published in Ps. ii. and quoted in Acts xiii. 33. Heb. i. 5; v. 5 (where in every place γεγέννηκά (*gegennēka*) should be read: "I have *brought Thee to the birth*"—and not "I have begotten Thee").

A reference to the list of Luke iii., p. 162, shows that the number of human names, beginning with the "First Adam" and ending with the "Last Adam" (the Lord Jesus) is 75 *, thus stamping upon the *human* links in the genealogy of our Lord, the number of Grace emphasised (viz., fifteen *fives* or 5 × 3 × 5).

But upon the list, as a whole, is impressed, as clearly, the number of spiritual perfection (7); the names in the list being 77. GOD heads the list (Luke iii. 23) and GOD ends it (Luke iii. 38), and must be reckoned in each case in the complete number (77).†

Upon the human side we have the number of Grace (5) culminating in JESUS—"the *completion* of Grace" (*plērēs*, John i. 14). Upon the total number of names in our Lord's genealogy in Luke, we have divinely stamped the number of spiritual perfection (77), including at either end (Luke iii. 23, 38) GOD, who is the beginning and end of all and every grace and spiritual perfection.

Num. xxxvi., where the daughters of Zelophehad, by Divine counsel, "were married to their father's brothers' sons . . . and their inheritance remained in the tribe of the family of their father" (*vv.* 11, 12). This is exactly what took place with Mary, who, according to the Jerusalem Talmud (*Chag.* 77, 4), is called the daughter of Heli, and by her marriage with Joseph, who was the real son of Jacob, caused Joseph to be called, *according to Law* (νομίζω), the son, or rather the son-in-law, of Heli.

* The name of the "Second Cainan" is undoubtedly an interpolation in certain copies of the Septuagint towards the close of the Fourth Century, A.D. "The evidence against his existence is, to the utmost possible degree, clear, full, and positive, and not liable to any mistake or perversion. On the contrary, the evidence for his existence . . . . . . is inferential, obscure, or open to the suspicion of falsification."—Lord A. Hervey on "*The Genealogies of Our Lord.*" Chap. viii. p. 195.

† It seems to be a fair inference that the "Second Cainan" came into existence in the endeavour to make up this number (77). Some copyist about the end of the Fourth Century, A.D., finding that the names numbered only 76, and not perceiving that GOD has to be reckoned *twice*, introduced this apochryphal Cainan into certain copies of the Septuagint, in order to make up the names to the number it was felt was the right one, viz. 77.

The names of the 5 kings omitted from the *regal* list in Matthew, viz., *Ahaziah*, *Joash*, *Amaziah*, *Jehoiakim* and *Jeconiah*, were all omitted "according to Law." The first three all died violent deaths, and were "blotted out" in fulfilment of GOD's declarations against, and "visiting" for, idolatry (Deut. xxix. 20).

The other two, *Jehoiakim* and *Jeconiah*, were also omitted from the *regal* list for the paramount reason that the kingdom, as an independent kingdom, *ended* with Josiah at Megiddo, when Judah passed under Gentile dominion. It was *Jehoiakim* who burnt the Roll, and brought on at once the declaration from Jehovah of Gentile supremacy. Also at his death, that which was found *on* him (according to the Rabbis an image engraved on his body) was, as stated by the Talmud, the reason why he is omitted in the Jewish genealogies. *Jeconiah* was "blotted out" for the sufficient reasons given in Jer. xxii. 24-30.*

These five kings were, therefore, not omitted by Matthew in his *regal* list in an arbitrary manner to produce an artificially constructed genealogy; but their names were ruled out in most strict accordance with Divine Law. We have

Names in Matt. i.	41
Names before Abraham (from Luke iii.) ...	19
Therefore in the royal line through Solomon ...	60 names.

So that while the Name "JESUS" is the 75th *human* name in the line through *Nathan*, as recorded in Luke, it is the 60th name in the line through *Solomon* in Matthew i.

We find, therefore, the numbers SIX and SEVEN divinely stamped upon the genealogy of Matthew—60 names (ten *sixes*, 10 × 6). Three sets of fourteen generations (two *sevens*, 7 × 2). Together *forty-two* generations (six *sevens*, 6 × 7).

His two names have the same significant stamp and seal: for Ἰησοῦς, JESUS, the birth name of His humiliation, as *Man*, is composed of *six* letters; while Χριστός, Christ, His Divine title as the anointed of God, is composed of *seven* letters.

This marvellous combination of *six* and *seven* stamps both genealogies with the Spirit's seal, and sets forth the human and Divine natures of our Lord, as perfect Man and perfect God.

* It is remarkable that in most of the lists given in the Commentaries *Jeconiah* appears twice instead of David. For the reasons above given, Jeconiah was "blotted out" of the regal list and only heads the *third* "fourteen generations"—after the "carrying away to Babylon."

We give the following complete list :—

MATTHEW.	MATTHEW & LUKE. *Names in Common.*	LUKE.
		GOD.
		1 Adam (Who was the Son of GOD, Lk. iii. 38).
		2 Seth
		3 Enos.
		4 Cainan.
		5 Maleleel.
		6 Jared.
		7 Enoch.
		8 Mathusala.
		9 Lamech.
		10 Noe.
		11 Sem.
		12 Arphaxad Cainan.*
		13 Sala.
		14 Heber.
		15 Phalec.
		16 Ragau.
		17 Saruch.
		18 Nachor.
		19 Thara.
	1 ABRAHAM.	20
	2 Isaac.	21
	3 Jacob.	22
	4 Judas.	23
	5 Phares.	24
	6 Esrom.	25
	7 Aram (or Ram).	26
	8 Aminadab.	27
	9 Naasson.	28
	10 Salmon.	29
	11 Booz.	30
	12 Obed.	31
	13 Jesse.	32
	14 DAVID—The King (in Hebron : 2 Sam. ii. 4, 11).	33
1 DAVID—THE KING ("Over all Israel." 2 Sam. v. 4, 5).		
2 SOLOMON (eldest surviving son of Bathsheba).		34 NATHAN (second surviving son of Bathsheba).
3 ROBOAM.		35 Mattatha.
4 ABIA.		36 Menan.
5 ASA.		37 Melea.
6 JOSAPHAT.		38 Eliakim.
7 JORAM.		39 Jonan.
AHAZIAH } "blotted out"		40 Joseph.
JOASH } "according		41 Juda.
AMAZIAH } to LAW."		42 Simeon.
		43 Levi.
8 OZIAS.		44 Matthat.

* See the notes (* †) on p. 160; and *The Companion Bible*, Appendix 99, p. 145.

MATTHEW.	MATTHEW & LUKE. *Names in Common.*	LUKE.
9 JOATHAM.		45 Jorim.
10 ACHAZ.		46 Eliezer.
11 EZEKIAS.		47 Jose.
12 MANASSES		48 Er.
13 AMON.		49 Elmodam.
14 JOSIAS.		50 Cosam.
. JEHOIAKIM, JECHONIAH } "blotted out" "according to LAW."		51 Addi.
		52 Melchi
1 Jechonias.		53 Neri.
2 Salathiel.*		54 Salathiel.*
3 Zorobabel.*		55 Zorobabel.*
		56 Rhesa.
4 Abiud.		57 Joanna.
		58 Juda.
5 Eliakim.		59 Joseph.
		60 Semei.
6 Azor.		61 Mattathias.
		62 Maath.
7 Sadoc.		63 Nagge.
		64 Esli.
8 Achim.		65 Naum.
		66 Amos.
9 Eliud.		67 Mattathias.
		68 Joseph.
10 Eleazar.		69 Janna.
		70 Melchi.
11 Matthan.		71 Levi.
		72 Matthat.
12 Jacob.		73 Heli.
13 JOSEPH { Son, "according to LAW" (*hōs enomizeto* Lk. iii. 23) of Heli by betrothal to Heli's daughter: therefore, also "according to LAW" (cp. MATT. i. 24, Lk. ii. 5, with Deut. xxii. 23, 24). 14		74 HUSBAND of MARY, of whom was born
	14 JESUS †	75 JESUS WHO IS CALLED MESSIAH THE SON OF ADAM (ὁ υἱὸς τοῦ ἀνθρώπου = בֶּן־הָאָדָם)‡ WHO WAS THE SON OF GOD (Luke iii. 22).

* The two Salathiels and Zorobabels are not to be *identified*—for it stands written, "Thus saith Jehovah, write ye this man (*i.e.* Jeconiah) childless, a man that shall not prosper in his days; for no man of *His seed* shall prosper, *sitting upon the throne of David, and ruling any more in Judah*" (Jer. xxii. 30). Therefore if the Salathiels and Zorobabels of Matthew and Luke are one and the same persons—then Christ was of "*the Seed*" of Jechonias; and in the face of the above ruling of Jehovah—*He could not be successor to the Throne.*

† The full number of names common to both lists is therefore 14 + 1 = 15 (5 × 3) Again the number of Grace.

‡ Not "the Son of man," but "the son of the [man] Adam."

Joseph was the husband of Mary, "of whom was born Jesus which is called Christ" (Matt. i. 16). That is to say, Joseph, who was the *real* son of Jacob (for it says "Jacob BEGAT Joseph," Matt. i. 16), could become the *legal* son of Heli only by his marriage with Heli's daughter Mary. Hence it does not say, in Luke iii. 23, that Heli begat Joseph, but that he was "*the son* of Heli." The words, "*the son*," it will be observed, are in italics, and being thus a wider expression, denotes that he was *legally* the *son-in-law* of Heli, by his marriage with Mary, Heli's real daughter.

While the Lord, therefore, was the real son of Mary, He could be reckoned as the legal son of Joseph, and was descended from Nathan through Heli, as well as from Solomon through Jacob.

THE SONS OF GOD.

Beni-ha-Elohim, "sons of God," occurs in *six* connections:—

1. Gen. vi. 2, 4.
2. Job i. 6; ii. 1.
3. Job xxxviii. 7.
4. Ps. xxix. 1.
5. Ps. lxxxix. 6.
6. Dan. iii. 25.

Beni-El-hai, "sons of the living God," *once*:—

7. Hos. i. 10.

Seven times in all, but not seven exactly alike. There are *six* in one form (used of angels*), and *one* in another (used of men), to mark the fact that the sons of God, whether angels or men, fell from the spiritual perfection of their original position.

This interesting illustration is not the only example of the contrasts presented between these two numbers, *six* and *seven*. Mr. Samuell † instances others:—

SHEM, HAM, AND JAPHETH.

The two names Shem and Japheth, who received their father's blessing, occur together *seven* times; but *six* of these are in connection with Ham whose posterity was cursed!

THE FOOD OF EGYPT

is given in *six* items (Num. xi. 5), viz., fish, cucumbers, melons, leeks, onions, and garlick; whereas the enumera-

* See *The Spirits in Prison*, by the same author and publisher.

† *Seven the Sacred Number*, by Richard Samuell, p. 438.

tion of the Divine provision of Emmanuel's land is marked by the number *seven* (Deut. viii. 8),—wheat, barley, vines, fig-trees, pomegranates, olives, and honey.

Israel's Lovers

are represented as giving to her *six* things (Hos. ii. 5),—bread water, wool, flax, oil, and drink; while Jehovah speaks of His own precious gifts of love to His people by contrast as being *seven* in number (*vv.* 8, 9),—corn, wine, oil, silver, gold, wool, and flax.

The Days of Creation and Rest.

In the Creation we have the *six* days and the *seven.* The *six* of labour and the *seventh* of rest.

The Two Lands.

2 Kings xviii. 32: Rabshakeh, in describing the land to which he would take the people captive, enumerated *six* things; but as he mentions them as being like their own land, there are *seven* as well:

"A land like your own land,
a land of corn
and wine,
a land of bread
and vineyards,
a land of oil olive
and of honey."

(the six lines from "a land of corn" to "and of honey" bracketed: 6; the whole: **7.**)

The Dominion of Man.

Psalm viii. 6-8: *Six* sets forth the perfection of human authority, and *seven* marks the fact that the *six* defined particulars were of Divine gift:

"Thou hast put all things under his feet:
all sheep
and oxen,
yea, and the beasts of the field;
the fowl of the air,
and the fish of the sea,
and whatsoever passeth through the paths of the seas."

(the six items from "all sheep" to "the paths of the seas" bracketed: 6; the whole: **7.**)

The Seven Spirits.

Isa. xi. 2: *Six* here marking that Christ would be perfect man, and *seven* that He was perfect God; the first statement being marked off from the rest by its form:—

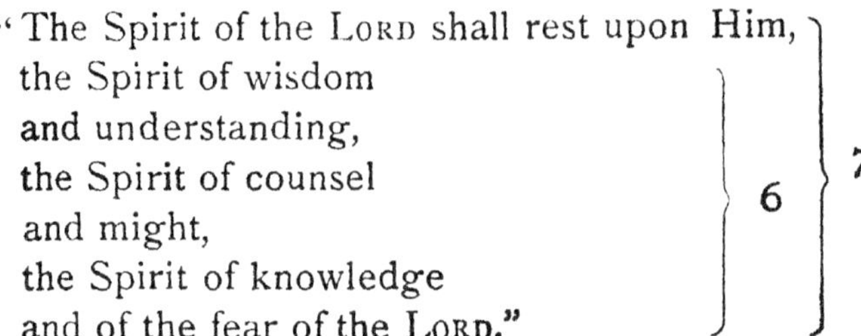

"The Spirit of the Lord shall rest upon Him,
the Spirit of wisdom
and understanding,
the Spirit of counsel
and might,
the Spirit of knowledge
and of the fear of the Lord."

6 7

The Spirit Poured Out.

Joel ii. 28, 29: The "all flesh" is the Divine inclusion; but *six* particulars mark the definition. It need hardly be added that this blessing refers (by interpretation) only to the house of Israel.

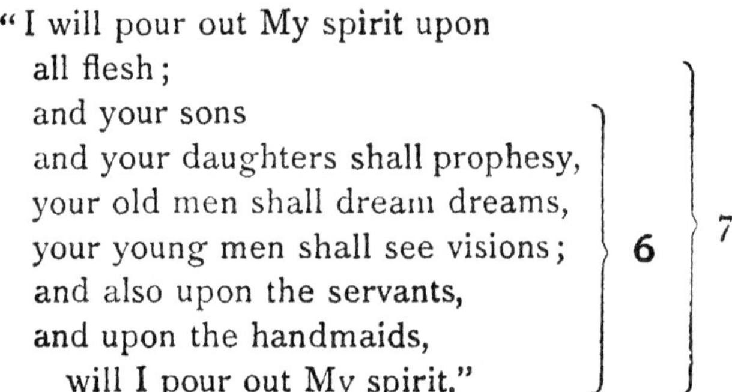

"I will pour out My spirit upon
all flesh;
and your sons
and your daughters shall prophesy,
your old men shall dream dreams,
your young men shall see visions;
and also upon the servants,
and upon the handmaids,
will I pour out My spirit."

6 7

Israel's Endowments.

Rom. ix. 4: The *one* defining who they were by Divine calling and standing, the *six* setting forth what pertained to them as men, thus called and blessed:—

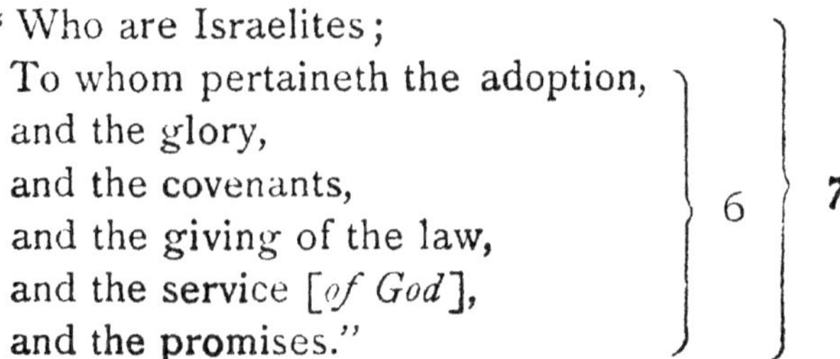

"Who are Israelites;
To whom pertaineth the adoption,
and the glory,
and the covenants,
and the giving of the law,
and the service [*of God*],
and the promises."

6 7

The Golden Candlestick

had *six* branches out of one central stem, making *seven* in all, marking, and in harmony with, the fact, that the light was the light of God's people in the world, but that its source was Divine.

The Panoply of God.

In Eph. vi. 14-18, the Christian's panoply consists of *six* pieces; but there is a *seventh*, without which they are of no avail, and that is *Prayer* :—

The Girdle of Truth, John xiv. 6; xvii. 17.
The Breastplate of Righteousness, Jer. xxiii. 6; Phil. iii. 9.
The Sandals of the Gospel, Eph. ii. 10.
The Shield of Faith (*i.e.*, Faith's shield, which is Christ), Gen. xvii. 1; Rom. xiii. 14; Ps. xci. 4.
The Helmet of Salvation, Ps. xxvii. 1.
The Sword of the Spirit (*i.e.*, the Spirit's sword, which is the Word of God), Rev. xix. 13.
Prayer—which keeps the armour bright and enables us to use it effectually.

Ezekiel's Temple.

In Ezek. xl. the measurements of God's Temple are given, which is yet to be erected in His land. The measuring rod used by "the man" was "*six* great cubits" in length (xli. 8). But the great cubit was one cubit and a hand-breadth long (xl. 5, R.V.); therefore as *six* hand-breadths went to one cubit, there were really *seven* ordinary cubits in "the full reed of *six* great cubits."

Thus whenever *six* and *seven* are used together the difference between their respective significations is most marked.

SEVEN, BY ITSELF.

But now turning to the number *Seven*, we must first consider the meaning of the word.

In the Hebrew, *seven* is שֶׁבַע (*shevah*). It is from the root שָׂבַע (*savah*), *to be full* or *satisfied, have enough of.* Hence the meaning of the word "seven" is dominated by this root, for on the *seventh* day God rested from the work of Creation. It was full and complete, and good and perfect. Nothing could be added to it or taken from it without marring it. Hence the word שָׁבַת (*Shavath*), *to cease, desist, rest,* and שַׁבָּת *Shabbath, Sabbath,* or day of *rest.* This root runs through various languages; *e.g.,* Sanscrit, *saptan;* Zend., *hapta;* Greek, ἑπτά (*hepta*); Latin, *septem.* All these preserve the "t," which in the Semitic and Teutonic languages is dropped out; *e.g.* Gothic, *sibun;* Germ., *sieben;* Eng., *seven.*

It is *seven,* therefore, that stamps with perfection and completeness that in connection with which it is used. Of *time,* it tells of the Sabbath, and marks off the week of seven days, which, artificial as it may seem to be, is universal and immemorial in its observance amongst all nations and in all times. It tells of that eternal Sabbath-keeping which remains for the people of God in all its everlasting perfection.

In the creative works of God, *seven* completes the colours of the spectrum and rainbow, and satisfies in music the notes of the scale. In each of these the *eighth* is only a repetition of the *first.*

Another meaning of the root שָׁבַע (*Shavagh*) is *to swear,* or *make an oath.* It is clear from its first occurrence in Gen. xxi. 31, "They sware both of them," that this oath was based upon the "seven ewe lambs" (*vv.* 28, 29, 30), which point to the idea of *satisfaction* or *fulness* in an *oath.* It was the *security, satisfaction,* and *fulness* of the obligation, or completeness of the bond, which caused the same word to be used for both the number *seven* and an *oath;* and hence it is written, "an oath for confirmation is an end of all strife." Beer-*sheba, the well of the oath,* is the standing witness of the spiritual perfection of the number *seven.* The number meets us on

The Fore-front of Revelation.

The first statement as to the original Creation in Gen. i. 1 consists of 7 words, and 28 letters (4×7).*

* But we ought to note in passing that the next statement, Gen. i. 2, which tells of the ruin into which this Creation fell, though it consists of 14 words, yet it has 52 letters. Now 52 is 4 times 13, and 13, as we shall see further on, is the number of apostasy. Thus the cause of that ruin is more than intimated by the number 13 appearing so significantly in the second verse.

The Words of Jehovah

are pure words. They are not angelic words (2 Cor. xii. 4, 1 Cor. xiii. 1), not words pertaining to heaven; but words used by men on this earth, human words, and therefore they have to be perfectly purified, as silver is purified in a furnace. In Ps. xii. 6, there is an ellipsis which requires the word "words" to be repeated from the previous clause. Then we can take the preposition ל, (*Lamed*), which means "to," in its natural sense. The A.V. translates it *of* ("a furnace of earth"); and the R.V. renders it *on* ("a furnace on the earth"). Both are wrong through not seeing and supplying the *ellipsis* which would have enabled them to translate the ל, *to*, or *pertaining to*, literally. Thus:—

a | The words of Jehovah are pure words,
  b | As silver tried in a furnace:
a | [*Words*] pertaining to the earth,
  b | Purified seven times.

Here we have the four lines complete, in which "a" corresponds to "*a*," the subject being the *words of Jehovah*. While in "b" and "*b*" we have *the purifying:* in "b" of silver, and in "*b*" of the earthly words which Jehovah uses.

Jehovah takes up and uses words "pertaining to this world," but they require purifying. Some words He does not use at all; some He uses with a higher meaning; others He uses with a new meaning: thus they are purified. Now, silver is refined "seven times." So these words have to be perfectly purified before they can be used as "the words of Jehovah."

Abraham's Seven-fold Blessing

in Gen. xii. 2, 3:—

"I will make of thee a great nation,
And I will bless thee,
And make thy name great;
And thou shalt be a blessing;
And I will bless them that bless thee,
And curse him that curseth thee:
And in thee shall all families of the earth be blessed."

With this we may compare

JEHOVAH'S SEVEN-FOLD COVENANT WITH ISRAEL

in Exod. vi. 6–8. Seven times does the expression, "I will" occur in these few verses, stamping the whole with *spiritual* perfection. These are preceded by "I have" three times repeated (*vv.* 4, 5), giving the *Divine* basis on which the blessing was based:—

> I have established My covenant with them, etc.
> I have also heard their groaning, etc.
> I have remembered My covenant.

Then follows the seven-fold blessing:—

> I will bring you out from Egypt.
> I will rid you of their bondage.
> I will redeem you.
> I will take you to Me for a people.
> I will be to you a God.
> I will bring you in unto the land.
> I will give it you.

"NOW HEBRON WAS BUILT SEVEN YEARS BEFORE ZOAN IN EGYPT"

(Num. xiii. 22). Egypt was "the house of bondage." Zoan was that city in it where its wise men were shown to be fools (Isa. xix. 11–13). It was also the place where God's miracles were performed which brought out the folly of that human wisdom (Ps. lxxviii. 12, 43).

But Hebron, which means *fellowship*, was a place in Canaan, the city of Abraham, "the friend of God," still called to-day the city of *El Khulil*, "*of the Friend.*" In its valley, Eschol, grew the finest fruit of Emmanuel's land.

"Now Hebron was built seven years before Zoan in Egypt." This phrase, thrown in parenthetically, at the moment when His people first discovered the existence of Hebron, contains the intimation of a deep spiritual truth, as shown by the significance of the number *seven.*

It shows that the sphere of Divine friendship and fellowship and of heavenly delights was established in eternity, seven years marking the spiritual perfection of time, before the wisdom of this world had any existence or place. (See

Ps. xc. 2; ciii. 17; Prov. viii. 22–31; Mic. v. 2; John xvii. 5–24; 1 Cor. ii. 7; Eph. i. 4—iii. 11; 2 Tim. i. 9; Titus i. 2; 1 Pet. i. 19, 20).

The Seven-fold Sprinkling

implies that it was perfectly and *spiritually* efficacious.

On the great Day of Atonement the blood was sprinkled "ON the mercy-seat eastward." This was Godward, and therefore it was *once* done and on the mercy-seat. But "BEFORE the mercy-seat" it was to be sprinkled *seven* times. *Before** the mercy-seat *seven* times, because this was the perfect testimony for the *people* that the atonement for their sins was accomplished.

The directions for the Day of Atonement are given in Lev. xvi.; but from other Scriptures we learn that there were *seven* sprinklings on that great day, to mark the perfection of accomplished atonement:—

1. On the mercy-seat (Lev. xvi. 14).
2. Before the mercy-seat (Lev. xvi. 14).
3. Before the veil (Lev. iv. 17).
4. On the horns of the golden altar (Exod. xxx. 10).
5. On the horns of the brazen altar (Lev. xvi. 18).
6. Round about upon the altar (Lev. xvi. 19).
7. The blood that was left poured out at the foot of the brazen altar (Lev. iv. 18).

The Psalms

are in many ways stamped with this number of spiritual perfection.

There are 126 Psalms which have titles. That is 7×18.

There are *seven* names mentioned in the titles as the authors of these Psalms, viz.:—

1. David, 56 (7×8).
2. The Sons of Korah, 11 (Pss. xlii., xliv.—xlix., lxxxiv., lxxxv., lxxxvii., lxxxviii).

---

* It was "directly before the *Tabernacle*" that the blood of the red heifer was sprinkled *seven* times, Num. xix. 4. The leper also was cleansed in the same place with a *seven* fold sprinkling of the blood of the killed bird (Lev. xiv. 7, 11).

3. Asaph, 12 (Pss. l., lxxiii. lxxxiii).
4. Heman the Ezrahite, 1 (Ps. lxxxviii).
5. Ethan the Ezrahite, 1 (Ps. lxxxix).
6. Moses, 1 (Ps. xc.).
7. Solomon, 1 (Ps. lxxii.).

There were 14 Psalms (2×7), all David's, which were written on historical occasions; viz., Pss. iii., vii., xviii., xxx., xxxiv., li., lii., liv., lvi., lvii., lix., lx., lxiii., and cxlii.

Seven Psalms are ascribed to David in the New Testament, specifically, by name:—

(1) Psalm ii. in Acts iv. 25, "Who by the mouth of Thy servant DAVID hast said, Why did the heathen rage and the people imagine a vain thing."

(2) Psalm xvi. in Acts ii. 25, "For DAVID speaketh concerning Him, I foresaw the LORD always before my face, for He is on my right hand that I should not be moved."

(3) Psalm xxxii. in Rom. iv. 6, "Even as DAVID also describeth the blessedness of the man unto whom God imputeth righteousness without works."

(4) Psalm xli. in Acts i. 16, "This Scripture must needs have been fulfilled which the Holy Ghost by the mouth of DAVID spake before concerning Judas."

(5) Psalm lxix. in Rom. xi. 9, "And DAVID saith, Let their table be made a snare, and a trap, and a stumbling-block, and a recompence unto them."

(6) Psalm xcv. in Heb. iv. 7, "He limiteth a certain day, saying in DAVID, To-day, after so long a time, as it is said, To-day if ye will hear His voice."

(7) Psalm cx. in Matt. xxii. 43, "How then doth DAVID in spirit call him Lord, saying, The LORD said unto my Lord," etc.

It will be observed that these *seven* quotations are arranged like the golden candlestick, in 2 threes with one in the centre, viz.:—

3 in the Acts,
1 in the Gospels, and
3 in the Epistles;

Or, like the candlestick—

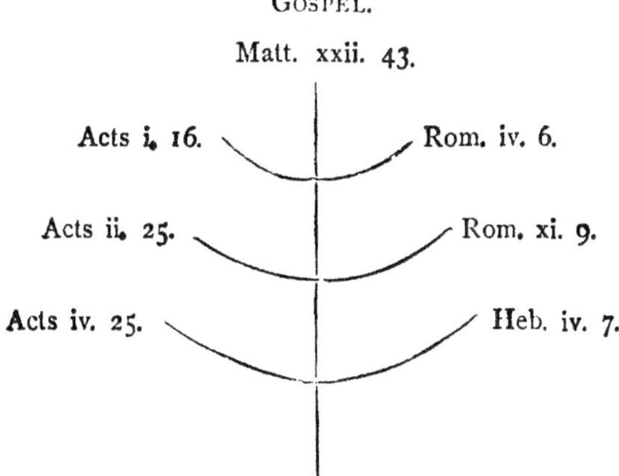

The Seven Quotations from Psalm lxix. in New Testament show that this Psalm is one of great importance, and mark its spiritual perfection, in connection with the Lord Jesus.

(1) Verse 4. The Lord Himself quotes this when the Eleven are gathered round Him just after the institution of the Supper, after telling them to expect the hatred of the world, because He had chosen them out of it. John xv. 18–25.

(2) Verse 9. Again, concerning the Lord, His disciples remembered that it was written. John ii. 13–17.

(3) Verse 9. The Holy Spirit uses it to hold up Christ as a pattern, even as Christ pleased not Himself. Rom. xv. 3.

(4) Verse 21. At the crucifixion this was fulfilled. Matt. xxvii. 34, 48.

(5) Verses 22 and 23. The Holy Spirit, referring to the fact that Israel had not obtained that which it sought for, but only the elect remnant, the rest being blinded, says Rom. xi. 7–10.

(6) Verses 24 and 27. Referring to the persecution of Christians by the Jews, the Holy Spirit says 1 Thess. ii. 15, 16.

(7) Verses 25 and 27. The Lord, in His last denunciation, closing His testimony against Jerusalem, says Matt. xxiii. 29–38.

This *seven* is divided into the usual *four* and *three ; four* of the quotations being in the Gospels, and *three* being in the Epistles. Further, they occur in the first and last of the Gospels, and in the first and last of the Epistles written to Churches. Thus they are stamped by the number of spiritual perfection.

In Matthew	2	4 in the Gospels	7.
In John	2		
In Rom.	2	3 in the Epistles	
In Thess.	1		

"Man of God."

There are *seven* so-called in the Old Testament:—

Moses, Deut. xxxiii. 1, and 5 other times.
David, 2 Chron. viii. 14, and twice.
Samuel, 1 Sam. ix. 6, and 3 times.
Shemaiah, 1 Kings xii. 22, and once (2 Chron. xi. 2).
Elijah, 7 times.
Elisha, 2 Kings iv. 7, and 29 times.
Igdaliah, once, Jer. xxxv. 4.

One in the New Testament on Resurrection ground (Timothy), making *eight* altogether.

Seven Weak Things in Judges,

used by God as instruments of deliverance, marking and stamping the spiritual perfection of His work :—

1. A left handed man (iii. 21),—Ehud delivering from Moab's oppression.
2. An ox-goad (iii. 31) in the hand of Shamgar, delivering from the Philistines.
3. A woman (iv. 4), and
4. A tent-peg in the hand of Jael (iv. 21) } delivering from Jabin, king of Canaan.
5. A piece of a millstone (ix. 53), thrown by another woman, and delivering the people from Abimelech's usurpation.
6. The pitchers and trumpets of Gideon's 300 (vii. 20), delivering from the hosts of Midian.
7. The jaw-bone of an ass (xv. 16), by which Samson delivered Israel from the Philistines.

And why all this in connection with the "saviour" (ii. 16–18), whom God raised up and used? To show that "no flesh shall glory in His presence" (1 Cor. i. 20).

So in later times, whenever God has "done wondrously," He has chosen "the weak things of the world to confound the things which are mighty" (1 Cor. i. 27). It was so in Apostolic days, and has been so in all ages. It was *Luther*, a miner's son, by whom God "shook the world." It was *Calvin*, a cooper's son in Picardy, by whom God built up His church in the Faith. It was *Zwingle*, a shepherd's son in the Alps, by whom God established the Reformation in Switzerland. It was *John Knox*, the son of a plain burgess in a country town, who caused Scotland to be known as "the Land of Knox."

And so through all the ages God has made it clear that it is He who is the worker, and that the instruments He chooses to use are nothing. He usually rejected man's first-born, and chose a younger son. He took David, the youngest, from the sheepfold, to be ruler over His people, as He had chosen Gideon, the least member of the poorest family in Manasseh, to deliver Israel from the Midianite hosts.

Seven-fold Qualification for Service.

This is seen in Gideon, Judg. vi.

1. *Conviction* as to his own humiliating condition, *v.* 11, as shown in *v.* 15.
2. An exercised heart, *v.* 13, as caused probably by the prophet's testimony, *v.* 8.
3. No confidence in the flesh, *v.* 15.
4. Peace with God through grace; the peace of God through gift, *vv.* 17, 18, 22, 23.
5. Worship, *v.* 24.
6. Obedience in small things, *vv.* 25–27.
7. Power for great things, *vv.* 33–35; and vii.

A careful study of Judg. vi. will yield spiritual profit, instructing us as to the ways of God in calling and qualifying His servants.

Seven Oak Trees

are mentioned in the Old Testament; the *seven* being divided into *four* and *three*—the first *three* being connected with burial.

Gen. xxxv. 4. Jacob buried teraphim.
Gen. xxxv. 8. Rachel's nurse.
2 Sam. xxxi. 13. At Jabesh Saul and his sons buried.
Josh. xxiv. 26. Joshua set up the stones of witness.
2 Sam. xviii. 9. Absalom's oak.
Judg. vi. 11. At Ophrah, where the angel appeared.
1 Kings xiii. 14. Where the man of God sat.

Seven of Jesse's Sons

passed before Samuel (1 Sam. xvi.) to show that the perfection of nature can yield nothing for God.

Seven Miracles in John's Gospel.

ii. The water turned into wine.
iv. 47. The nobleman's son.
v. 4. At the pool of Bethesda.
vi. The feeding of the 5,000.
ix. 1. The man born blind.
xi. The raising of Lazarus.
xxi. The draught of fishes.

These formed the spiritual perfection of the "signs" that Jesus was the Christ.

The Seven Words to the Woman of Samaria

in John iv. are full of interest, and the perfection of Christ's dealings with her is thus stamped.

(1) *v.* 7. Attracting her attention by His question, "Give Me to drink"?
(2) *v.* 10. Leading her to ask it of Him.
(3) *vv.* 13, 14. Describing the water which He gives
(4) *v.* 16. The arrow of conviction, "Go," "call," and "come."
(5) *v.* 17. Increasing the conviction.
(6) *vv.* 21–24. Answering her questions and her doubts.
(7) *v.* 26. Revealing Himself.

THE SEVEN APPEARANCES OF ANGELS *

during the life of Jesus on earth.

1. To the shepherds (Luke ii. 9).
2. To Joseph (Matt. ii. 13).
3. To Joseph (Matt. ii. 19).
4. After the Temptation (Matt. iv. 11).
5. In Gethsemane (Luke xxii. 43).
6. At the Resurrection (Matt. xxviii. 2).
7. At the Ascension (Acts i. 10).

THE SEVEN THINGS WHICH SPIRITUALLY DEFILE.

They come "out of the heart," and complete the picture of spiritual defilement, emphasising the fact that spiritual defilement is caused, not by that which goeth "into the mouth," but by that which cometh "out of the heart" (Matt. xv. 19).

There is no end to the mere enumeration of the groups of *seven* things which are to be found in the Bible. Many students have noted them, and some have published lists of their discoveries. This part of our subject is so well-known and well-trodden, that we may here leave it, merely noting a few miscellaneous examples. Mr. Samuell † points out some curious facts in connection with

THE TEN COMMANDMENTS.

These were written with the finger of God, and would, therefore, be specially stamped with this symbol of spiritual perfection.

1. *Seven* of them commence with the word לא, *not.*
2. The word יום, *day*, occurs *seven* times.
3. The preposition ב, *in, seven* times.
4. The preposition ל, *to*, 14 times.
5. "Upon" and "above" together, *seven* times.

* There were *three* appearances *before* the birth of Jesus :—(1) to Zacharias (Luke i. 1); (2) to Mary (Luke i. 26); (3) to Joseph (Matt. i. 20). Altogether there were *ten*, which completes the perfection of Divine order. It would prove a fruitful source of profit to make a close study of all the words and sayings of angels.

† In his work, *Seven, the Sacred Number.*

6. "Serve," "servant," "maidservant," together, *seven* times.
7. The relationship of "father," "mother," "son," "daughter," "wife," together, *seven* times.
8. The numbers "third," "fourth," "six," "seventh," and "thousands," together, *seven* times.
9. "Lord" and "God," together, 14 times.
10. There are *seven* different pronouns used, in all 49 times (7^2).*
11. The 3rd pers. sing. pronoun occurs *seven* times.
12 The conjunction "and" *seven* times in Com. II.
13. The definite article *seven* times in Com. IV.
14. Com. IV. forbids the doing of any work on the *seventh* day to *seven* persons and things.
15. Com. X. forbids coveting to *seven* persons and things.
16. Com. III. contains 21 (7 × 3) simple words.
17. Com. IX. contains 7; and
18. Com. X. contains 28 (7 × 4).

THE DIVISION OF SEVEN INTO FOUR AND THREE

is generally noticeable. It is specially so in the Apocalypse

The Promises to the Churches

are *seven* in number. Each contains the solemn exhortation, "He that hath an ear, let him hear what the Spirit saith unto the churches." In the first *three* epistles the promise (which refers to the *past* in its imagery) *follows* this exhortation; while in the latter *four* the promise (which has reference to *future* blessings) precedes it.

Our attention is thus called to this great exhortation. It tells us that when these epistles were sent, the Church and the churches had all failed in their corporate capacity. They are addressed not to the churches, but to individuals; and all through, individuals are exhorted. It is the same with John's Epistles, written, like his Gospel and the Apocalypse, at the close of the first century. So that we must not and cannot do as we are bidden on every hand,—"Go back to the first three centuries," and "hear the voice of the Church"; for

---

* Omitting "thy" before "stranger" (Com. IV.) with LXX. and Vulg.

before the close of the first century we are bidden to hear not what the church or the churches say, but to "*hear what the Spirit saith unto the churches.*"

The Seven Seals

are thus divided; the first four being marked by the command "Come,"* given to the horseman, while the latter three are altogether different.

The Seven Trumpets

are also divided into three and four, the first four being severed from the latter three by the angel flying saying, "Woe, woe, woe."

The Seven Parables of Matthew xiii.

are also thus marked, as already shown on page 128.

The division is still further marked by the *three* commencing with the word "Again" (*vv.* 44, 45, and 47), while the *four* are separated by the word "Another"; thus indicating that in the *four* we have four different revelations in their relation to the *world*, while in the *three* we have a repetition of the one truth in different forms† in its relation to God's people.

MISCELLANEOUS EXAMPLES.

The *seven* gifts of Rom. xii. 6–8.
The *seven* unities of Eph. iv. 4–6. (See p. 59.)
The *seven* characteristics of wisdom, James iii. 17.
The *seven* gifts of Christ in John's Gospel:
His flesh, vi. 51.
His life, x. 11.
His example, xiii. 15.
The comforter, xiv. 16.
"My peace," xiv. 27.
His words, xvii. 8, 14.
His glory, xvii. 22.

* The verb means "to come," or "go."
† See *The Kingdom and the Church*, by the same author.

The *seven* "better" things in Hebrews:
Testament, vii. 22.
Promises, viii. 6.
Substance, x. 34.
Hope, vii. 19.
Sacrifices, ix. 23.
Country, xi. 16.
Thing, xi. 35.

The *seven* titles of Christ in Hebrews:
Heir of all things, i. 2.
Captain of our salvation, ii. 10.
Apostle, iii. 1.
Author of salvation, v. 9.
Forerunner, vi. 20.
High Priest, x. 21.
Author and finisher of faith, xii. 2.

The *seven*-fold "once," ἅπαξ (*hapax*). *Once for all*, in Hebrews (ix. 7, 26, 27, 28; x. 2; xii. 26, 27).

The *seven* exhortations in Hebrews, "Let us," x. 22, 23, 24; xii. 1, 28; xiii. 13, 15.

The *seven* graces of 2 Pet. i. 5-7.

The *seven*-fold ascriptions of praise in Rev. v. 12; vii. 12, etc.

The *seven* "eternal" things in Hebrews:
A priest for ever, v. 6.
Eternal salvation, v. 9.
,, judgment, vi. 2.
,, redemption, ix. 12.
,, spirit, ix. 14.
,, inheritance, ix. 15.
Everlasting covenant, xiii. 20.

The *seven* firstfruits of—
Resurrection, 1 Cor. xv. 20-23.
The Spirit, Rom. viii. 23.
New creation, James i. 18.
Israel, Rom. xi. 16.
The "redeemed from the earth," Rev. xiv. 5.
Missions, Rom. xvi. 5.
Ministry, 1 Cor. xvi. 15.

The *seven* parables of Matt. xiii.*

The *seven-fold* "blessed" in Revelation: i. 3; xiv. 13; xvi. 15; xix. 9; xx. 6; xxii. 7, 14.

The *seven* "mysteries" or secrets:

The kingdom, Matt. xiii. 11; Mark iv. 11; Luke viii. 10.

The partial blindness of Israel, Rom. xi. 25.

The Church or Body of Christ, Rom. xvi. 25; Eph. iii. 3 4, 9; v. 32; vi. 19; Col. i. 26, 27; Rev. i. 20.

The first Resurrection, 1 Cor. xv. 51.

The secret purpose of God, Eph. i. 9; Col. ii. 2; Rev. x. 7.

The secret purpose of the devil, 2 Thess. ii. 7.

Babylon, Rev. xvii. 5, 7.

The *seven* steps in the humiliation of Jesus and the *seven* in His exaltation in Phil. ii.

The *seven* words of Jesus from the Cross:

"Father, forgive them, for they know not what they do," Luke xxiii. 34.

"Verily, I say unto thee to-day: Thou shalt be with Me in Paradise," Luke xxiii. 43.

"Woman, behold thy son . . . . Behold thy mother," John xix. 26.

"My God! my God! why hast Thou forsaken Me," Matt. xxvii. 46.

"I thirst," John xix. 28.

"It is finished," John xix. 30.

"Father, into Thy hand I commend my spirit," Luke xxiii. 46.

Seven-fold occurrence of the expression "in Christ," in 2 Tim.: i. 1, 9, 13; ii. 1, 10; ii. 12, 15.

The mystery of God is completed in the *seventh* vial of the *seventh* trumpet of the *seventh* seal.

The "*seventh*" man "from Adam" "*was not*, for God took him" (Gen. v. 24).

The day of atonement was in the *seventh* month (Lev. xvi. 29).

The clean beasts were taken into the Ark by *sevens* (Gen. vii. 2). (The others were taken by twos, vi. 19).

Seven steps lead up to the temple in Ezek. xl.

---

* See *The Kingdom and the Church*, by the same author.

The Lord's Prayer contains *seven* petitions. These are divided into four and three. The first three relate to God, the four to man.

Seven washings are typical of our complete spiritual cleansing (2 Kings v. 14).

NUMBERS OF WORDS AND OCCURRENCES.

Turning now to another department we come to a large subject, which has already been touched upon (see pp. 23-44).

Some writers see *seven* everywhere and in everything in the Bible.* But this is to deny, practically, the significance of all other numbers, and to lose all their instruction. Still we must admit that in the structure and outward form of Holy Writ, as being the special work of the Holy Spirit, we do see this stamp of *spiritual perfection* in a very remarkable manner. Mr. Samuell calls attention to the number as we see it:

1. In the occurrences of single *words*.
2. In the occurrences of important *phrases*.
3. In groups of words from the *same root*.
4. In groups of words from *different* roots, but with similar meaning.

And this not merely in the Bible as a whole, but sometimes very markedly:

1. In the Old Testament.
2. In the Hebrew or Chaldee portions of the Old Testament.
3. In the New Testament.
4. In a particular book.
5. In all the books of a particular writer.
6. In a particular section of a book referring to a special subject.

Let us look at a few examples, and first of the number of words used for a particular thing. We have already seen an example of this under the number *six*.

SEVEN WORDS FOR GOLD.

As *brass* is symbolical of judgment (seen in the brazen altar), so *gold* is symbolical of glory, and glory is grace

* See *Seven the Sacred Number*, by Richard Samuell.

consummated. "The Lord will give grace and glory" (Ps. lxxxiv. 11). "Whom He justified them He also glorified" (Rom. viii. 30).

Hence the number of spiritual perfection in the words used for gold:

1. זהב (*zah-hahv*), from root *to shine, glitter,* like gold. Hence the common name for gold. This is earthly gold, than which the Word of God is more to be desired (Ps. xix. 7–10).

2. פז (*pahz*), *fine* or *refined gold.* "More to be desired are they than gold (זהב), yea, than much fine gold (פז)," Ps. xix. 10.

   "Therefore I love Thy commandments above gold (זהב); yea, above fine gold (פז)," Ps. cxix. 127.

   "Thou settest a crown of pure gold (פז) upon his head" (Ps. xxi. 3).

   This word is therefore rightly used of the perfections of the living and the written Word. For He "knew no sin" (2 Cor. v. 21). He "did no sin" (1 Pet. ii. 22). "In Him was no sin" (1 John iii. 5).

3. בצר (*betzer*), Job xxii. 24, 25, and בצר (*b'tzar*), *gold ore* or *dust,* from root *to dig out* or *cut off.* Hence used of gold broken up.

   The sense of Job xxii. 24, 25 is completely lost in the A.V. In the R.V. it reads, *v.* 22:

   > "Receive, I pray thee, the law from His mouth,
   > And lay up His words in thine heart.
   > If thou return to the Almighty, thou shalt be built up;
   > If thou put away unrighteousness far from thy tents.
   > And lay thou thy treasure (בצר) in the dust,
   > And the gold of Ophir among the stones of the brooks;
   > And the Almighty shall be thy treasure (בצר),
   > And precious silver unto thee."

   Hence, if we have His Word abiding in us, He Himself is our treasure and our defence. "His truth shall be thy shield" (Ps. xci. 2).

4. חרוץ (*chah-rootz*), from חרץ (*charatz*), *to chop* or *cut off short;* then of the instrument which the *stone-cutter* uses; then of the *pieces cut off.* Hence gold in

pieces or parts, as preserved in the word *carats*, specially applied to gold.*

As applied to God's "workmanship" we are cut off and *tried* as gold and precious stones. "When He hath tried me I shall come forth as gold" (Job xxiii. 10). "The furnace is for gold, but God trieth the hearts" (Prov. xvii. 3).

5. כתם (*keh-them*), from כתם (*kah-tham*), *to cut in, engrave* (only in Jer. ii. 22, "Mine iniquity is marked before me"). As used of gold it implies that it is true and sterling, having the stamp or mark graved upon it.† As a title of the Psalms it is used with the prefix מ, *mem*. מכתם (*michtam*), *writing*, especially writing cut in or engraved with a stylus (like the LXX. στηλογραφία, "a sculptured writing"‡). מכתב, *michtahv*, means simply *a writing*.§ A writing of David concerning David's Son and David's Lord.

6. סגור (*s'gohr*), from סגר (*sāh-gar*), *to shut up, enclose*, used of gold as being *solid*, 1 Kings vi. 20, "he overlaid it with *pure* (marg., shut up) gold," *i.e.* gold plates, not merely gold leaf or wash. Occurs in Job xxviii. 15, "It cannot be gotten for gold," *i.e.* the wisdom of God's Word. "Every word of God is pure." "Add thou not unto His words."

7. דהב (*d'hav*, Chald.), meaning same as זהב (see No. 1); occurs only in Ezra and Daniel.

Thus the fact of there being *seven* words for gold speaks to us of the spiritual perfection of the Word of God, which is so often compared to it.

Seven different Names for Palestine.

In Old Testament only:

1. "The Holy Land," Zech. ii. 12 (אדמת הקדש, *Admath Ha-kadosh*; LXX., ἡ γῆ ἡ ἅγια; early Christian writers,

* Job xli. 30; Ps. lxviii. 13; Prov. iii. 14; viii. 10, 19; xvi. 16; Isa. xxviii. 27; xli. 15; Dan. ix. 25; Joel iii. 14; Amos i. 3; Zech. ix. 3.

† It occurs Job xxviii. 16, 19; xxxi. 24; Ps. xlv. 9; Prov. xxv. 12; Song v. 11; Isa. xiii. 12; Lam. iv. 1; Dan. x. 5.

‡ στήλη (*steelee*) was the word for *grave-stone*. Hence these Psalms point to *Resurrection*, Ps. xvi., lvi., lvii., lviii., lix., lx.

§ See Ex. xxxii. 16; xxxix. 30; Deut. x. 4; 2 Chron. xxi. 12; xxxv. 4; xxxvi. 22; Ezra i. 1; Isa. xxxviii. 9.

Terra sancta). Very common in Middle Ages, now used only geographically.

2. "The Land of Jehovah," only in Hosea ix. 3. Compare Lev. xxv. 23; Ps. lxxxv. 1; Isa. viii. 8; Joel i. 6; iii. 2; Jer. xvi. 18.

In New Testament only:

3. "The Land of Promise," Heb. xi. 9. This title is based of course on the Old Testament and other Scriptures. Compare Gen. xiii. 15; Deut. xxxiv. 1–4; Gen. l. 24; Ezek. xx. 42; Acts vii. 5.
4. Judea, or the Land of Judah, ארץ יהודה. This name was at first used only of the territory of the Tribe of Judah (2 Chron. ix. 11); but after the Captivity it was used of the whole land, even including the East of the Jordan, Luke i. 5; xxiii. 5; Matt. xix. 1; Acts xxviii. 21.

In Old and New Testaments:

5. "The Land," הארץ, *Ha-ahretz*, Ruth i. 1; Jer. xii. 11; Luke v. 25; Matt. xxvii. 45. This was a strictly Jewish name.
6. "The Land of Israel," ארץ ישראל. First used in 1 Sam. xiii. 19, and occasionally in later books (2 Kin. v. 2; vi. 23). In Ezekiel oftener than in all the rest of the Bible. Matt. ii. 21. This name is also essentially Jewish.
7. "Canaan," כנען (*K'naan*). So called after the son of Ham, by whose descendants it was at first inhabited (Gen. ix. 18; x. 15–19). It is therefore the oldest name, and was confined to the country west of the Jordan. See Exod. vi. 4; xv. 15; Lev. xiv. 34; Deut. xxii. 39; Josh. xiv. 1; Ps. cv. 11; Gen. xvii. 8.

The name *Palestine* and *Palestina*, when the A.V. was made, was equivalent to *Philistia*. See Ps. lx. 8; lxxxvii. 4; cviii. 9. It is never used of the whole land, but only of "Philistia." See Kitto, vol. iii. p. 386.

Some Words which Occur Seven Times.

(1) *Old Testament.*

אזור (*Eh-zōr*), a girdle, 14.

אזכרה (*az-kah-rah*), memorial, 7.

אכר (*ik-kar*), husbandman, 7.

אנף (*ah-naph*), to be angry, 14.

אסר (Chald., *esahr*), a decree, 7 (all in Dan. vi.).

אפק (*ah-phak*), to restrain, 7.

בקר (*bah-kar*), to search, 7.

בר (*bar*), clean, 7.

בר (*bar*) and בר (*bahr*), corn, 14.

ברי (*b'ree*) and בריא (*bah-ree*), fat, 14.

ברית (*b'reeth*), covenant; 7 in Gen. ix. of God's covenant with Noah, and 14 in Gen. xv. and xvii. of God's covenant with Abraham.

גולה (*goh-lah*), captivity, 42 (7 being in the simple form, and 7 with the preposition ב, *into*, prefixed).

גזה (*gizzah*), a fleece, 7 (all in Judg. vi. 37–40).

גן (*gan*), a garden, 42 (14 being in Genesis, and 28 elsewhere).

דשא (*deh-sheh*), grass, 14.

זקק (*zah-kak*), to refine, 7.

חי (*chah'y*), living: In Chaldee, 7.

In Hebrew, 168, viz.:—

Leviticus ...	35	
Numbers ...	7	
Deuteronomy...	21	168 (7 × 8 × 3).
Samuel ...	49	
Solomon's ...	56	

In Chaldee it occurs 7 times (Ezra vi. 10; Dan. ii. 30; iv. 17, 34; vi. 20, 26; vii. 12).

טירה (*tee-rah*), an enclosure, or castle, etc., 7.

טף (*taph*), little children, 42:

Deuteronomy ...	7	
Rest of Pentateuch	21	42 (6 × 7).
Elsewhere	14	

יהודי (*y'hudee*), a Jew (singular)	10	14.
Jehudi (proper name) ...	4	

ילד (*yah-lad*), to beget, 28 in Gen. v.

יצחק (*yitz-chahk*) and ישחק (*yis-chahk*), Isaac, 112:

Deuteronomy ...	7	
Rest of Pentateuch	91	112 (7 × 8 × 2).
Elsewhere	14	

כהן (*Koh-heyn*), priest, 7 in Genesis.

כהנה (*K'hoonnah*), the priest's office, 14.

לבונה (*l'voh-nah*), frankincense, 21 (7 being in Leviticus).

מן (*mahn*), manna, 14.

נא (*nah*), I pray, or vow, 406 (7 × 58).

נגינה (*n'gee-nah*), a song, 14:

In Psalm titles, 7.

Elsewhere, 7.

נגן (*nah-gan*), to play on a stringed instrument, 7 in 1 Sam. xvi.—xix., all spoken of David.

צאצאים (*tzeh-tzaheem*), offspring, 7 in Isaiah.

צום (*tzoom*), to fast, 21.

קהלת (*kō-he-leth*), a preacher, 7, all in Ecclesiastes:

3 in beginning, i. 1, 2, 12.

1 in middle, vii. 27.

3 at the end, xii. 8, 9, 10.

נעם (*noh-gam*), beauty, Ps. xxvii. 4; xc. 17; Zech. xi. 7, 10: pleasantness, Prov. iii. 17: pleasant, Prov. xv. 26; xvi. 24.

נתן (*n'than*), to give or bestow, Ezra iv. 13; vii. 20 twice; Dan. iv. 16; iv. 17, 25, 32.

עלמה (*al-mah*), a maiden, Gen. xxiv. 43; Exod. ii. 8; Ps. lxviii. 25; Prov. xxx. 19; Song i. 3; vi. 8; Isa. vii. 14.

שרף (*sah-raph*), fiery serpents, Num. xxi. 6, 8; Deut viii. 15; Isa. vi. 2, 6; xiv. 29; xxx. 6.

רמה (*rim-mah*), a worm, 7.

שטן (*sah-tahn*), Satan, 14 in Job.

תור (*tohr*), a turtle dove, 14.

El-Shaddai * (God Almighty), Gen. xvii. 1; xxviii. 3; xxxv. 11; xliii. 14; xlviii. 3; Exod. vi. 36; Ezek. x. 5.

(2) *New Testament.*

ἁγνίζω (*agnizō*), to purify.

ἀήρ (*aeer*), air, 7.

ἀνάστασις (*anastasis*), resurrection; 42 times, 21 of which have the article, and seven are in the dative case.

ἀπάτη (*apatee*), deceit.

ἄπειμι (*apeimi*), to be absent, 7.

---

* *Shaddai* (Almighty) without *El* occurs 48 times (4 × 12), a number which speaks of perfection of dominion over the earth. (See p. 53.)

ἀργύριον (*argurion*), pieces of silver money } 7, in connection with Judas.
ἀστήρ (*asteer*), a star, 14 in Revelation.
ἄφθαρτος (*aphthartos*), incorruptible, 7.
βασιλεύω (*basileuō*), to reign, 21 (*seven* being in Revelation; 14 elsewhere).
δοῦλος (*doulos*), servant, 14 in Revelation.
ἐπίσταμαι (*epistamai*), to know, 14.
ἐπιστάτης (*epistatees*), master, 7 (all in Luke).
ἐπιταγή (*epitagee*), commandment, 7.
ἡγέομαι (*hegeomai*), to be chief, 28.
ἄμωμος (*amōmos*), 7:

  without blemish, Eph. v. 27; 1 Pet. i. 19.
  without spot, Heb. ix. 4.
  without fault, Rev. xiv. 5.
  without blame, Eph. i. 4.
  faultless, Jude 24.
  unblameable, Col. i. 22.

παρουσία (*parousia*), presence or coming, 7 times in 1 and 2 Thess. (4 times in the first Epistle and 3 times in the second).
Σιών (*Siōn*), Zion, 7 times.
φίλημα (*phileema*), a kiss, 7.
ᾠδή (*ōdee*), a song, 7.
ψαλμός (*psalmos*), psalm, 7.

PHRASES.

(1) *Old Testament.*

אל קנא (*El quannah*) ... 5 } a jealous God.
אל קנוא (*El quannoh*) ... 2 }
הנה ימים באים (*Hinneh yahmim baheem*), Behold, the days come, 21.*
טהור הוא (*tahōr hu*), he or it (is) unclean, 7 (all in Lev. xi. and xiii.).
טמא הוא (*tamey hu*), he or it (is) unclean, 7 in Lev. xiii.
טמא הוא לכם (*Tamey hu lahkem*), he or it is unclean unto you, 7 (all in Lev. xi. and Deut. xiv.).

* "Lo" in Jer. xxx. 3; Amos iv. 2, instead of "Behold."

יברכך יהוה אלהיך (*Y'bahrek'kah Y'hovah Eloheka*), the LORD thy God shall bless thee, 7; Deut. xiv. 24, 29; xv. 10; xvi. 10, 15; xxiii. 20; xxiv. 19.*

יהוה צבאות (*Y'hovah Ts'baioth*), the LORD of hosts, 7 in the Psalms and 14 in Haggai.

כי יהוה דבר (*Kee Y'hovah dibber*), for the LORD hath spoken, 7; 1 Kings xiv. 11; Isa. i. 2; xxii. 25; xxv. 8; Jer. xiii. 15; Joel iv. 8; Obad. 18.

"As I live saith the Lord GOD," 14 (all in Ezekiel).

"As I live" (spoken by God), 7; Num. xiv. 28; Isa. xlix. 18; Jer. xxii. 24; xlvi. 18; Ezek. xvii. 19; xxxiii. 27; Zeph. ii. 9.

"Daughter of Jerusalem," 14 (7 in sing. and 7 in plur.).

"Rising up early and sending" (spoken of God), 7 (viz., 2 Chron. xxxvi. 15, and 6 times in Jeremiah).

"Shadrach, Meshach, and Abednego" (Chald.), 14 in Dan. ii. 49—iii. 30.

"The land which [the LORD] sware unto . . . Abraham, to Isaac, and to Jacob," 7; Gen. l. 24; Exod. xxxiii. 1; Num. xxxii. 11; Deut. i. 8; vi. 10; xxx. 20; xxxiv. 4.

"The tree of life," 7 (3 in Gen. lit.; and 4 in Prov., fig.).

"The voice of the LORD," 7 times in Ps. xxix.

"And it came to pass in the days of" ויהי בימי (*Vay'hee Beemaye*), 7 times; always indicating a time of sorrow and distress, (ויהי (*Vayhee*) sounding like the Greek *οὐαὶ, woe;* Lat., *væ*), followed by a manifestation of delivering grace.

(1) Gen. xiv. 1. The war which brought sorrow to Lot and distress to Abraham ends in the blessing of Melchisedek.

(2) Ruth i. 1. The famine and bereavement ending in blessing, marriage, and redemption.

(3) 2 Sam. xxi. 1. A famine again ending in divine deliverance (*v.* 14).

(4) Isa. vii. 1. The confederacy against Jerusalem ending in the promise of Messiah's birth (*v.* 14).

(5) Jer. i. 3. The captivity of Judah followed by the promise of restoration.

* Not always translated in the same way.

(6) Esther i. 1. The danger and distress of the Jewish nation ending in a complete and happy deliverance.

(7) Luke ii. 1. The enrolment of Cæsar Augustus, showing that the land and the people were tributary to Rome, followed by the birth of the Lord Jesus.

Jehovah is said to "Dwell between the cherubim" 7 times: 1 Sam. iv. 4; 2 Sam. vi. 2; 2 Kin. xix. 15; 1 Chron. xiii. 6; Ps. lxxx. 1; xcix. 1; Isa. xxxvii. 16.

(2) *New Testament.*

"As it is written,"* 28 (4 × 7).

καθὼς γέγραπται	... 24	28	Gospels	...	7
ὡς γέγραπται	... 4		Romans	...	14
			Elsewhere	...	7

"From the foundation of the world," ἀπὸ καταβολῆς κόσμου (*apo katabolees kosmou*), 7 times, because relating to God's work of *grace;* while the phrase "before the foundation of the world" occurs 3 times,† because relating to the act of Divine sovereignty. The *seven* occurrences are 3 in the Gospels and 4 elsewhere: Matt. xiii. 35; xxv. 34; Luke xi. 50; Heb. iv. 3; ix. 26; Rev. xiii. 8; xvii. 8.

"The Sabbath day," 7.

"After the order," κατὰ τὴν τάξιν (*kata teen taxin*), 7 (all in Hebrews).

"The first day of the week," μια (του) Σαββάτων (*mia* (*ton*) *sabbatōn*), 7.

πιστός (*pistos*), *faithful,* followed by ὁ λόγος (*ho logos*), *the word* or *saying*, 7 (all in the Pastoral Epistles, 1 Tim. i. 15; iii. 1; iv. 9, 12; 2 Tim. ii. 11; Tit. i. 9; iii. 8‡).

"Children of Israel," 14.

"There shall be weeping and gnashing of teeth," 7.

---

* τὸ ῥηθέν (*tō reethen*), "that which was spoken," occurs 12 times (omitting Matt. xxvii. 35 and Mark xiii. 14 with R.V.). For the *writing* was given by inspiration of the Spirit (7); while the *speaking* was in Divine sovereignty and government. (See p. 37.)

† John xvii. 24; Eph. i. 4; 1 Pet. i. 20. See pages 120, 121.

‡ This "faithful saying" does not refer to what follows it, but to what precedes it in verses 3–7. The affirmation of this is to be made "*in order that* (ἵνα) they which have believed in God might be careful to maintain good works."

Words from the same Root.

(1) *Old Testament.*

אשד (*eshed*), a stream 1, and אשדות (*ashedōth*), springs, 6. Total, 7.

גנזים (*g'nah-zeem*), treasuries, 3; גנזין (*ginzeen*, Chal.), treasure, 3; and גנזך (*ganzak*), a treasury, 1. Total, 7.

כשב (*kesev*), a lamb, 13; כשבה (*kisbah*), a ewe-lamb. 1. Total, 14.

סוף (*sooph*), to have an end, Heb., 8; Chald., 2: סוף (*sōph*), the end, Heb., 5; Chald., 5: סופה (*suphah*), a whirlwind, Heb., 15.

Total, Hebrew ...	28	35 in all.
Chaldee ...	7	

רקם (*rahqam*), to embroider, 9; רקמה (*riqmah*), broidered work, 12. Total, 21.

שמט (*shamat*), to release, etc., 9; שמטה (*sh'mittah*), a release, 5. Total, 14.

(2) *New Testament.*

ἀστήρ (*asteer*), a star, 24; ἄστρον (*astron*), a star, 4. Total, 28.

βάσανος (*basanos*), torment, 3; βασανίζω (*basanizō*), to torment, 12; βασανισμός (*basanismos*), torment, 5; βασανιστης (*basanistees*), a tormentor, 1. Total, 21.

Γαλατία, Galatia, 4 times: 1 Cor. xvi. 1; Gal. i. 2; 2 Tim. iv. 10; 1 Pet. i. 1. Galatians, once: Gal. iii. 1. Of Galatia, twice: Acts xvi. 6; xviii. 23. Total, 7.

ἐλεύθερος (*eleutheros*), free, 23; ἐλευθερία (*eleutheria*), freedom, 11; ελευθεροω (*eleutheroō*), to set free, 7; ἀπελεύθερος (*apeleutheros*), a freed-man, 1. Total, 42.

In Romans	7	42.
In St. John's Gospel and Revelation ...	7	
Elsewhere	28	

ἦχος (*eechos*), a sound, 3; ἠχέω (*eecheō*), to sound, 2; ἐξηχέομαι (*exeecheomai*), to sound forth, 1; κατηχεω (*kateecheō*), to teach by sound (or word of mouth), 8. Total, 14.

WORDS FROM A DIFFERENT ROOT, BUT WITH SIMILAR MEANING.

Word	Occurrences	Total
ברוש (*b'rosh*), fir ...	20	21
ברותים (*b'rot.eem*), fir ...	1	
גת (*gath*), winepress ...	5	21
יקב (*ye-kev*), wine vat ...	16	
יצק (*yah-tzak*), to cast (of metal)	53	58
יצקה (*y'tzoo-kah*), a casting... ...	1	
מוצק (*moo-tzak*), a casting	2	
מוצקת (*moo-tze-keth*), a hollow pipe...	2	
צוק (*tzook*), to pour out, cast	3	5
מצוק (*mah-tzook*), a pillar	2	
		63 (7×9)
כוה (*kah-vah*), to be burned	2	10
כי (*kee*), burning	1	
כויה (*k'veey-yah*), burning	2	
מכוה (*mik-vah*), burning	5	
צרב (*tzarav*), to be burned	1	4
צרבת (*tzah-re-veth*), burning	3	
		14 (2×7)

Word	Occurrences	Subtotal	Total
ἄῤῥην (*arreen*), man	3*	11	21
ἄρσην (*arseen*), male	6		
ἀρσενοκοίτης (*arsenokoitees*), sodomite ...	2		
θήλεια (*theeleia*), female	2	10	
θηλάζω (*theelazō*), to give suck	5†		
θῆλυ (*theelu*), female	3		
ἀμνός (*amnos*), lamb	4	35 (5×7)	
ἀρήν (*areen*), lamb (Luke x. 3)	1		
ἀρνίον (*arnion*), lamb	30		
γελάω (*gelaō*), to laugh	2	6	
γέλως (*gelōs*), laughter	1		
καταγελάω (*katagelaō*), to laugh to scorn	3		
μυκτηρίζω (*mukteerizō*), to mock	1	3	
ἐκμυκτηρίζω (*ek-mukteerizō*), to deride	2		

* The R.V. with the textual editors read ἄρσην (*neut.*) for ἄῤῥην in these three passages: Rom. i. 27; Rev. xii. 5, 13.

† Reading τρέφω, "to nourish," in Luke xxiii. 29 with R.V. and editors.

ἐμπαίζω (*empaizō*), to mock	13	17
ἐμπαιγμός (*empaigmos*), mocking ...	1	
ἐμπαιγμονή (*empaigmonee*), mockery	1*	
ἐμπαίκτης (*empaiktees*), a mocker ...	2	
χλευάζω (*chleuazō*), to mock	2†	2
Total of the four roots		28 (4×7)
ὁρμή (*hormee*), onset	2	20
ὁρμάω (*hormaō*), to rush	5	
ὅρμημα (*hormeema*), a mighty fall	1	
ἀφορμή (*aphormee*), occasion	7	
κονιορτός (*koniortos*), dust	5	
παροτρύνω (*par-otrunō*), stir up		1
		21 (3×7)

Sometimes a single chapter or separate portion may be taken and dealt with by itself, and thus form a fruitful subject of Bible study. We give an example ‡ of

Ezekiel xxxvi.

I. *Seven things concerning Israel to-day*:—
1. Unclean in the sight of God (*v.* 29).
2. Possessed of stony hearts (*v.* 26).
3. Profaning God's holy Name (*vv.* 20, 22).
4. Scattered among the heathen (*v.* 19).
5. Covered with infamy and shame (*vv.* 3-6).
6. Subject to heathen rule (*v.* 6).
7. Desolate, forsaken, and a reproach (*vv.* 3, 4, 30).

II. *Seven things God will do to Israel's oppressors* (*Anti-semites*):—
1. Speak in jealousy against them (*v.* 5).
2. Turn their glory into shame (*v.* 7).
3. Dispossess them of their occupation in the land (*vv.* 10, 11).
4. Give them to Israel for a possession (*v.* 12).
5. Break their power to crush Israel (*vv.* 13, 14).
6. Vindicate and glorify His own name among them (*v.* 22).
7. Teach them that He is God (*vv.* 36, 38).

* This word is added by the Textual Editors and R.V. in 2 Pet. iii. 3, which would thus read "scoffers with scoffing."

† All the authorities read διαχλευάζω in Acts ii. 13.

‡ Suggested by Rev. W. H. Walker, jun., in *The Faithful Witness.*

III. *Seven things God will do for Israel :—*

1. Gather them out of all countries (*v.* 24).
2. Bring them into their own land (*v.* 24).
3. Cleanse them from filth and idols (*v.* 26).
4. Give them new hearts and minds, and His spirit (*vv.* 26, 27).
5. Make them again His people (*v.* 28).
6. Cause them to flourish and multiply (*v.* 30).
7. Make their end better than their beginning (*v.* 11).

IV. *Seven things Israel themselves will do :—*

1. Remember their past evil (*v.* 31).
2. Loathe themselves for their iniquity (*v.* 31).
3. Be ashamed and confounded (*v.* 32).
4. Walk in Jehovah's statutes (*v.* 27).
5. Keep His judgments (*v.* 27).
6. Dwell for ever in the land (*v.* 33).
7. Pray for the accomplishment of all these blessings (*v.* 37).

Gematria.

One or two examples may be given of the numbers in names, etc., though many more are given elsewhere.

Enoch, "the seventh from Adam" = 84 (7 × 12).
"Heirs of God," in the Greek = 1071 (7 × 153).
"The Lamb," in Greek = 651 (= 7 × 93 or 7 × 3 × 31).

The Multiples of Seven

as a rule partake of the same spiritual significance, and therefore we have not treated all of them specially, but only where they have a peculiar significance arising from the power of the other factor, as is the case with 42, 49, 70, etc.

As an example of one of the other multiples we may take

The Ass.

The "ass" is the only animal that man is compared to: see Job xi. 12, "For vain man would be wise, though man be born a wild ass's colt."

In Exod. xiii. 13 the first-born of man is classed with the firstling of an ass. Both must be redeemed with a lamb.

This is repeated in Exod. xxxiv. 20. Nothing less than a sacrificial redemptive act could bring such a being to God.

There are 28 (4×7) asses separately spoken of, and with these may be compared the 28 (4×7) "times" connected with "vain man" in Eccles. iii. 1–8.

1. Balaam's ass (Num. xxii. 21), "a time to speak."
2. Achsah's ass (Josh. xv. 18), "a time to get," when she lighted off her ass to make her request and get what she asked.
3. Samson's (Judg. xv. 15), "a time to war."
4. The Levite's (Judg. xix. 28), "a time to be silent," when "none answered," and he sent his desperate, silent message throughout Israel.
5. Abigail's (1 Sam. xxv. 20), "a time of peace," when she met David and made peace for Nabal.
6. Her second ass (*v.* 42), "a time to love," when she went to meet David and became his wife.
7. Ahithophel's (2 Sam. xvii. 23), "a time to die," when he saddled his ass and went and hanged himself.
8. The "old prophet's" ass (1 Kin. xiii. 13, 27), "a time to kill," when he found "the man of God" killed by the lion.
9. The "man of God's" ass (*v.* 28), "a time to mourn," when the old prophet laid him thereon "to mourn and to bury him."
10. The Shunamite's ass (2 Kin. iv. 24), "a time to heal," when she rode to Elisha, who restored her son.
11. Mephibosheth's (2 Sam. xix. 26), "a time to embrace," when he would go and salute David.
12. Shimei's (1 Kin. ii. 40), "a time to die."
13. Jesse's (1 Sam. xvi. 20), "a time to live" (21).
14. Moses's (Exod. iv. 20–26), "a time to kill," when he incurred the judgment of Gen. xvii. 14.
15. Abraham's (Gen. xxii. 3), "a time to get and a time to lose," when God demanded back the son He had given.
16. The Saviour's ass (Matt. xx. 5), "a time to laugh," when the daughter of Jerusalem rejoiced.
17. The young, its foal (Matt. xxi. 5).

18–28. The asses of Jacob's sons (Gen. xliv. 13), filling up the other "times."

EIGHT.

In Hebrew the number eight is שמנה (*Sh'moneh*), from the root שמן (*Shah'meyn*), "to make fat," "cover with fat," "to super-abound." As a participle it means "one who abounds in strength," etc. As a noun it is "superabundant fertility," "oil," etc. So that as a numeral it is the superabundant number. As *seven* was so called because the seventh day was the day of completion and rest, so *eight*, as the eighth day, was over and above this perfect completion, and was indeed the *first* of a new series, as well as being the *eighth*. Thus it already represents two numbers in one, the *first* and *eighth*. Let us first consider the connection between

EIGHT AND SEVEN TOGETHER.

Just as we saw the connection between the numbers *six* and *seven* together (pp. 158–167), so we must note the remarkable connection between *seven* and *eight* when used together.

Seven means, as we have seen, according to its etymology, that which is spiritually complete or satisfying; while *eight* denotes that which is superabundant or satiating. Hence we often find these two numbers associated with these distinctions.

Jehovah's Covenants with Abraham

were *eight* in number; seven before Isaac was offered up, and the eighth when he had been received "in a figure" from the dead.

1. Gen. xii. 1–3, sovereignty.
2. Gen. xii. 7, the seed.
3. Gen. xiii. 14–17, Divine assurance, rising and walking on resurrection ground.
4. Gen. xv. 13–21, the limits of the land; the 400 years; the 4th generation.
5. Gen. xvii. 1–22, invincible grace.
6. Gen. xviii. 9–15, human failure and imperfection.
7. Gen. xxi. 12, Spiritual blessing headed up in the seed.
8. Gen. xxii. 15–18, resurrection blessing.

The first *three* are marked off from the others by the words "after these things," xv. 1. The next *four* are marked off from the eighth by similar separating words, repeated in xxii. 1.

It will be noted that each covenant blessing is stamped with the character of its numerical significance.

JOSEPH'S TYPICAL COMMUNICATIONS WITH HIS BRETHREN

were *eight* in number. *Seven* times before Jacob's death, and an *eighth* time after.

1. In Gen. xxxvii. 6, he tells his dream about the sheaves of wheat (earthly glory).
2. His second dream about the sun, moon, and stars (heavenly glory, completing the double witness of John iii. 12).
3. His message of love to them from his father, when he is rejected and cast into the pit, but raised (unknown to them) to the right hand of power.
4. They are compelled to go to Joseph, Gen. xlii.
5. Again they go, Gen. xliii. 15.
6. A third time (Gen. xliv. 13), when Joseph proclaims himself. Three times they had denied him. Three times they have to go to him; and the third time, after deep exercise of heart, reach the place of blessing. But it is (like the No. 6) incomplete. It needs the
7. "And Israel (no longer Jacob) took his journey with all that he had" (Gen. xlvi.). Nothing more is to be desired, so he says, "Now let me die, since I have seen thy face," etc. (*v.* 30). The history is spiritually complete; but there remains another communication.
8. Jacob has passed away, and they are face to face with Joseph, a type of Christ in resurrection glory (Gen. l. 15, etc.).

EXODUS XXI. 23-25.

There are eight particulars in connection with punishment; but seven stand in a different category, not being possible if the eighth were inflicted, viz., "Life for life."

1. Life for life,
2. Eye for eye,
3. Tooth for tooth,
4. Hand for hand,
5. Foot for foot,
6. Burning for burning,
7. Wound for wound,
8. Stripe for stripe.

(Items 2–8: 7; items 1–8: 8)

Exodus xl.

Seven times we have the phrase "As the Lord commanded Moses,"* and *once* (*v.* 16), "according to all that the Lord commanded him."

The Feast of Tabernacles

was the only feast which was kept eight days. The eighth is distinguished from the seventh. See Lev. xxiii. 39, and compare verses 34–36; Num. xxix. 39, and Neh. viii. 18.

2 Chronicles vi.

Eight appeals of Solomon for his prayer to be heard. Seven times, "Hear Thou from heaven," and once (*v.* 21), "Hear Thou from thy dwelling-place, from heaven." Similarly in 1 Kings viii., the parallel passage.

Isaiah v. 1, 2.

There are eight sentences describing the vineyard, but *seven* give the characteristics, and *one* the result.

The Steps in Ezekiel's Temple.

Seven led into the outer court (xl. 22, 26), and eight led from the outer to the inner (xl. 31, 34, 37).†

The *seven* led from labour to rest, the eight from rest to worship.

The Lord Jesus was on a Mountain

eight times.‡ *Seven* times were before the cross, but the *eighth* time after He rose from the dead.

---

* Verse 23, "had commanded," is the same as the other six in the Hebrew.

† How many led into the Temple the Hebrew Text does not say. The Septuagint says there were ten. See *v.* 49, R.V. text and margin.

‡ Omitting of course the scene in the Temptation.

Ephesians iv. 4–6.

Seven unities, but the seventh is two-fold—"God and Father"—making *eight* in all.

Colossians iii. 12, 13.

There are seven graces, but (*v.* 14) over all these there is "love," which is the bond of perfectness, the upper garment which completes and unites the others.

James iii. 17.

"The wisdom that is from above" is enumerated in *seven* particulars, but the fifth is double, making *eight* in all ("full of mercy and good fruits").

Abraham's Sons

were eight in number; but *seven* were "born after the flesh," while one, the *eighth*, was "by promise."

The Consecration of Aaron and his Sons

was on the *eighth* day, after abiding "at the door of the Tabernacle of the Congregation day and night *seven* days" (Lev. viii. 35; ix. 1).

In Solomon's Temple

there were *eight* classes of furniture, while in the Tabernacle there were *seven*:—

Temple.	Tabernacle.
1 Ark.	1 Ark.
1 Mercy-seat.	1 Mercy-seat.
1 Altar of Incense.	1 Altar of Incense.
10 Candlesticks.	1 Candlestick.
10 Tables of shewbread.	1 Table of shewbread.
1 Altar of burnt-offering.	1 Altar of burnt-offering.
10 Lavers.	1 Laver.
1 Brasen Sea.	
35 (5×7).	7

The Sabbath to be Kept Holy.

There were *eight* commands in all. *Seven* by Jehovah (Exod. xx. 8; Deut. v. 12, repetition; xxiii. 12;

xxxi. 13; xxxiv. 21; Lev. xix. 3, 30; xxiii. 3: *one* by Moses, Exod. xxxv. 2).

David was the Eighth Son of Jesse

according to 1 Sam. xvi. 6, etc., and 1 Sam. xvii. 12; but owing doubtless to the death of one son without issue, and hence excluded from the genealogies, David would be called in 1 Chron. ii. 15 "*the seventh.*"

These will suffice to show the connection between the numbers *seven* and *eight*. Let us now consider the number

EIGHT BY ITSELF.

It is 7 *plus* 1. Hence it is the number specially associated with *Resurrection* and *Regeneration*, and the beginning of a new era or order.

When the whole earth was covered with the flood, it was Noah "the eighth person" (2 Pet. ii. 5) who stepped out on to a new earth to commence a new order of things. "Eight souls" (1 Pet. iii. 20) passed through it with him to the new or regenerated world.

Hence, too, circumcision was to be performed on the *eighth* day (Gen. xvii. 12), because it was the foreshadowing of the true circumcision of the heart, that which was to be "made without hands," even "the putting off of the body of the sins of the flesh by the circumcision of Christ" (Col. ii. 11). This is connected with the new creation.

The first-born was to be given to Jehovah on the eighth day (Exod. xxii. 29, 30). But

Resurrection

is the great truth which is signified. Christ rose from the dead on "the *first* day of the week," that was of necessity the *eighth* day. And it is remarkable that the Bible contains the record of

Eight individual Resurrections

(other than the Lord and the saints):

3 in the Old Testament.
3 in the Gospels.
2 in Acts ix. and xx.
} 8.

The three in the Old Testament correspond to the three raised by our Lord.

1. The son of a widow—
   Zarepta (1 Kings xvii. 17–25) and
   Nain (Luke vii. 11–18).

2. The child of a rich person—
   Son of the woman of Shunem (2 Kings iv. 32–37),
   The daughter of Jairus (Mark v. 35; Luke viii. 49).

3. A full grown man . . . . after burial—
   In Elisha's tomb (2 Kings xiii. 20, 21),
   Lazarus (John xi.).

The Feast of Tabernacles

lasted *eight* days, with a special reference to the Incarnation (John i. 14).

The Transfiguration

also took place on the eighth day (inclusive reckoning) after the first announcement of Christ's "sufferings," and it was the showing forth of the "glory" which should follow at His coming again.

The First Cube.

Eight is the first *cubic* number, the cube of *two*, 2 × 2 × 2. We have seen that *three* is the symbol of the first *plane* figure, and that *four* is the first *square*. So here, in the first *cube*, we see something of transcendent perfection indicated, something, the length and breadth and height of which are equal. This significance of the *cube* is seen in the fact that the "Holy of Holies," both in the Tabernacle and in the Temple, were *cubes*. In the Tabernacle it was a *cube* of 10 cubits. In the Temple it was a cube of 20 cubits. In Rev. xx. the New Jerusalem is to be a cube of 12,000 furlongs. Dr. Milo Mahan is inclined to believe that the Ark of Noah, too, had a kind of sacred Shechinah in "the window finished in a cubit above"—a cube of *one*. If so, we have the series of *cubes*:—

1 = The Ark.
10^3 = 1,000, The Tabernacle.
20^3 = 8,000, The Temple.
$12{,}000^3$ = 1,728,* 000,000,000, the New Jerusalem.

EIGHT SONGS IN THE OLD TESTAMENT

outside the Psalms:

1. Redemption, Exod. xv.
2. Supply and maintenance, Num. xxi. 17.
3. Moses witnessing to the grace of God and the unfaithfulness of man, Deut. xxxii.
4. Victory over oppression, Judg. v.
5. David, God's elect, delivered from all his foes, 2 Sam. xxii.
6. The Song of Songs.
7. The song of the well-beloved touching Israel, God's vineyard, Isa. v.
8. This (the *eighth*) waits to be sung on resurrection ground (Isa. xxvi.), for it does not come till after "death is swallowed up in victory," xxv. 8.

THE MIRACLES OF ELIJAH

were *eight* in number, marking the Divine character of his mission:

1. The shutting up of heaven, 1 Kings xvii. 1; James v. 17; Luke iv. 25.
2. Multiplying the widow's meal, 2 Kings xvii. 14–16.
3. Raising the widow's son, *vv.* 17–23.
4. Causing fire to come down from heaven, 1 Kings xviii. 37, 38.
5. Causing rain to come down from heaven, *vv.* 41–45.
6. Causing fire to come down from heaven, 2 Kings i. 10.
7. The same, *v.* 12.
8. Dividing the Jordan, 2 Kings ii. 8.

THE MIRACLES OF ELISHA

were *double* in number, viz. *sixteen*, for his request was, "Let a double portion of thy spirit be upon me," 2 Kings ii. 9:

* This 1728, too, is a remarkable number, viz., $8^2 \times 3^3$.

1. Dividing the Jordan, 2 Kings ii. 14.
2. Healing the waters, *v.* 21.
3. Cursing the young men,* *v.* 24.
4. Procuring water for the three kings, 2 Kings iii. 16–20.
5. Multiplying the widow's oil, 2 Kings iv. 1–7.
6. Raising the widow's son, iv. 37.
7. Healing the deadly pottage, *v.* 38.
8. Feeding the hundred men, *vv.* 42–44.
9. The healing of Naaman, 2 Kings v. 1–19.
10. The smiting of Gehazi, *vv.* 20–27.
11. Causing the iron to swim, 2 Kings vi. 1–7.
12. Opening the eyes of his servant, *v.* 17.
13. Smiting the Syrian army with blindness, *v.* 18.
14. Restoring their sight, *v.* 20.
15. Arresting the king's messenger, *vv.* 30–33.
16. A dead man raised by touching his bones, 2 Kings xiii. 20, 21.

The use and significance of the number *eight* in Scripture is seen to recur in marvellous exactitude. It may indeed be said that

EIGHT IS THE DOMINICAL NUMBER,

for everywhere it has to do with the LORD. It is the number of His name, ΙΗΣΟΥΣ, Jesus:—

Ι	=	10
Η	=	8
Σ	=	200
Ο	=	70
Υ	=	400
Σ	=	200
		888

It is the number stamped upon the Old Testament, the numbers of its books in all the MSS. being 24 (3 × 8). See p. 25.

In the book which relates to His great Apocalypse or Revelation, there are in the introduction which sets forth the

* The word is used of Isaac, aged 28; Joseph when 39; Rehoboam when 40; Shadrach and his companions in Babylon.

glory of the Lord, to be revealed in the day of the Lord, *eight* references to the Old Testament on which the claims of His Lordship are based.

The Eight References to the Old Testament in Revelation i.

It will be noted, moreover, that these are not given at haphazard. Our attention is called to their importance by the order in which they are given. They are arranged in the form of an *epanodos*, the first being from the same book as the eighth, the second corresponding in the same way to the seventh, the third to the sixth, and the fourth to the fifth. Thus the Divine seal of superabundant perfection is there set on the Scriptures which declare the Lordship of Jesus:

A | 5. Isa. lv. 4.
  B | 7-. Dan. vii. 13.
    C | -7. Zech. xii. 10.
      D | 8. Isa. xli. 4; xliv. 6; xlviii. 12.
      D | 11. Isa. xli. 4; xliv. 6; xlviii. 12.
    C | 12. Zech. iv. 2.
  B | 13-15. Dan. vii. 9, 13, 22; x. 5, 6.
A | -16-. Isa. xlix. 2.

Other Dominical Names of Jesus

are also marked by gematria and stamped with the number *eight* as a factor:

Χριστός, Christ, 1480 (8 × 185).
Κύριος, Lord, 800 (8 × 100).
Κύριος ἡμῶν, Our Lord, 1768 (8 × 221).
Σωτήρ, Saviour, 1408 (8^2 × 22).
'Εμμανουήλ, Emmanuel, 25600, (8^3 × 50).
Μεσσίας, Messiah, 656 (8 × 82).
Υἱός, Son, 880 (8 × 110).

We ought also to note that the other factors, beside the prevailing *eight*, are full of significance.

All this speaks to us, if we have "ears to hear," that "God hath glorified His Son Jesus" (Acts iii. 13), and "hath made that same Jesus . . . both Lord and Christ" (Acts ii. 36).

But here we must consider the two numbers

EIGHT AND THIRTEEN TOGETHER

that we may afterwards compare and contrast the two. For this purpose we must consider the number *thirteen* here, and out of its otherwise proper order.

As to the significance of *thirteen*, all are aware that it has come down to us as a number of ill-omen. Many superstitions cluster around it, and various explanations are current concerning them.

Unfortunately, those who go backwards to find a reason seldom go back far enough. The popular explanations do not, so far as we are aware, go further back than the Apostles. But we must go back to *the first occurrence* of the number *thirteen* in order to discover the key to its significance. It occurs first in Gen. xiv. 4, where we read "*Twelve* years they served Chedorlaomer, and the *thirteenth* year they REBELLED."

Hence every occurrence of the number *thirteen*, and likewise of *every multiple* of it, stamps that with which it stands in connection with *rebellion, apostasy, defection, corruption, disintegration, revolution*, or some kindred idea.

The second mention of *thirteen* is in connection with Ishmael, Gen. xvii. 25. He was *thirteen* years old when Abraham circumcised him and admitted him into the covenant to which he was a stranger in heart, and which ended in his rebellion and rejection.

We see it stamped upon the very fore-front of Revelation. For while the opening statement of Gen. i. 1 is composed of seven words and twenty-eight letters (4 × 7), the second verse consists of fourteen words, but fifty-two letters; fifty-two being 4 × 13 tells of some *apostasy* or rebellion which caused the ruin of which that verse speaks.

But it is when we come to

GEMATRIA

that the most wonderful results are seen. These results may be stated thus, briefly: That the names of the LORD's people are multiples of *eight*, while the names of those who apostatised, or rebelled, or who were in any sense His enemies, are multiples of *thirteen*. This statement, if it be proved, is one of the greatest evidences of verbal inspiration which the world has yet seen. The discovery of the great principle is due, we believe, to the late Dr. Milo Mahan, of New York, who has given many examples of it in his work already referred to, now long out of print. The effect of this law can hardly be estimated in establishing the presence of an ever-present working of the Holy Spirit in inditing the very words and even the letters of Scripture. No human foresight or arrangement could have secured such a result beforehand; no human powers could have carried it out in such perfection. No matter where we look, we find the working of the law without cessation, without a break, without a flaw from beginning to end. Only one conclusion is possible, and that is that the Bible has but one Author, an eternal, omniscient Author, designing, superintending, working, and carrying out His own infinite plans.

Let us take a survey of this wondrous field.

THE SETH AND CAIN LINES.

The numerical value of the Seth line of names collectively is a multiple of **8**; whilst those of the *Cain* line collectively is a multiple of **13**.

The Seth Line of Names.

Name	Value	Total
Adam	45	
Seth	700	
Enos	357	
Cainan	210	
Mahalaleel	136	
Jared	214	3168 (**8** × 396).
Enoch	84	
Methuselah	784	
Lamech	90	
Noah	58	
Japheth *	490	

* Japheth was the eldest son of Noah, though Shem was chosen for the genealogy of Jesus Christ.

Taking the Noah group separately, we have:

Name		
Noah	58	936 (**8** × 9 × **13**).
Shem	340	
Ham	48	
Japheth	490	

Without Ham, the three names, Noah, Shem, and Japheth, equal 888. With Ham they equal 936, as above; but this, though it is a multiple of 8, is at the same time a multiple of **13**, and of 9 also, the number of judgment.

The gematria of the whole Scripture, Gen. v. 6–24, which contains the record of these names, amounts to 62960 (or **8** × 7870).

The Cain Line of Names.

Name		
Adam	45	2223 (**13** × 9 × 19)
Cain	160	
Enoch	84	
Irad	284	
Mehujael	95	
Methusael	777	
Lamech	90	
Jabal	42	
Jubal	48	
Tubal Cain	598	

The family of Lamech is also significant if looked at separately:

Lamech and Adah	169 (13^2).
The two wives, Adah and Zillah ...	611 (**13** × 47).
Jabal, his firstborn, the father of the Bedouin	42 { the No. of Antichrist.
Tubal Cain	598 (**13** × 46).
The whole family, including the daughter, Naamah ...	= 1924 (or **13** × 148).

The history of the Cain family is given in Gen. iv. 1–25, and spreads over 130 years (**13** × 10). See Gen. v. 3.

Further, the whole Scripture which records the history, Gen. iv. 1–25, yields by gematria 76882 (**13** × 5914). There is, however, a remarkable exception which "proves the rule." Verse 25 records the birth of Seth, and its value is 6560 (**8** × 820); verse 26, also, which records the birth of his son Enos, and tells how men began then to "call upon the name of the LORD," yields 3064 (**8** × 383).

Contrast this with verse 1, where the numerical value of the words "and she conceived and bare Cain" is 1612 (**13** × 124).

The years of Adam during the days of Cain, before the birth of Seth, were 130 (**13** × 10): see Gen. v. 3. While after the birth of Seth he lived 800 years (**8** × 100), Gen. v. 4.

THE GEMATRIA OF LAMECH'S SONG

in Gen. iv. 23, 24, is 4667 (**13** × 359); while the sentence pronounced on Cain in *v.* 10-13 is 10283 (**13** × 791).

GENESIS VI.

The record in Gen. vi., which gives the apostasy of man, leading up to the judgment of the Flood, is stamped and branded throughout with significant numbers:

Verses 1-3 amount to 7272 (6 × 1212).

Verse 2 amounts to 3198 (**13** × 6 × 41).

Verse 4, "the same were mighty men which were of old, men of renown" = 1703 (**13** × 131).

Verses 5-7, which speak concerning the corruption, = 10335 (**13** × 795).

Verses 1-7 = 21672 (6^2 × 602).

But now contrast *vv.* 8-10 concerning Noah—"But Noah found grace in the eyes of the LORD," etc., 7008 (**8** × 876):

Verses 11-17, the end of all flesh, the command to build the ark, and the threat of the Flood, = 33540 (**13** × 2580).

Verses 14-16, concerning the ark, = 17668 (4 × 4417).

Verses 12, 13, and 17 together, concerning the violence and corruption, = 13320 (666 × 20).

Verses 18-22, which speak of the covenant to save Noah and his house, while they are stamped with the number 13 (which is the number of *atonement* as well as of *sin*, see below), are stamped also with the triple *five*, the 15 of perfect grace by which Noah was called, and by the number 2, which tells of incarnation and deliverance. The gematria of these verses is 15002 (**13** × 1154).

GENESIS X. 15–18.

The Canaanite names:

Name		Value	Total
Canaan	... ...	190	
{ And	... ...	6	
{ Sidon	... ...	154	
Heth ...	... ...	408	
The Jebusite	...	93	
The Amorite	...	256	
The Girgashite	...	521	3211 (**13**^{2} × 19).
The Hivite ...	...	29	
The Arkite ...	...	385	
The Sinite ...	...	135	
The Arvadite	...	226	
The Zemarite	...	345	
The Hamathite	...	463	

THE DESCENDANTS OF JOKTAN (Gen. x. 25–29)

Name		Value
Joktan (the 13th from Shem)	...	169 (**13**^{2})
Peleg (his brother)	... ...	113
Salah (his grandfather) ...	...	338 (**13**^{2} × 2)

His 13 sons—

Name		Value
Almodad ...	... ...	85
Sheleph ...	... ...	410
Hazarmaveth	... ...	744
Jerah ...	... ...	218
Hadoram ...	... ...	255
Uzal ...	... ...	44
Diklah ...	... ...	139
Obal ...	... ...	108
Abimael ...	... ...	84
Sheba ...	... ...	303
Ophir ...	... ...	287
Havilah ...	... ...	59
Jobab ...	... ...	20
		2756 (**13** × 212).

The whole passage (Gen. x. 25–29) yields the number 10647 (**13**^{2} × 63). Such are the pains taken to emphasise the rise of the progenitors of the Saracens, for Joktan settled in S. Arabia, while Ishmael settled in Arabia Petrea.

THE LINE OF ARPHAXAD (Gen. xi. 10–27).

Name		Value	Subtotal	Total
Shem	...	340	1944 (**8** × 243)	3568 (**8** × 446).
Arphaxad		605		
Salah	...	338		
Eber	...	272		
Peleg	...	113		
Reu	...	276		
Serug	...	509	1624 (**8** × 203)	
Nahor	...	264		
Terah	...	608		
Abram	...	243		

NAHOR'S FAMILY.

Name		Value	Total
Nahor	...	264	1264 (**8** × 158).
Haran	...	255	
Lot	...	45	
Sarai	...	510	
Milcah	...	95	
Iscah	...	95	

Thus the entire generation is 4832 (**8** × 604).

THE GENERATIONS OF ABRAHAM.

Abraham had eight sons. Seven of them were born "after the flesh," while the *eighth* was "by promise" (see p. 199).

Name		Value	Total
Abraham		248 (**8** × 31)	456 (8 × 57).
Isaac	...	208 (**8** × 2 × **13**)*	
Jacob	...	182 (7 × 2 × **13**)	

JACOB'S FAMILY.

Name		Value	Total
Jacob	...	182	456 (**8** × 57).
Leah	...	36	
Rachel	...	238	

Leah's Six Sons.

Name		Value	Total
Reuben	...	259	1726 (**13** × 2 + 1700).
Simeon	...	466	
Levi	...	46	
Judah	...	30	
Issachar	...	830	
Zebulon	...	95	

* Isaac's household was a divided one, as well as Jacob's; hence we have the 13 as a factor as well as 8.

Add parents' names (Jacob 182, and Leah 36), and we have 1944 (**8** × 243).

*Rachel's Two Sons.**

Joseph ...	...	156	308 (77 × 4).
Benjamin	...	152	

Rachel's Maid.

Bilhah ...	...	42	666.
Dan ...	...	54	
Naphtali...	...	570	

Leah's Maid.

Zilpah ...	...	122	666.
Gad ...	...	7	
Asher ...	...	501	
Add Leah	...	36	

The whole family of Jacob, including Ephraim (331) and Manasseh (395) = 4512 ($\mathbf{8}^3$ + 4000).

THE TWELVE TRIBES

are enumerated in some 18 (3 × 6) different ways, in which one is always omitted. For there were 12 tribes; but there were also 13, telling of God's design for perfect government, and of man's apostasy from that government.

In Deut. xxxii. Simeon is left out.

In Rev. vii. Dan and Ephraim are omitted (Joseph and Levi being inserted).

Generally it is Levi that is omitted.

Arranged in their 4 camps, as in Num. ii., their value is 3736 (**8** × 467).

Arranged as in Rev. vii., the value (according to the Greek spelling, of course) is 8480 (**8** × 1060).

Arranged as in Num. xiii. 3–16, in connection with the rebellion on the return of the 12 spies, we see defection at once; for all the representatives of the tribes failed except Caleb and Joshua (788).

The whole passage = 17654 (**13** × 1358).

From verse 4–16 = 12038 (**13** × 926).

* The spelling is taken as in Gen. xxxv. 22–26.

To go back, however, to Genesis, we now take

ISHMAEL'S TWELVE SONS (Gen. xxv. 12-17).

Now these ...	40	1327	4836 (**13** × 12 × 31).
The generations of	836		
Ishmael	451		
Nebaioth	462	3509	
Kedar	304		
Abdeel	38		
Mibsam	382		
Mishmah	450		
Dumah	55		
Massa	341		
Hadar	212		
Tema	451		
Jetur	225		
Naphish	440		
Kedemah... ...	149		

THE ELEVEN DUKES OF EDOM.

Gen. xxxvi. 40-43 is by gematria 9880: thus—

Verse 40	= 5453	9880 (**13** × 760).
" 41	= 670	
" 42	= 1340	
" 43	= 2417*	

The word אלוף (*al-luph*), "duke," amounts to 117 (**13** × 9).

And *eleven* times repeated, it is still a multiple of 13, viz., 1287 (**13** × 99).

THE ABRAHAM-KETURAH GROUP (Gen. xxv. 1, 2).

Abraham ...	248 (8 × 31)	2249 (**13** × 173).
Keturah ...	320 (8 × 40)	
Zimran	297	
Jokshan	460	
Medan	94	
Midian	104	
Ishbak	412	
Shuah	314	

* As far as "he is Esau."

THEIR DESCENDANTS IN GEN. XXV. 3.

Shebah	303	481 (**13** × 37).
Dedan	58	
Sons of Dedan ...	120	
Asshurim	547	1053 (**13** × 81).
Letushim	385	
Leummim	121	

THE SONS OF MIDIAN (Gen. xxv. 4).

Sons of Midian ...	166	936 (**13** × 72).
Ephah	165	
Epher	350	
Hanoch	58	
Abidah	87	
Eldaah	110	

The phrase which concludes the lists, "All these are the sons of Keturah," has for its value 468 (**13** × 36), making with the numbers above 5213 for the whole group, or **13** × 401.

The whole passage is also a multiple of **13**.

THE INCESTUOUS CHILDREN OF LOT (Gen. xix.).

Ammon	166	286 (**13** × 22).
Ammi	120	

Beni-Ammi (children of Ammi) = 182 (**13** × 14).

The whole passage (Gen. xix. 31–38) is a multiple of 13.

GENESIS XIX.

"And there came two angels to Sodom at even," 640 (**8** × 80).

"And Lot sat in the gate of Sodom" * = 1313.

Verse 1. The whole verse, 4299, significant of Antichrist (42) and judgment (9).

Verses 1–25 = 90441 (**13** × 9 × 773).

Verses 26–29, describing the results of the overthrow = 14274 (**13** × 9 × 122).

Verses 1–29, the entire account = 104715 (**13** × 9 × 895).

Lot's words in verse 7 = 777.

Verse 25. The work of the LORD in the overthrow = 2888.

The account in the Second Epistle of Peter = 6999.

It will be observed how we have here not only the number *thirteen*, but also the number *nine*, which we shall presently see is the number of judgment.

* Even the expression in 2 Pet. ii. 7, "and righteous Lot," is 1326 (**13** × 102).

THE DESTRUCTION OF JERICHO

is also stamped with the number *thirteen*, though not by gematria, for the city was compassed once each day for six days, and *seven* times on the *seventh* day, making 13 times in all (6 + 7). Jericho, יריחו, is 234, which is (**13** × 2 × 9) (*nine* being the number of judgment; see below, under that number).

THE TWELVE JUDGES

who were raised up as saviours in a time of apostasy and rebellion exhibit *both* these factors, 8 and 13.

Othniel	561	3848 (**8** × **13** × 37).
Ehud	16	
Shamgar ...	543	
Barak	302	
Gideon	133	
Tola	506	
Jair	221	
Jephthah ...	498	
Ibzan	143	
Elon	97	
Abdon	132	
Samson	696	

Abimelech the usurper (Judg. ix.) by his name

Ben ...	52 (**13** × 4)	364 (**13** × 28).
Jerubbaal	312 (**13** × 24)	

The Judges period ends under Samuel, 377 (**13** × 29), and the last three names which come before us are—

Eli, Hophni, and Phinehas, which together amount to 462 (42 × 11 *).

THE SAUL GROUP OF NAMES (1 Sam. xiv. 49-51).

Saul	337	3900 (**13** × 300).
Kish	760	
Sons of Saul ...	399	
Jonathan	516	
Ishui	326	
Melchishua ...	476	
Ahinoam	179	
Merab	242	
Michal	100	
Abner son of Ner	565	

* See under these two numbers for their respective significance.

THE JUDAH AND ISRAEL LINES OF KINGS
are stamped in a remarkable manner with these numbers.

There are two periods specially marked with regard to Israel.

The number 65 is associated with the separate existence of the Ten Tribes in Isa. vii. 8, "Within *threescore and five* years shall Ephraim be broken, that it be not a people." From that time, that is to say, from the utterance of the prophecy to the carrying away of Israel was exactly 65 years, or 5 times **13**, which characterised the disintegration which was going on in the nation.

But, more than this, the number 390 was also stamped upon Israel as being the whole duration of the separate existence of the Ten Tribes from the day they *rebelled* against Rehoboam to the day they were led away captive. This we see from Ezek. iv. 4, 5, where the command was given to Ezekiel, "Lie thou upon thy left side, and lay the iniquity of the house of Israel upon it; according to the number of the days that thou shalt be upon it, thou shalt bear their iniquity. For I have laid upon thee the years of their iniquity according to the number of the days, *three hundred and ninety* days; so shalt thou bear the iniquity of the house of Israel."

Now 390 is *thirteen times thirty*,* and the duration of Israel's rebellion is sufficiently and appropriately branded upon it.

On the other hand, when we turn to Judah we see the number 8 pervading it. For the same prophet, in the next verse, is commanded to lie on his *right* side *forty days* to bear the iniquity of the house of Judah—each day for a year. We ought to note in passing that the name of Ezekiel, who foretells the duration and end of this apostasy, is 156 (**13** × 12); while the words of the prophecy, Ezek. iv. 1–6, amount to 36673 ($\mathbf{13}^2$ × 7 × 31), and the whole passage, iv. 1–8, to 43069 (**13** × 3313).

The fulfilment ought also to be noted. The 390 years were to signify not only the years of apostasy, but were also to signify the 390 *days* of the siege of Jerusalem; viz., 13 months (30 × **13**). The siege commenced on the 10th day of the 10th month of the 9th year of Zedekiah (2 Kings xxv. 1–4), and it was taken on the 9th day of the 4th month of the

* Commentators entirely miss the point when they say that 390 = 10 × 39, instead of **13** × 30!

11th year of the same king. This gives a period of 18 months. But the siege was raised for about 5 months (see Jer. xxxvii.), while Nebuchadnezzar's army was withdrawn for fear of Pharaoh, king of Egypt, who had come up to meet him.

Thus we have the two numbers stamped by the history; upon Judah 8, and upon Israel 13.

Now look at

The List of Judah's Kings.*

> Of the 20 successors of Solomon, 7 were good, and 13 stained with apostasy. Ahaz was the 13th from Solomon.

King		Value	Group	Total
Rehoboam	...	320		
Abijam	...	53		
Asa † ...	...	62		
Jehoshaphat	...	410		
Jehoram	...	261		
Ahaziah	...	37	2424 (**8** × 303)	
Athaliah	...	515		
Jehoash	...	322		
Amaziah	...	152‡		
Azariah (Uzziah) §	...	292		
Jotham	...	456		
Ahaz ...	...	16	608 (**8** × 76) ‖	4400 (**8** × 550).
Hezekiah	...	136		
Manasseh	...	395		
Amon ...	...	97	824 (**8** × 103)	
Josiah ...	...	332		
Jehoahaz	...	37		
Jehoiakim	...	181	544 (**8** × 68)	
Jehoiachin	...	111		
Zedekiah	...	215		

* The spelling, which sometimes varies, is taken according to the first occurrence of the name.

† In the 39th (3 × 13) year of his reign he forsook the Lord (2 Chron. xvi. 12).

‡ Amaziah = 146 or 152 according to the spelling. If 146, then the total will be 4394 (13^2 × 2). But if we add Saul 337, David 14, and Solomon 375, it is 5120 (8^3 × 10).

§ He had reigned 52 (4 × 13) years when he apostatized (2 Chron. xxvi. 3, 21). He was the 13th king reckoning from Saul.

‖ These three are peculiarly associated in 2 Chron., where their action with regard to the house of God is noted :—Jotham (xxvii. 1, 2) "entered not into the Temple"; Ahaz (xxviii. 1, 24) "shut up the doors"; Hezekiah (xxix. 1, 3) "opened the doors of the house of the Lord."

THE ISRAELITE KINGS.

> There were 13 kings before the anarchy, and 6 after it.

Jeroboam I.	322	
Nadab	56	
Baasha	373	
(or 429 (13 × 33))*		
Elah	36	
Zimri	257	
Omri	320	
Ahab	12	
Ahaziah	37	
Jehoram	261	
(or 923 (13 × 71))		
Jehu	22	3900 (13 × 300).
Jehoahaz	37	
Joash	317	
Jeroboam II.... ...	322	
(or 676 (13^2 × 4))		
Zachariah	242	
Shallum	376	
Menahem	138	
Pekahiah	203	
Pekah...	188	
Hoshea	381	
(or 910 (13 × 70))		

THE LEADERS WHO RETURNED FROM BABYLON.

Ezra ii. 2.

Zurubbabel	241	
Jeshua	386	
Nehemiah	113	
Seraiah	515	
Reelaiah	315	
Mordecai	274	3008 (8^2 × 47)
Bilshan	382	
Mizpar †	380	
Bigvai	21	
Rehum	254	
Baanah	127	

* The alternative numbers are caused by another spelling, but, as it will be seen, the result is the same.

† In the Hebrew Text מספר, *Mizpar*, is repeated again after Baanah. If we count this in, then the total, instead of 3008, will be 3388, which though not a multiple of 8 is very significant.

Other chiefs mentioned in other connections are—

Shesbazzar, the prince of Judah	892	
Ezra the scribe	619	1624 (8 × 203).
Nehemiah	113	

It is difficult to observe a strict order in the presentation of these phenomena, because the results are best shown by direct contrast. For example, if we take out the names of the adversaries who came in direct opposition to the Lord, the law will be more clearly seen.

THE ADVERSARIES OF EZRA (iv. 7-9).

Bishlam	372	
Mithredath	1044	
Tabeel	42	
"And the rest of their companions"	989	3913 (13 × 301).
Rehum the chancellor ...	475	
Shimshai the scribe	991	

These Companions (Ezra iv. 9) are the—

Dinaites	75	
Apharsathchites	772	
Tarpelites	330	
Apharsites	352	
Archevites	237	2665 (13 × 205).
Babylonians	45	
Susanchites	687	
Dehavites	16	
Elamites	151	

Together they all make 6578 (13 × 506).

The men who took strange wives (Ezra x. 17–44) were in number 113. The gematria of their names is 38194 (13^2 × 226).

THE ADVERSARIES OF NEHEMIAH

as mentioned and named in ii. 19; iv. 7; and xiii. 4:

Sanballat the Horonite ...	424	
And Tobiah the servant, the Ammonite	294	
And Geshem the Arabian ...	636	2717 (13 × 209)
And the Arabians	333	
And the Ammonites	221	
And the Ashdodites	376	
Eliashib the priest	433	

With this we may note the 6-fold nature of their opposition as shown on p. 153.

DANIEL AND HIS COMPANIONS.

(*Daniel* i. 6.)

Daniel	95	888.
Hananiah	120	
Misael	381	
Azariah	292	

But their *Chaldean* names, given by Nebuchadnezzar, make a number of no significance whatever.

THE ENEMIES OF GOD AND HIS PEOPLE

as named in Scripture are generally multiples of *thirteen.*

Let us begin with the great enemy himself, always remembering that though we may give the English for the sake of clearness, the gematria always refers to the original Hebrew or Greek:

Satan, in Hebrew = 364 (**13** × 28).

Satan, in Greek = 2197 (**13**³).

"That old serpent, even Satan" (ὁ ὄφις ὁ ἀρχαῖος . . . καὶ ὁ Σατανᾶς) = 2756 (**13** × 212).

"A spirit of Python" (Acts xvi. 16) = 1339 (or 1300 + 3 × **13**).

Beelzebub (with art.) = 598 (**13** × 46).

Belial = 78 (**13** × 6).

Δράκων (*Drakōn*), Dragon (Rev. xii. 9), = 975 (**13** × 75).

Ὄφις (*Ophis*), Serpent, = 780 (**13** × 60).

Murderer = 1820 (**13** × 140).

Tempter = 1053 (**13** × 81).

ὁ δαίμων, The demon, = 975 (**13** × 75).

The Lion (Ps. xci. 13) = 338 (**13** × 26).

"As a Lion" (1 Pet. v. 8) = 1885 (**13** × 145).

"The Power of the Enemy" (Luke x. 9) = 2509 (**13** × 193).

"Your adversary, the Devil, as a roaring lion" = 6032 (**13** × 464).

Fowler (Ps. xci. 3) = 416 (**13** × 32).

"Who is called the Devil and Satan" (ὁ καλούμενος διάβολος καὶ ὁ Σατανᾶς) = 2197 (**13**³).

"Seven Devils" = 572 (**13** × 44).

"Because the Prince of this world is judged" (John xvi. 11) = 5577 (**13**² × 33).

"When he speaketh a lie he speaketh of his own, for he is a liar" (John viii. 44) = 7072 (**13** × 544).

Genesis iii.,

where the Devil is first mentioned and revealed. The opening words:

"The Serpent was more subtle than all the beasts of the field" = 1521 ($\mathbf{13}^2$ × 9).

The history of the Temptation, *vv.* 1–7 = 24011 (**13** × 1847).

The *second* section (*vv.* 8–11) = 49478 ($\mathbf{13}^2$ × 1903).

The *third* section (*vv.* 22–24), which records the expulsion from Eden, = 10894 (**13** × 838).

The whole chapter = 84383 (**13** × 6491).

Eve's confession (*v.* 13) = 3692 (**13** × 284).

Verse 8, which describes the act of the LORD God, is, on the contrary, 4064 (**8** × 508).

Verse 21, which records the Divinely prepared clothing in grace, = 2856 (7 × **8** × 51).

Verse 15, which we might expect to find significant, being the great primeval prophetic promise, is 4266 (3^3 × 158); where we have the 42, the 66, of Antichrist, and the 9 of judgment.

Verse 16, containing the hope of the promised seed, added to *v.* 15 = 8512 (8000 + $\mathbf{8}^3$).

Isaiah xxvii. 1.

"The piercing Serpent, even Leviathan" = 1170 (**13** × 90).

"That crooked Serpent" = 1014 ($\mathbf{13}^2$ × 6).

"The Dragon that is in the sea" = 1469 (**13** × 113).

Isaiah xiv. 29.

"Rejoice not thou, whole Palestina, because the rod of him that smote thee is broken: for out of the serpent's root shall come forth a cockatrice (marg. *adder*), and his fruit shall be a fiery flying serpent" = 5369 (**13** × 413).

Psalm lxxv. 15.

"Thou smotest the heads of Leviathan in pieces, and gavest him for meat for the people in the wilderness" = 3510 (**13** × 270; or **13** × 6 × 45; or **13** × 3^3 × 10).

Revelation ix. 11.

The whole verse = 12090 (**13** × 930).
The locusts = 351 (**13** × 3^3).
"They have a king, the angel of the abyss" = 3978 (**13** × 306).

Ephesians ii. 2.

"According to the course of this world, according to the prince of the power of the air" = 9178 * (**13** × 706).
"The power of the air" = 2600 (**13** × 200).

Luke x. 18.

"Lightning from heaven" = 2626 (**13** × 202).
"And He said, I beheld Satan as lightning fall from heaven" = 6903 (**13** × 531).

Ephesians vi. 12.

"But against principalities, against powers, against the rulers of the darkness of this world, against spiritual wickedness in high places" = 16211 (**13** × 1247).

Matthew xvi. 23.

"An offence unto me" (*σκανδαλόν μου*) = 936 (**13** × 72).

THE HUMAN ADVERSARIES

present the same peculiar phenomena:
Asshur = 169 (**13**^{2}).†
"The man of sin" = **13**182 (**13**^{3} × 6).
"The man who took not God for his strength" = 2197 (**13**^{3}). ‡

THE BOOK OF ESTHER

reveals the same law in operation. Having diligently *cast the horoscope* (as *Pur*, פּוּר, means: see Isa. xlvii. 13), Haman found the most favourable time for carrying out his designs as "the Jews' enemy." §

---

* Ninety-one hundred being **13** × 700; and 78 being **13** × 6.

† Nimrod exhibits a number connected with Antichrist, being 294, or 7 × 42.

‡ The whole of Psalm lii. = 19572 (**42** × 466).

§ A term applied to none but Haman. See Esth. iii. 10; vii. 6; viii. 1; ix. 10, 24.

Est. iii. 7 tells us that for 12 months the horoscope was consulted "in the *first* of the month. . . . from day to day, and from month to month, to the *twelfth* month." Then (*v.* 12) on the *thirteenth* day of the first month (*i.e.*, the *thirteenth* month from the time they commenced) the favourable day was found. Then (iii. 13) the letters were prepared, and upon "one day, even upon the *thirteenth* day of the twelfth month" (at the end of the second year), the Jews were all to be put to death. On that day came the deliverance (viii. 12, etc.). Thus we have three *thirteens* connected with this gigantic effort of the great enemy to destroy the Lord's people, and with them, of course, the promised seed. This is the ultimate object of the great enemy in all his designs against God's people.

On the other hand, we see the multiples of the dominical *eight* in the Lord's people:

Mordecai (ii. 5)	274	
Son of Jair ...	273	
Son of Shimei...	472	1912 (8×239).
Son of Kish ...	462	
Benjamite ...	431	

אתהדסה היא אסתר (*Eth-Hadassah hee Esther*) (ii. 7).

Eth-Hadassah...	475	1152 (8×12^2).
That is Esther	677	

Purim (ix. 26), 336 (8×42).

On the other hand we have:

Bigthan (ii. 21) ... 455 (13×35).
Haman the Agagite 117 (13×9).
Zeresh (his wife) ... 507 ($13^2 \times 3$).

Haman's sons present a curious phenomenon. In every Hebrew manuscript these names are presented thus (ix. 7–9):

and (*v'eth*)	Parshandatha.
and (*v'eth*)	Dalphon.
and (*v'eth*)	Aspatha.
and (*v'eth*)	Poratha.
and (*v'eth*)	Adalia.
and (*v'eth*)	Aridatha.
and (*v'eth*)	Parmashta.
and (*v'eth*)	Arisai.
and (*v'eth*)	Aridai
and (*v'eth*)	Vajezatha.

This peculiarity has been preserved not only in all the manuscripts, but in every printed edition of the Hebrew Text. No scribe or editor has ventured to change this form of their presentation.

Various conjectures have been made both by the ancient Jewish and modern commentators as to the reason why these names are always presented thus; but no one seems to have looked upon the names as an addition sum (regarding of course each letter as a figure). Treated thus the sum of the names amounts to 10244 or **13** × 788.

The whole family is 10868 or **13** × 836.

The Adversaries of Christ.

"The Scribes" = 780 (**13** × 60).

"The Scribes and Pharisees, hypocrites" = 2704 (**13**² × 16).

"Woe!" = 481 (**13** × 37).

"Leaven of Pharisees and Sadducees" = 3718 (13² × 22).

"A wicked and adulterous generation" = 1365 (**13** × 105).

The Scriptures concerning Barabbas.

Matt. xxvii. 20: "But the chief priests and elders persuaded the people that they should ask Barabbas, and destroy Jesus" = 10127 (**13** × 779).

The elders = 1352 (**13** × 104).

The multitude = 2340 (**13** × 180).

Matt. xxvii. 16: "And they had then a notable prisoner, called Barabbas" = 2743 (**13** × 211).

Mark xv. 6: "Now at that feast he released unto them one prisoner, whomsoever they desired" = 910 (**13** × 70).

Luke xxiii. 18: "And they cried out all at once, saying, Away with this man, and release unto us Barabbas" = 9347 (**13** × 719).

John xviii. 40: "Then cried they all again, saying, Not this man, but Barabbas. Now Barabbas was a robber." In this verse we have—

"Then cried they all again"	= 2600 (**13** × 200).
"Not this man, but Barabbas. Now Barabbas was a robber"	= 1300 (**13** × 100).
	= 1833 (**13** × 141).
	5733 (**13** × 441).

The Scriptures concerning Judas Iscariot.

Luke xxii. 3: "Then entered Satan into Judas surnamed Iscariot, being of the number of the twelve" = 8359 (**13** × 643).

Verse 47, "And he that was called Judas, one of the twelve" = 3458 (**13** × 266).

John xii. 4: "Judas Iscariot, he that should betray Him" = 4511 (**13** × 347).

John xiii. 26: "Jesus answered, He it is to whom I shall give a sop, when I have dipped it. And when He had dipped the sop, He gave it to Judas Iscariot, the son of Simon" = 19435 (**13** × 1495).

The last clause ("When," etc.) = 7371 (**13** × 567).

Matt. xxvi. 48: "Now he that betrayed Him gave them a sign, saying, Whomsoever I shall kiss, that same is He; hold Him fast" = 9867 (**13** × 759).

So with Acts i. 16; Mark xiv. 44, 45, and all the corresponding passages.

Acts iv. 25–27.

Verse 25, "Why did the heathen rage?" = 1560 (**13** × 120).

Verse 26, "The kings of the earth stood up, and the rulers were gathered together against the Lord, and against His Christ" = 12467 (**13** × 959).

Verse 27, "Both Herod and Pontius Pilate with the Gentiles" = 3926 (**13** × 302).

OTHER ADVERSARIES.

Simon Magus (with art.) = 1170 (**13** × 90).

Elymas = 676 ($\mathbf{13}^2$ × 4).

"Certain sons of one Sceva, a Jew, and chief of the priests, seven" (Acts xix. 14) = 4953 (**13** × 381).

The Adversaries named by St. Paul.

Hermogenes (2 Tim. i. 15)=481 (13 × 37).
Philetus (2 Tim. ii. 17)=1118 (13 × 86).

The Whole Group.

Hymenæus and Alexander (1 Tim. i. 20) Phygellus and Hermogenes (2 Tim. i. 15) Hymenæus and Philetus (2 Tim. ii. 17) Demas (2 Tim. iv. 10)	5226 (13 × 402).

John in his Epistles and the Apocalypse.

Rev. ii. 20: "That woman Jezebel" = 1573 (13 × 121).
Rev. iii. 1: Sardis = 520 (13 × 40).
1 John ii. 18–22: Antichrists = 1651 (13 × 127).
The Antichrist = 1911 (13 × 147).
"The last time" = 2015 (13 × 155).
"This is that spirit of Antichrist" = 4836 (13 × 372).
1 John iv. 3: "And every spirit that confesseth not that Jesus Christ is come in the flesh, is not of God: and this is that spirit of Antichrist" = 17329 (13 × 1333).
1 John ii. 22: "That denieth the Father" = 1963 (13 × 151).
"But he that denieth that Jesus is the Christ" = 4992 (13 × 384).
2 John 7: "The many deceivers" = 611 (13 × 47).
"This is the deceiver" = 2106 (13 × 162).
"The Antichrist" = 1911 (13 × 147).
πλάνη (*planee*), deceiver (*i.e.*, error or deception) = 169 (13^2).

The Apocalypse.

xiii. 1: "The sand of the sea" = 1716 (13 × 132).
"The sea" = 1157 (13 × 89).
"A beast rise up out of the sea" = 1664 (13 × 128).
θήρ (*theer*), a wild beast = 117 (13 × 9).
Verse 11, The whole verse = 6318 (13 × 486).
θηρίον (*theerion*), beast = 247 (13 × 19).
ἄλλο θηρίον (*hallo theerion*), another beast = 378 (9 × 42).

"He had two horns" = 1521 (13^2 × 9).

"And he had two horns like a lamb" = 2704 (13^2 × 16).

Verse 15, "The image of the beast" = 1482 (**13** × 114).

Verse 18, "The mark of the beast" = 2483 (**13** × 191).

"The number of the beast" (acc. with article) = 2067 (**13** × 159).*

xvii. 1: "The great whore" = 403 (**13** × 31).

Verse 5, "The mother of harlots" = 2756 (**13** × 212).

"Mystery, Babylon the great, the mother of harlots and abominations" = 8138 (**13** × 626).

xix. 20: "The beast . . . and with him the false prophet who doeth wonders before him" = 8489 (**13** × 653).

"The harlot, the beast, and the false prophet" = 3510 (**13** × 270). The false Trinity is marked by 3 × 3 × 3 × 10 × **13**.

The whole verse = 25441 (**13** × 1957).

xxii. 15: "Dogs, and sorcerers, and whoremongers, and murderers, and idolaters, and whatsoever loveth and maketh a lie" = 8710 (**13** × 670).

viii. 10: "A great star" = 858 (**13** × 66).

viii. 11: "Wormwood" = 1040 (**13** × 80).

xx. 8: "Gog" = 806 (**13** × 62). (Greek.)

"Magog" = 52 (**13** × 4). (Hebrew.)

Ezekiel's Prophecy of Gog.

xxxviii. 2: "The chief prince of Meshech" (the title of Gog) = 1222 (**13** × 94).

xxxix. 11: "Hamon-Gog" (the burying place of Gog) = **113**.

"All his multitude" = 156 (**13** × 12).

The whole prophecy of Ezekiel concerning him (Ezek. xxxviii. 2 and xxxix. 29) = 204256 (**13** × 15712).

The last portion, xxxix. 16–29, = 55887 (**13** × 4299).

Jude.

Verses 3–9 = 230464 (**13** × 17728).

Verses 14 and 15 = 30940 (**13** × 2380).

---

* In Nom. without article = 1027 (**13** × 79).

Verse 15, "Judgment" (Κρίσιν, *noun*) = 390 (**13** × 30).
"The error of Balaam" * = 1014 ($\mathbf{13}^2$ × 6).
"Kore" † = 195 (**13** × 15).

2 Thessalonians ii. 3.

"The apostasy" = 871 (**13** × 67).
"The man of sin" = 1963 (**13** × 151).
"The son of perdition" = 1807 (**13** × 139).
"Son of perdition" with *v.* 4 = 13182 ($\mathbf{13}^3$ × 6).

Thus, no matter in what way we look at the recurrence of these two numbers, we see the same law pervading the history. A few miscellaneous examples must suffice :—

In Gen. x. we have the scattering of the nations, and their division through the earth. It happened in the days of Peleg, the gematria of whose name is one hundred and *thirteen.* The Scripture recording it (Gen. x. 25–29) = 10647 (**13** × 63).

Salah (Peleg's grandfather) was 338 ($\mathbf{13}^2$ × 2).

When Uzziah apostatised (2 Chron. xxvi.) it was after he had reigned 52 years (4 × **13**).

Jeroboam II. had 40 years of prosperity, and then 12 of apostasy = 52 (4 × **13**).

Joash reigned 39 years (3 × **13**), and then apostatised (2 Chron. xxiii., xxiv.).

In the **13**th year of Josiah, Jeremiah began to prophesy against the apostasy of Judah.

Cain has no chronology, and Saul has none, except the last year, which was the first of David's, and of which 13 is a factor.

Solomon was **13** years building his *own* house, which was so full of apostasy. (But he was 7 years building the Lord's house.)

The Number of those who died in Korah's Rebellion

was 250 + 14700 = 14950 (**13** × 1150). See Num. xvi. 35, 49.

The Valley of Hinnom

(or of the son or children of Hinnom) occurs 13 times. It was the scene of the idolatrous and inhuman rites of Moloch

---

* Compare Josh. xiii. 22, Balaam. "Did the children of Israel slay with the sword among the slain" = 1183 ($\mathbf{13}^2$ × 7).

† Num. xvi. 1–4 = 12909 (**13** × 993).

introduced by Solomon (1 Kings xi. 7). The casting of children into the fire in that valley made it the fit symbol of the future punishment of sinners, who are to be cast into the lake of fire, and gave rise to the word γεέννα (*Gehenna*), from the Hebrew גֵיא הִנֹּם (*Gee-Hinnom*), Valley of Hinnom. The 13 occurrences, which contain the whole history of the valley, are worthy of connected study (Josh. xv. 8, 18; xviii. 16, twice; 2 Kings xxiii. 10; 2 Chron. xxviii. 3; xxxiii. 6; Neh. xi. 30; Jer. vii. 31, 32; xix. 2, 6; xxxii. 35).

Thus the two numbers **8** and **13** are like two threads—gold and crimson—which run through the whole of Divine Revelation, continually crossing and recrossing each other.

There is, however, one very important branch of this part of our subject still remaining, and that is:—

The Connection of the Number Thirteen with Substitution and Atonement.

The Saviour, though without sin, was "made sin," or a sin-offering, for His people. He was "wounded for our transgressions," and bruised for their iniquities. He was, in fact, "NUMBERED WITH THE TRANSGRESSORS" (Isa. liii. 12).

Therefore this number is not only the all-pervading factor of SIN, but also of sin's atonement. It is not only the number which brands the sinner as a rebel against God, but it is the number borne by the sinner's Substitute.

His very names in the Old Testament, before the work of Atonement was entered on or accomplished, are all multiples of **13**, just as His names, afterwards in the New Testament and when the work of Atonement was carried out, are all multiples of **8**. See these names on p. 204.

The Old Testament names are:—

- Jehovah = 26 (**13** × 2).
- Adonai = 65 (**13** × 5).
- Ha-Elohim = 91 (**13** × 7).
- Messiah, as given in Psalm ii., a form in which it occurs 10 times, "His Anointed" = 364 (**13** × 28)—the very number of Satan himself (*Ha-Shatan*).

But note here the marvellous combination of the other factors, 2, 5, and 7, the significance of which we need not dwell upon after all that we have said about them as indicating *incarnation, grace,* and *spiritual perfection.*

Truly, it is written, "Cursed is every one that hangeth on a tree." Hence the numerical value of the very word, ἀνάθεμα (*anathema*), curse, is 546 (**13** × 42), and it occurs 6 times.

Genesis iv. 4,

which records the first type of this Lamb of God, the sinner's substitute, exhibits the number **13.**

"And Abel, he also brought of the firstlings of his flock, and of the fat thereof. And the LORD had respect unto Abel and his offering." The verse amounts to 2093 (**13** × 161).

Verse 7, where we have a further reference to this offering, = 5421 (**13** × 3 × 139).

Abel suffered; Cain sinned; Seth was the substitute for Abel. Hence the three names are:—

Abel	...	37	897 (**13** × 69).
Cain	...	160	
Seth	...	700	

Their whole history (Gen. iv. 1–25) amounts to 76882 (**13** × 5914).

Leviticus xvi.

The great chapter on Atonement is most remarkable. We cannot give the whole chapter; but note—

Verses 2–4, which describe Aaron's preparations, = 15015 (**13** × 5 × 7 × 33).

Verses 5–11, the choosing of the victims, down to the sacrificing of the bullock, = 24739 (**13** × 1903).

Verses 12–14, the burning of the sweet incense, and the seven-fold sprinkling of the blood before the mercy-seat, = 13377 (**13** × 3 × 7^3). With this we may compare the words in Eph. v. 25, 26, "And gave Himself for it, that He might sanctify it" = 4459 (**13** × 7^3).

Verses 15, 16, the atonement of the holy place, = 13637 (**13** × 1049).

Verses 17–34, the high priest entering alone, ending with the everlasting statute, = 80613 (13^2 × 3^2 × 53).

Verses 20–23, the scape-goat's dismissal, = 20670 (**13** × 5 × 6 × 53).

Verses 24–27, the purification of the priest and his assistants, = 18993 (**13** × 3 × 487).

The latter two together (verses 20–27) = 39663 (**13** × 3^3 × 113).

The scape-goat = 585 (**13** × 45).

Verse 20, the choosing of the goat, = 3575 (**13** × 5 × 55).

Verses 21–23, the driving of the goat, = 17095 (**13** × 1315).

Verses 24–27, the rest of the atonement, = 18993 (3 × **13** × 487).

Numbers xxi. 8, 9.

It may be observed that the serpent (*Ha-Seraph*) is also 585, exactly the same number as the scape-goat.

Verses 6, 7, which speak of the sin, the judgment, and the prayer, = 7241 (**13** × 557).

Verse 8. "And the LORD said unto Moses, make thee a fiery serpent" = 1664 (**8** × **8** × 2 × **13**).

"And set it upon a pole; and it shall come to pass that every one that is bitten" = 1430 (**13** × 110).

Verses 8, 9 = 8886.

John iii. 14.

The Lord's own reference to Num. xxi. = 2366 ($\mathbf{13}^2$ × 14).

Isaac,

who was the type of Christ in substitution, has, as the factor of his name, **13** as well as **8**. It is 208 (**13** × **8** × 2).

Isaac's history, too, in Gen. xxii. 1–19 (the eighth of the Divine interviews and covenants), amounts to 54808, or (**13** × **8** × 17 × 31).

The Sacrifice of Job for his Friends.

Job xlii. 8 = 6721 (**13** × 517).

The Atonement after Korah's Rebellion,

Num. xvi., "When Aaron stood between the living and the dead."

Verses 45–47 = 8138 (**13** × 2 × 313).

Verses 45–50 = 20501 (**13** × 19 × 83).

Isaiah liii.

Verses 2-4 = 7995 (**13** × 15 × 41).
Verses 1-5 = 13286 (**13** × 1022).
Verses 6-8 = 8749 (**13** × 673).

lii. 14—liii. 10 = 36582 (**13** × 42 × 67).
lii. 1-12 also equals 36582. Thus the lifting up of the voice of joy in Zion, and the lifting up of the Son of Man, present the very same number.
lii. and liii. = 84123 (**13** × 9 × 719).

Isaiah vii. 7-16.

Verse 7 = 1391 (**13** × 107).
Verse 8. "Damascus" = 444.
Verse 9 = 4017 (**13** × 309).
Verse 10 = 712 }
Verse 11 = 1778 } 2490 (2 × 15 × 83). Where the No. 2 = Incarnation. No. 15 = Divine grace.

The Day of Atonement.

Lev. xxiii. 26, 27, = 6526 (or **13** × 502, or **13** × 5 + 2 × 13).
Lev. xxiii. 27, 28, = 5187 (**13** × 399).

Daniel ix. 25-27.

The three verses = 21164 (**13** × 4 × 407), or (**13** × 1628).
"Abomination of desolation" = 966 (42 × 23).
"Abomination" = 546 (42 × **13**).
"Desolation" = 420 (42 × 10).
Verse 26. Messiah shall be cut off = 988 (**13** × 76).
Verse 25. "Unto Messiah" = 432 (2 × **8** × 3^3).
Verse 25. "Messiah the Prince" = 425 (5^2 × 17).
Verse 24. "To anoint the most holy" = 1242.
Verse 24. "The most holy" = 858 (**13** × 66).
The entire prophecy = 43554 (42 × 17 × 61*).

Compare Matt. xxiv. 15 in the Greek.
"Abomination" = 855 (9 × 19 × 5).
"Desolation" = 2158 (**13** × 166).

---

* 61 is the *nineteenth* prime number.

While the phrase, "abomination of desolation" = 2666,
The whole quotation, "the abomination of desolation spoken of by Daniel the prophet, standing in the holy place" = 9373 (**13** × 721).

1 *Corinthians xv.* 3.

"Christ died for our sins" = 5616 (**13** × **8** × 2 × 3^3).

2 *Corinthians v.* 17–21.

The whole passage is 53365, or (**13** × 4105).

John xiii. 31, 32.

"Now is the Son of Man glorified" = 3887 ($\mathbf{13}^2$ × 23).
"God is glorified in Him" = 2197 ($\mathbf{13}^3$).
"God shall glorify Him in Himself" = 3016 (**13** × **8** × 29).

Romans vi. 6–8.

Verse 6. "He died for the ungodly" = 1794 (**13** × 6 × 23).
Verse 8. "We being sinners" = 4290 (**13** × 330).
Verse 9. "Being justified now by His blood" = 4602 (**13** × 3 × 118).
Verse 9. "From wrath" = 1040 (**13** × 80).
Verse 9. "Through whom we have now received the atonement" = 1989 (**13** × 153).

1 *Corinthians ii.* 2.

"Him crucified" = 3211 ($\mathbf{13}^2$ × 19).

Galatians vi. 14.

"But God forbid that I should glory, save in the cross of our Lord Jesus Christ, by whom the world is crucified unto me, and I unto the world" = 16367 (**13** × 1259).

Philippians ii.

Verse 8. "Obedient unto death, even the death of the cross" = 4745 (**13** × 5 × 73).
Whole of verse 8 = 11804 (**13** × 908).

Verse 7. "He made Himself of no reputation" = 1911 (**13** × 3 × 7^2).
Verse 7. "The form of a servant" = 1742 (**13** × 134).
Verses 5-9 = 42328 (**13** × **8** × 407).

Colossians ii. 14, 15.

The whole of these verses = 22282 (**13** × 1714).
"Blotting out the handwriting of ordinances that was against us" = 4407 (**13** × 3 × 113).
"Which was contrary to us, even it He took out of the way, nailing it to His cross; and having spoiled principalities and powers" = 13065 (**13000** + 5 × **13**).
"He made a show of them openly, triumphing over them in it" = 5018 (**13** × 386).

Turning once more to the number *eight*, it is remarkable that:—

THE RISEN CHRIST

was seen by 512 persons. And 512 is the cube of 8 (8^3).

THE NUMBER OF THE DISCIPLES

gathered in the upper room (Acts i. 15) was 120 (**8** × 15).

I PETER III.

Verse 20. "A few ...	193	= 1480, the No. of Χριστός	6016 (8^2 × 94).
were saved"	1287		
"that is eight souls"	= 4536		

On the other hand we have:—
"The days of Noah" = 1209 (**13** × 31 × 3).
Verse 22. "Who is on the right hand of God" = 2224 (**8** × 278).

LUKE I. 35.

The angel's words = 5688 (**8** × 711).

"Nazareth," the scene of the Annunciation, = 464 (**8** × 58).
But "Jesus of Nazareth" = 2197 (13^3).

Eight in the Apocalypse.

We see not only the number *seven* stamping the book throughout with spiritual perfection, but as it contains also the history which leads up to resurrection and the new heavens and earth, the number *eight* is also seen.

There are 24 elders (3 × **8**).

Four beasts, each with six wings, = 24 (3 × **8**).

Twelve thousand from each tribe, 12000 = (**8** × 15 × 100).

144000 for all the tribes = $\mathbf{8}^2 \times 15^2 \times 10$; the same number of virgins who follow the Lamb.

1600 furlongs, the measure of the wine press (**8** × **8** × 25), or ($\mathbf{8}^2 \times 5^2$).

The 1000 years (**8** × 125).

The 12000 cubits' length of the "four-square" city (**8** × 15 × 100).

The Number of Occurrences

of the word ζύμη (*zumee*), "leaven," in the New Testament is *thirteen*, and it is significant of its connection with corruption, as denoting apostasy from the truth.

It is surely impossible to explain all this evidence on the doctrine of chances. There must be design. And design so perfect, so uniform, so significant can only be Divine. And being Divine is an unanswerable argument in favour of the verbal and even literal inspiration of the Scriptures of Truth.

NINE.

The number *nine* is a most remarkable number in many respects. It is held in great reverence by all who study the occult sciences; and in mathematical science it possesses properties and powers which are found in no other number.*

It is the *last* of the digits, and thus marks the *end;* and is significant of the *conclusion* of a matter.

It is akin to the number *six*, six being the sum of its factors ($3 \times 3 = 9$, and $3 + 3 = 6$), and is thus significant of the *end of man*, and the summation of all man's works. *Nine* is, therefore,

THE NUMBER OF FINALITY OR JUDGMENT,

for judgment is committed unto Jesus as "the Son of man" (John v. 27; Acts xvii. 31). It marks the completeness, the end and issue of all things as to man—the judgment of man and all his works.

It is a *factor* of 666, which is 9 times 74.

The gematria of the word "Dan," which means a judge, is 54 (9×6).

"τῇ ὀργῃ μου" (*tee orgee mou*), my wrath, =999 (Heb. iii. 11).

The solemn ἀμήν (*ameen*), *amen*, or "verily," of our Lord, amounts also to 99, summing up and ending His words.

The sum of the 22 letters of the Hebrew alphabet is 4995 (5×999). It is stamped, therefore, with the numbers of *grace* and *finality*.

The sum of the Greek alphabet is 3999.

THE FIRST CONTEST (Gen. xiv.)

is a battle between the 4 kings and 5 (= 9).†

* Among others may be mentioned (1) that the sum of the digits which form its multiples are themselves always a multiple of *nine; e.g.*, $2 \times 9 = 18$ (and $1 + 8 = 9$); $3 \times 9 = 27$ (and $2 + 7 = 9$); $4 \times 9 = 36$ (and $3 + 6 = 9$); $5 \times 9 = 45$ (and $4 + 5 = 9$), etc., etc.; and so with the larger numbers: $52843 \times 9 = 475587$ (and $4 + 7 + 5 + 5 + 8 + 7 = 36$, and $3 + 6 = 9$. (2) The sum of its multiples through the nine digits = 405, or 9 times 45.

† The Gematria of verses 3 and 4, Gen. xiv., which describe the *rebellion* and the *battle*, is 5655 (13×435). And verses 4 and 5, which describe the coming of the four kings, = 5590 (13×430). Thus the *rebellion* verse binds the war and its cause together. Verse 9, also, which describes the *battle*, is 4732 ($13^2 \times 28$).

The swift vengeance of Abram, verses 13–16, = 10738 ($13 \times 7 \times 118$).

The standing of Abram before Melchisedech = 19019 ($13 \times 7 \times 11 \times 19$). Thus with Abram we find not only the 13, but 7 marking the spiritual character of himself and his mission.

Sodom.

Gen. xix., recording the judgment of Sodom, is marked by multiples of *nine*. Verses 4–29 amount to 89550 (9 × 9950, or 9 × 50 × 199). The same is seen if we divide it into sections:—

Verses 4–18. From the riot in Sodom to Lot's plea for Zoar is 50733 (9 × 3 × 1879).

Verses 19–25. From Lot's plea to the overthrow is 24543 (9 × 9 × 303).

Verses 26–29. From "Lot's wife" to the end of the history is 14274 (9 × 2 × 13 × 61).*

We see the same phenomena in the account as given in the Second Epistle of St. Peter. As we do also in the judgment pronounced upon Jerusalem.

The Sieges of Jerusalem

have been 27 in number, or three times *nine*, and they are stamped with the number of Divine completeness (3) and the number of judgment (9). As the significance of other numbers is involved and illustrated in these 27, we give a complete list of all Jerusalem's sieges.

1. By the children of Judah against the Jebusites (Judg. i. 8) about 1425 B.C., and as this is the *first*, we may note the solemn words which so vividly stamp, from the first, what was to be the after history of the city,—"Now the children of Judah had fought against Jerusalem, and had taken it, and smitten it with the edge of the sword, and set the city on fire." This was about 1400 B.C., or 700 years before Rome was founded. This siege was only partial, for in David's reign we still find the Jebusites occupying the citadel.

2. By David against the Jebusites (2 Sam. v. 6–10; 1 Chron. xi. 23–39), about 1046 B.C.

3. By Shishak, king of Egypt, against Rehoboam (2 Chron. xii. 9; 1 Kings xiv. 25, 26), about 971 B.C. To this there was only a feeble resistance, and the Temple was plundered.

---

* It is interesting to note that in the midst of all this, the words which refer to the deliverance of Lot, "Haste thee" (*v.* 22) to "out of the midst" (*v.* 29), give a multiple of 8, the Dominical Number; it is 25304 (8 × 3163); while four of the verses of this section (25–28) are each separately multiples of 8; their total sum being 11312 (8 × 1414). The sum of the whole chapter is a multiple of 13.

4. By the Philistines, Arabians, and Ethiopians against Jehoram (2 Chron. xxi. 16), about 887 B.C. In this siege the royal palace was sacked, and the Temple again plundered.

5. By Jehoash, king of Israel, against Amaziah, king of Judah (2 Kings xiv. 13, 14), about 826 B.C. The wall was broken down and the city and Temple pillaged.

6. Rezin, king of Syria, and Pekah, king of Israel, against Ahaz (2 Chron. xxviii.), about 841 B.C. The city held out, but Ahaz sought the aid of Tiglath-Pileser, king of Assyria, who stripped the Temple.

7. By Sennacherib, king of Assyria, against Hezekiah (2 Chron. xxxii.), about 713 B.C. In this case the siege was raised by a Divine interposition, as foretold by Isaiah the prophet. (See the significance of this No. below).

8. Nebuchadnezzar, king of Babylon, against Jehoiakim (2 Chron. xxxvi. 7), about 606 B.C., when the Temple was partly pillaged.

9. By Nebuchadnezzar again, against Jehoiachin (2 Chron. xxxvi. 10), about 599 B.C., when the pillage of the Temple was completed and 10,000 people carried away.

10. By Nebuchadnezzar, B.C. 590–588, against Zedekiah (2 Chron. xxxvi. 17–20), when the overthrow was complete, the Temple burnt with fire,* and the city lay desolate for 50 years. After some 58 years, it was again besieged

11. By Ptolemy Soter, king of Egypt, against the Jews (320 B.C.). More than 100,000 captives were taken to Egypt.†

12. By Antiochus the Great, about 203 B.C.

13. By Scopus, a general of Alexander, about 199 B.C., who left a garrison.

14. By Antiochus again, 168 B.C., the worst siege since No. 10. The whole city was pillaged, 10,000 captives taken, the walls were destroyed, the altar was defiled, ancient manuscripts perished, the finest buildings were burned, and

* It was in the *ninth* year of Zedekiah that the house of God was burnt; and on the *ninth* day of the fourth month that the famine prevailed (2 Kings xxv.). It may be noted also here, that it was in the *ninth* year of Hoshea that the King of Assyria took Samaria, and carried Israel away (2 Kings xvii. 6).

† Where the Septuagint Version was afterwards made for Philadelphus, the successor of Ptolemy Soter.

the Jews were forbidden to worship there. This was the *Preteritist* fulfilment of Daniel's prophecy (ix. and xi.), and a foreshadowing example of what the *Futurist* fulfilment will yet be.

15. By Antiochus again, about 162 B.C., against Judas Maccabæus. This time honourable terms were made, and certain privileges were secured.

16. By Antiochus Sidetes, king of Syria, against John Hyrcanus, about 135 B.C.

17. By Hyrcanus (son of Alex. Jannæus) and the Priest Aristobulus. The siege was raised by Scaurus, one of Pompey's lieutenants, about 65 B.C.

18. By Pompey, against Aristobulus, about 63 B.C. The machines were moved on the Sabbath, when the Jews made no resistance. Only thus was it then reduced; 12,000 Jews were slain.

19.* Herod with a Roman army besieged the city in 39 B.C. for five months.

20. By Titus A.D. 70. At this memorable siege the conquest was complete. The *Second* Temple (Herod's) was burnt (in spite of Titus's orders). The tenth legion was left to carry out the work of destruction, and for another 50 years the city again disappears from history, as it did after the *tenth* siege.

21. The Romans had again to besiege the city in 135 A.D. against the false Messiah, Bar-Cochebas, who had acquired possession of the ruins. Not much is known of this, perhaps the most awful of all the sieges. So great and severe was the struggle, that Hadrian, in announcing to the Roman Senate the conclusion of the war, refrained from using the usual congratulatory phrase. The city was now obliterated. Its very name was changed, and it was renamed *Ælia Capitolinus*. A Temple was erected to Jupiter, and a statue of Hadrian placed on the site of the Holy of Holies. For 200 years the city passed out of history, no Jews being permitted to approach it.†

* Antigonus, son of Aristobulus, with a Parthian army took the city in 40 B.C.; but there was no siege, the city was taken by a sudden surprise.

† So great was the relief which Rome experienced by this suppression of Jerusalem and the Jews, that the toast became common at Roman feasts, "Hierosolyma Est Perdita," "Jerusalem is destroyed," the guests immediately greeting it with the shout *Hurrah*. This is the origin of our "Hep!

This siege was foretold by our Lord in Luke xix. 43, 44 and xxi. 20–24.

22. After 400 years of so-called Christian colonization, Chosroes the Persian (about 559 A.D.) swept through the country; thousands were massacred, and the church of the Holy Sepulchre was destroyed. The Emperor Heraclius afterwards defeated him, and restored the city and the church.

23. The Caliph Omar, in 636–7 A.D., besieged the city against Heraclius, and after a feeble resistance, followed by capitulation on favourable terms, the city passed into the hands of the Turks, thus marking one of the most important events connected with it and with chronology.*

24. Afdal, the Vizier of the Caliph of Egypt, besieged the two rival factions of Moslems, and pillaged the city in 1098.

25. In 1099 it was besieged by the army of the first Crusade.

26. In 1187 it was besieged by Saladin for seven weeks.

27. The wild Kharezmian hordes, in 1244, captured and plundered the city, slaughtering the monks and priests.

It seemed necessary to give this brief outline, because of several points which arise out of it. The list was made, in the first instance, without any reference whatever to "Number in Scripture." It was not till some time after, in considering the number *nine* as the number of *judgment,* that we noted the fact, that the number of these sieges was 27, or three times *nine*, and thus we saw the significance of the number.

Then, without looking at the list, we anticipated that there would be something peculiar about the numbers 10 and 20, *ten* being the number of *ordinal perfection,* and marking some cycle of completeness. So it proved on examination, for both the *tenth* and *twentieth* sieges were marked by the destruction of the Temple by fire! The *tenth* witnessed the destruction of Solomon's Temple by Nebuchadnezzar; the *twentieth* saw the destruction of Herod's Temple under Titus!

Hep! Hurrah," H, E, P, being the abbreviation of the three words, formed by their initial letters (on the principle known as *Notarica*, or *Notricon*). To this day *Hep* or *Hip* is said by only one person, the rest joining in the shout which greets it!

* See *The Witness of the Stars,* by the same author and publisher, page 186.

It was next felt that *seven* being the number of *spiritual perfection*, there would be something to mark off the *seventh*, *fourteenth*, and *twenty-first* sieges from all the others, and to connect them in some way with the perfection of Divine Revelation. So it proved on examination. These three were each the subject of Divine *Prophecy!* The *seventh* in 2 Chron. xxxii.; the *fourteenth* in Dan. xi.; the *twenty-first* in Luke xix. 43, 44. And there is a siege yet future—a *twenty-eighth* siege—which is also *foretold* in Scripture (see Zech. xiv., etc.). These four form an *epanodos*, the *first* corresponding to the *fourth* (the *first* and *fourth* sieges in each case being raised by Divine interposition); while the *second* corresponds to the *third* in the terrible character of each, thus:

A | The 7th—Sennacherib. The siege raised by a miraculous interposition by an angel from heaven. (2 Chron. xxxii.)

  B | The 14th—Antiochus (Dan. xi.)—one of the most awful.

  B | The 21st—Hadrian (Luke xix. 43, 44)—one of the most complete.

A | The 28th—Antichrist. Yet future. But the siege will be raised by a glorious deliverance, not by an angel, but by the Lord Himself coming from heaven. (Zech. xiv).

Thus, *four* are the subjects of *prophecy*—the 7th, 14th, 21st, and 28th.

Two mark complete cycles—the 10th and 20th, when the Temple was destroyed, each being followed by fifty years of silence.

Fourteen (7 × 2) are recorded in the Scripture.

Thirteen are non-Biblical, and are recorded only in profane history.

Surely there is something more than *chance* in the occurrence of these significant numbers.

The Judgments

of God in Hag. i. 11 * are enumerated in nine particulars:

"And I called for a drought upon the land,
and upon the mountains,

* Note in this verse an illustration of two figures of language—*Zeugma* and *Polysyndeton*.

and upon the corn,
and upon the new wine,
and upon the oil,
and upon that which the ground bringeth forth,
and upon men,
and upon cattle,
and upon all the labour of the hands."

There are nine words used from the root δίκη, *right* or *judgment* :—

1. δίκη (*dikee*), right, right proceeding, judgment (Acts xxv. 15; xxviii. 4; 2 Thess. i. 9; Jude 7).
2. δίκαιος (*dikaios*), right, just as it should be.
3. δικαιόω (*dikaioō*), to make δίκαιος (No. 2), to account righteous.
4. δικαιοσύνη (*dikaiosunee*), the state, or quality, or condition of him who is δίκαιος (*dikaios*).
5. δικαίως (*dikaiōs*), justly, rightly.
6. δικαίωμα (*dikaiōma*), a righteous act or requirement.*
7. δικαίωσις (*dikaiōsis*), is the action of the judge in promulgating a decree, in declaring or recognizing a person as δίκαιος (Rom. iv. 25; v. 18).

---

* It is important to distinguish the 10 occurrences of this word, which is variously translated, but which should be thus rendered:—

Luke i. 6, righteous ordinance.
Rom. i. 32, the righteous sentence of God.
,, ii. 26, the righteous requirement of the Law.
,, v. 16, righteous acquittal.
,, v. 18, righteous act.
,, viii. 4, righteous requirement.
Heb. ix. 1, 10, righteous ordinances.
Rev. xv. 4, righteous sentence.
,, xix. 8, righteous awards given.

The difference between δικαίωμα (*dikaiōma*) and δικαιοσύνη (*dikaiosunee*) points us to the fact that the latter word relates either to the quality, attribute, or condition of those acceptable before God, or to God's own relative attribute of righteousness; while the former word shows that the righteous requirement of the Law is fulfilled by those who are not under the Law, either for condemnation or a rule of life, but who are, as the apostle was, ἔννομος Χριστοῦ (*ennomos Christou*), *i.e.*, under obedience to Christ's commands (see pp. 88, 89, and 1 Cor. ix. 20, R.V., where the Apostle distinctly says he was not ὑπὸ νόμον (*hupo nomon*), *i.e.*, under law-principle, the word law not having the article). The Law condemned every one under it. But Christians who realize (subjectively) that they died with Christ and live as those alive from the dead, walking in the Spirit and in the power of Christ, carry out practically (though with many failures, doubtless) *the righteous requirement* of the Law.

8. δικαστής (*dikastees*) is the judge (Luke xii. 14; Acts vii. 27. 35).

9. δικαιοκρισία (*dikaiokrisia*) is the righteous judgment of the judge (Rom. ii. 5).

OCCURRENCES OF WORDS.

The following words, among others, occur 9 times, and are all connected in some way with *judgment* :—

ἄβυσσος (*abussos*), bottomless pit, or deep.
ἀσεβής (*asebees*), ungodly.
ἀσέλγεια (*aselgeia*), lasciviousness.
ἀστραπή (*astrapee*), lightning.

All calling for, or connected with judgment.

Enough has been said to show that the signification of the number *nine* is *judgment*, especially divine judgment, and the conclusion of the whole matter so far as *man* is concerned.

But *nine* is the square of three, and *three* is the number of Divine perfection, as well as the number peculiar to the Holy Spirit. It is not surprising, therefore, to find that this number denotes *finality* in divine things.

"*Fruit* (not fruits) *of the Spirit*" comprises nine (3^2) graces: (1) love, (2) joy, (3) peace, (4) longsuffering, (5) gentleness, (6) goodness, (7) faith, (8) meekness, (9) temperance,* while

THE GIFTS OF THE SPIRIT

in 1 Cor. xii. 8–10 are also *nine* in number, viz. :—

The word of wisdom,
The word of knowledge,
Faith,
Healing,
The working of miracles,
Prophecy,
Discerning of spirits,
Divers kinds of tongues,
The interpretation of tongues.

---

* It will be noticed that in this fruit of the Spirit "temperance" is put last; while in the "*works of the flesh*" (verses 19–21), which are *sixteen* in number (4^2, the earth number), "drunkenness and revellings" are put last! Truly man's ways are not God's ways, nor God's thoughts man's thoughts (Isa. lv. 8).

TEN.

It has been already pointed out that *ten* is one of the perfect numbers, and signifies *the perfection of Divine order*, commencing, as it does, an altogether new series of numbers. The first decade is the representative of the whole numeral system, and originates the system of calculation called "decimals," because the whole system of numeration consists of so many *tens*, of which the first is a type of the whole.

Completeness of order, marking the entire round of anything, is, therefore, the ever-present signification of the number *ten*. It implies that nothing is wanting; that the number and order are perfect; that the whole cycle is complete.

NOAH

completed the antediluvian age in the *tenth* generation from God.

THE TEN COMMANDMENTS

contain all that is necessary, and no more than is necessary, both as to their number and their order, while

THE LORD'S PRAYER

is completed in *ten* clauses.*

THE TITHES

represent the whole of what was due from man to God, as marking and recognising God's claim on the whole.

THE REDEMPTION MONEY

was *ten* gerahs, and thus was acknowledged both what God claimed, and what man was responsible to give. Now ten

---

* These clauses have the significance of their respective numbers :—
The *first*, God's *sovereignty*.
The *second*, Jehovah's manifested Name.
The *third*, the *realization* of God's kingdom.
The *fourth* first mentions the *earth*.
The *fifth*, the gift of grace supplying our need.
The *sixth* treats of *man's* sin.
The *seventh* pleads for *spiritual* guidance.
The *eighth* pleads for final deliverance from all evil.
The *ninth* sums up the *divine* glory (3^3), while
The *tenth completes* the eternal cycles.

gerahs was half a shekel (Exod. xxx. 12–16; Num. iii. 47). Every male that was numbered, over 20 years of age, must pay this sum and meet God's claim.*

But the *first-born* were to pay ten times as much; for when God took the Levites instead of the first-born of Israel, there were found

22,273 first-born males, but only
22,000 Levites. So that

273 had to pay the ransom money,

which amounted to *ten* times *ten* gerahs. Thus, though the five shekels looked like a variation, the significance of *ten* is sustained, for the five shekels were *ten* times the "half shekel." (See Num. iii. 12, 13, 40–51).†

THE TEN PLAGUES

were representative of the complete circle of God's judgments on Egypt. Exod. ix. 14, "I will . . . send all my plagues."

ANTICHRIST'S WORLD-POWER

is comprised in the *ten* kingdoms, symbolized by the *ten* toes on the feet of the image of Nebuchadnezzar's dream (Dan. ii. 41), and by the *ten* horns of the fourth beast of Daniel's vision (Dan. vii. 7, 20, 24, etc.; Rev. xii. 3; xiii. 1; xvii. 3, 7, 12).

TEN NATIONS

imply the whole of the nations which are to be the scene of Abraham's covenant possessions (Gen. xv. 19).

ABRAHAM'S FAITH

was proved by a completed cycle of *ten* trials:—

1. His departure from Haran.
2. His flight to Egypt from the famine.
3. In the seizure of Sarah.
4. In his war to rescue Lot.

* When David *numbered* the people (2 Sam. xxiv. and 1 Chron. xxi.), this payment was not made and God's claim was not met. Hence the judgment which followed.

† We may note, in passing, that the number of the males over was 273 (13 × 21), while the amount of the shekels was 1,365 (13 × 105) (Num. iii. 50). For the significance of this, see under the number "Thirteen."

5. In his taking Hagar.
6. In his circumcision.
7. In the second seizure of Sarah at Gerar.
8. In the expulsion of Ishmael.
9. In the expulsion of Hagar.
10. In the offering of Isaac.

THE TEN REBELLIONS

of Israel in the wilderness (Num. xiv. 22) mark the completed series of Israel's perversities.

THE SILVER SOCKETS

which formed the foundation of the Tabernacle were 10 × 10 (Exod. xxxviii. 27). These were made of silver, and silver is significant of *redemption* (1 Pet. i. 18, 19).*

FIRE CAME DOWN FROM HEAVEN

ten times, *six* of which were in judgment :—

Gen. xix. 24, on Sodom.
Lev. ix. 24, on the first offerings.
" x. 2, on Nadab and Abihu.
Num. xi. 1, on the murmurers at Taberah.
" xvi. 35, on Korah and his company.
1 Kings xviii. 38, on Elijah's offering at Carmel.
2 Kings i. 10, on Elijah's enemies.
" " 12, " "
1 Chron. xxi. 26, on David's sacrifice.
2 Chron. vii. 1, on Solomon's sacrifice.

TEN TIMES THE PEOPLE SHOUTED FOR JOY.

Lev. ix. 24, when the fire from heaven consumed the first sacrifices.
Josh. vi. 20, at the taking of Jericho.
1 Sam. iv. 5, when the Ark was brought into the camp.
" x. 24, when Saul was chosen king.
" xvii. 20, when Israel went to fight the Philistines.
" " 52, when pursuing them.
2 Sam. vi. 15 (1 Chron. xv. 28), when the Ark was brought back from the house of Obed-edom.

---

* *Ten* also completed the number of the curtains (Exod. xxvi. 1).

2 Chron. xiii. 15, when God smote Jeroboam before Abijah.
2 Chron. xv. 14, when Asa and the people heard Oded's prophecy.
Ezra iii. 11, when the foundation of the second Temple was laid.

The Ten Virgins

represent the whole of the nation of Israel (as distinct from the elect remnant, which is the Bride);* while the *five* denotes those who by *grace* will be able to say, "This is our God, we have waited for Him."

God's Righteous Curses

are completed in a series of ten :—

Gen. iii. 14, 15, on the serpent.
„ „ 17, the ground.
„ iv. 11, Cain.
„ ix. 25, Cainan.
Josh. vi. 17, Jericho.
„ „ 28, } Achan.
„ vii. 12, }
„ ix. 23, Gibeonites.
Judg. ix. 57, Shechemites.
1 Kings xvi. 34, Hiel the Beth-elite.
Mark xi. 21, The Fig-tree.

"I have Sinned."

Ten† persons complete the series of those who uttered this confession, and acknowledged their desert of divine judgment :—

Pharaoh, Exod. ix. 27; x. 16.
Balaam, Num. xxii. 34.

* The popular interpretation of this parable cannot be the correct one, for we cannot, in one parable, take two totally different classes of persons as representing one and the same person. It is impossible to take *the Church* as represented by both the Ten Virgins and the Bride! If the Church is the Bride, then it cannot be the Virgins. If the Church is represented by the Ten Virgins, then it cannot be the Bride. The only escape from the dilemma is not to *read into* the Gospel of Matthew that which was the subject of a subsequent revelation (Rom. xvi. 25, 26; Eph. iii. 1-11; Col. i. 26, 27); but to interpret Matthew by what was already the subject of previous revelation in the Old Testament about the Bride. See under the number *One*, "*First occurrences*" (p. 61).

† Of these *ten*, 6 were individual (the number of *man*), while 4 were on behalf of the nation—"We."

Achan, Josh. vii. 20.
Saul, 1 Sam. xv. 24, 30; xxvi. 21.
David, 2 Sam. xii. 13; xxiv. 10, 17; 1 Chron. xxi. 8, 17; Pss. xli. 4; li. 4.
Shimei, 2 Sam. xix. 20.
Hezekiah, 2 Kings xviii. 14 (rendered "offended").
Job vii. 20.
Micah vii. 9.
Nehemiah i. 6.

THE TABERNACLE

is spoken of *ten* times as the "Tabernacle of Witness," or "Tabernacle of Testimony." Of these, *five* are מִשְׁכָּן (*mish-kahn*), Exod. xxxviii. 21; Num. i. 50, 53 (twice); x. 11. This has special reference to the Tabernacle as the dwelling-place of God, from שָׁכַן (*shahcan*), "to dwell." *Mish-kahn* means the dwelling-place of God (Exod. xxv. 8), and is therefore never used by the Holy Spirit of "whole congregation."

The other *five* are אֹהֶל (*oh-el*), Num. xvii. 7, 8, 10; xviii. 2; 2 Chron. xxiv. 6. *Oh-el* means simply a tent, and has special reference to the meeting-place of the people by appointment or at appointed seasons. This is the word which is used by the Holy Spirit of the "tent of the congregation."

THE TEN WORDS OF PSALM CXIX.

complete the cycle of the Divine description of His Word. One or other of these *ten* words occurs in every verse (except 122), viz., Way, Testimony, Precepts, Commandments, Saying, Law, Judgment, Righteousness, Statutes, Word. These, the Massorah says, "correspond to the Ten Commandments." *

THE TENTH GENERATION

completed and represented the whole existence of the family or nation. In Deut. xxiii. 3 we read that "an Ammonite or Moabite shall not enter into the congregation of the LORD; even to their tenth generation shall they not enter into the congregation of the LORD for ever." The reason is given in verses 4 and 5. See also Neh. xiii. 1.

* See *A Key to the Psalms*, by the Rev. Thomas Boys, edited by the same author, p. 122. This refers to the Hebrew numbering of the verses, not the verses of the English Bible.

THE PARABLES OF THE KINGDOM

are ten in number in the Gospel of Matthew. *Seven* in ch. xiii., and *three* in chaps. xxii. and xxv.

THE UNRIGHTEOUS WHO SHALL NOT ENTER

the kingdom of God are enumerated in *ten* particulars (1 Cor. vi. 9, 10).

THE SECURITY OF THE SAINTS

is set forth in a ten-fold enumeration, which completes the whole cycle of assurance to all who are "in Christ" (see under *Seventeen*), Rom. viii. 38, 39. They are given in two fives:—

"For I am persuaded, that
{ neither death, nor life,
{ nor angels, nor principalities, nor powers;
{ nor things present, nor things to come,
{ nor height, nor depth, nor any other creature."

THE TEN I AM'S OF JESUS IN JOHN.

"I am the Bread of Life" (vi. 35).
"I am the Bread of Life which came down from heaven" (vi. 41).
"I am the Living Bread" (vi. 51).
"I am the Light of the world" (viii. 12).
"I am One that bear witness of Myself" (viii. 18).
"I am the Door of the sheep" (x. 7, 9).
"I am the Good Shepherd" (x. 14).
"I am the Resurrection and the Life" (xiv. 6).
"I am the Way, the Truth, and the Life" (xiv. 6).
"I am the True Vine" (xv. 1, 5).

THE REPEATED* NAMES.

Ten completes the perfect cycle of the repeated Names. Moreover we shall note that these are divided signifi-

* The 14 *changed* names would form a profitable subject of Bible-study, there being 10 examples in the Old Testament, and 4 in the New Testament. Of these fourteen, 5 were changed by Divine authority, whilst 9 were apparently changed by man. See *The Repeated Name*, by the Rev. James Smith, of Dufftown, N.B., published by A. & R. Milne, Aberdeen.

cantly. Of these *ten*, seven are spoken directly to individual human beings, while *three* are spoken by the Lord in different connections. Of these seven, four are in the Old Testament, and three are in the New Testament.

1.	Abraham, Abraham, Gen. xxii. 11.	Old Test. (4)	Used by God to men (7)
2.	Jacob, Jacob, Gen. xlvi. 2.		
3.	Moses, Moses, Exod. iii. 4.		
4.	Samuel, Samuel, 1 Sam. iii. 10.		
5.	Martha, Martha, Luke x. 41.	New Test. (3)	
6.	Simon, Simon, Luke xxii. 31.		
7.	Saul, Saul, Acts ix. 4.		
8.	Lord, Lord, Matt. vii. 21, 22; xxv. 11; Luke vi. 46; xiii. 25.	Used under other circumstances.* (3).	
9.	Eloi, Eloi, Mark xv. 34, Matt. xxvii. 46; Ps. xxii. 1.		
10.	Jerusalem, Jerusalem, Matt. xxiii. 37; Luke xiii. 34.		

WORDS AND PHRASES WHICH OCCUR TEN TIMES.

Among these may be mentioned :—

זֵר (*zair*), the crown of the Ark of the Covenant.

כִּיוֹר (*keeyōr*), Laver, *ten* times in Exodus and Leviticus with regard to the Tabernacle; and *ten* times in Kings and Chronicles with regard to the Temple.

כֵּן (*kain*), the foot or base of the Laver.

ἁγιασμός (*hagiasmos*), holiness.

ἅγιον (*hagion*), holy (7 of these are in the plural for the Holy of Holies).

δικαίωμα (*dikaiōma*), righteous requirement. (See p. 241).

παντοκράτωρ (*pantokratōr*), Almighty, used only of God. (9 times in Revelation).

καταβολὴ κόσμου (*katabolee kosmou*), the foundation of the world. (See pp. 120 and 190.)

λέγει κύριου (*legei kuriou*), saith the Lord (omitting Heb. x. 30 with R.V., T., Tr., W. & H., and R.V.).

---

* Each of these three is unique, viz. :—
In No. 8 it is the name of the Lord by human beings.
In No. 9 it is the name of God by Jesus.
In No. 10 it is God's city and people by Jesus.

THE TALMUD

calls attention to the fact that there are—

Ten different words used for Idols.

Ten for Prophet, viz., Ambassador, Faithful, Servant, Messenger, Seer, Watchman, Seer of Vision, Dreamer, Prophet, Man of God (*Avoth*, ch. xxxiv.).

Ten designations are applied to the Word of God, viz., Scripture, Proverb, Interpretation, Dark Saying, Oracle, Utterance, Decree, Burden, Prophecy, Vision.

Ten different words for Joy.

Ten generations from Adam to Noah; and

Ten from Noah to Abraham.

Abraham was tried with *ten* trials (*Av. d. R.N.* 33, *Pd. R.E.* 26). See page 244.

ELEVEN.

If *ten* is the number which marks the perfection of Divine *order*, then *eleven* is an *addition* to it, subversive of and undoing that order. If *twelve* is the number which marks the perfection of Divine *government*, then eleven falls short of it. So that whether we regard it as being 10 + 1, or 12 − 1, it is the number which marks *disorder*, *disorganization*, *imperfection*, and *disintegration*.

There is not much concerning it in the Word of God, but what there is is significant, especially as a *factor* and from what we have already seen on pp. 22–44.

The Dukes of Edom

were *eleven* in number (Gen. xxxvi. 40–43), and Edom, though closely related to Israel, was different from [illegible] in order and government, while the bitterest hatred exist[illegible] them. The word for "Duke" is a multiple of [illegible] p. 212.

The Eleven Sons of Jacob

told of the disintegration and disorganization in Jacob's family, which made it possible for it to be said "one is not."

From Horeb to Kadesh Barnea

was a journey of *eleven* days (Deut. i. 2). One more day would have carried them to the complete administration of all those wonderful laws which God had given them.

Eli, Hophni, and Phinehas

have for their *gematria* the number 462, the *factors* of which are 11 and 42; both significant of the disorder in Eli's house, and of disintegration in Israel.

Jehoiakim Reigned Eleven Years,

when Nebuchadnezzar came up and began his disintegrating work on Jerusalem (2 Kings xxiii. 36; xxiv. 1; and 2 Chron. xxxvi. 5, 6).

Zedekiah Reigned Eleven Years,

when Nebuchadnezzar completed the work by putting an end to Israel's rule in Jerusalem (2 Chron. xxxvi. 11; Jer. lii. 1), for "in the eleventh year the city was broken up" (Jer. xxxix. 2).

THE ELEVENTH YEAR

in which Ezekiel prophesied against Tyre (Ezek. xxvi. 1) and against Egypt (xxx. 20 and xxxi. 1) was the *eleventh* year of Zedekiah, in which Jerusalem was broken up. And the threefold repetition of it is to impress us with the fact that Tyre and Egypt should be broken up, as Jerusalem had been.

THE ELEVEN APOSTLES

witness of disintegration even amongst the Twelve (Acts ii. 14, etc.); while

THE ELEVENTH HOUR

(Matt. xx. 6, 9) is proverbial as being contrary alike both to what is right in order and arrangement.

THE LIFE OF OUR LORD ON EARTH

was *about* 33 years (3 × 11), and then He was "cut off," and "we see not yet all things put under Him" (Dan. ix. 26; Heb. ii. 8).

ELEVEN HUNDRED

occurs only twice, both referring to days of defective administration, marked by the fact that there was "no king":

(1) Judg. xvi. 5, the Philistine bribe which deprived Israel of their mighty judge and deliverer, Samson.

(2) Judg. xvii. 2, etc., connected with the introduction of idolatry into Israel, which brought with it trouble and disintegration; added to God's order and ordinances for them; and in the end caused the ruin and loss of all government.

Dan and Ephraim were the two offending tribes, for Micah, who made the image with the *eleven hundred* shekels, was an Ephraimite, and the tribe that stole it and his priest was the Tribe of Dan. Both are omitted from the tribes in Rev. vii., according to the declaration of Jehovah in Deut. xxix. 18–20, that the "man, woman, family, or tribe" which should introduce idolatry into Israel, "the LORD shall BLOT OUT HIS NAME." But though omitted from the Ecclesiastical or *spiritual* blessings of the *sealing* (Rev. vii.), they have their Political or *territorial* blessing in the land (Ezek. xlviii. 1, 5).

TWELVE

is a perfect number, signifying *perfection of government*, or of *governmental perfection*. It is found as a multiple in all that has to do with *rule*. The sun which "rules" the day, and the moon and stars which "govern" the night, do so by their passage through the *twelve* signs of the Zodiac which completes the great circle of the heavens of 360 (12 × 30) degrees or divisions, and thus govern the year.

Twelve is the *product* of 3 (the perfectly Divine and heavenly number) and 4 (the earthly, the number of what is material and organic).

While *seven* is composed of 3 *added* to 4, *twelve* is 3 *multiplied by* 4, and hence denotes that which can scarcely be explained in words, but which the spiritual perception can at once appreciate, viz., *organization*, the products denoting production and multiplication and increase of all that is contained in the two numbers separately. The 4 is generally prominently seen in the *twelve*.

There were Twelve Patriarchs

from Seth to Noah and his family, and *twelve* from Shem to Jacob.

The Twelve Tribes of Israel.

Though actually thirteen in number, there are never more than *twelve* named in any one list. There are about 18 enumerations altogether, but in each list one or other is omitted. Generally it is Levi, but not always. In Rev. vii. both Dan and Ephraim are omitted (see p. 211), but the enumeration is still *twelve*, Levi and Joseph being introduced for this special sealing of the remnant which shall go unscathed through the great tribulation.

Then there were *twelve* Judges or Saviours (see p. 214).

The Temple of Solomon

has the number *twelve* as one of its great factors in contrast with the Tabernacle, which had the number five. This agrees with the *grace* which shines in the Tabernacle, and with the *glory* of the kingdom which is displayed in the Temple.

When we come to the New Testament we find the same great principle pervading the Apostolic government as we see in the Patriarchal and National, for we have:

The *twelve* Apostles.
The *twelve* foundations in the heavenly Jerusalem.
The *twelve* gates.
The *twelve* pearls.
The *twelve* angels.

The Measurement of the New Jerusalem

will be 12,000 furlongs square, while the wall will be 144 (12 × 12) cubits, Rev. xxi. 16, 17.

The number of the sealed in Rev. vii. 4 will be 144,000, and all that has to do with the *Twelve* Tribes is necessarily pervaded by this number, such as the stones in the High Priest's breastplate, the stones taken out of the Jordan, the number of the spies, etc. etc., and therefore we have not referred to all such reference in these pages.

Twelve Persons were Anointed

for government of various kinds. Of course, all kings, priests, prophets, and healed lepers were anointed; but the circumstances of the anointing of *twelve* individuals is specially recorded. Of these, five were priests (Aaron and his four sons, Exod. vi. 23) and seven were kings:

1.	Aaron, Exod. xxix. 7, 9, etc. ...	Priests (5).	12
2.	Nadab ,, ...		
3.	Abihu ,, ...		
4.	Eleazar ,, ...		
5.	Ithamar ,, ...		
6.	Saul, 1 Sam. x. 1	Kings (7).	
7.	David,* 1 Sam. xvi. 13		
8.	Absalom, 2 Sam. xix. 10 ...		
9.	Solomon, 1 Kings i. 39		
10.	Jehu, 2 Kings ix. 6		
11.	Joash, 2 Kings xi. 12		
12.	Jehoahaz, 2 Kings xxiii. 30 ...		

* David was anointed *three* times, viz.:
by Samuel, 1 Sam. xvi. 13;
by the men of Judah, 2 Sam. ii. 4;
by the elders of Israel, 2 Sam. v. 3.

It will be observed from the above list that Saul, the man of *man's choice*, is thus stamped with the number 6. David, the man of *God's choice*, is stamped with the number *seven.* For Saul and David are the sixth and seventh respectively in order. The words, "a man after God's own heart," mean simply *a man of God's choice*, and not, as infidels are never tired of asserting, that God approved of all the sins which David fell into.

Twelve Years

of age was Jesus when He first appears in public (Luke ii. 42) and utters His first-recorded words (see p. 52).

Twelve Legions

of angels mark the perfection of angelic powers (Matt. xxvi. 53).

The Half of Twelve

sometimes denotes interruption or defect in human government, while

The Number of Occurrences

of words agrees with its signification, *e.g.*, αὐλή, *aulee*, "palace," occurs *twelve* times.

THIRTEEN.

This number has been considered in connection with the number *eight,* to which the reader is referred (see pages 205-232).

FOURTEEN,

being a multiple of *seven,* partakes of its significance; and, being double that number, implies a double measure of spiritual perfection.

The number *two* with which it is combined (2 × 7) may, however, bring its own significance into its meaning, as in Matt. i., where the genealogy of Jesus Christ is divided up and given in sets of 14 (2 × 7) generations, *two* being the number associated with incarnation.

The same principle may be applied to other multiples of *seven,* and Bible students can find their own illustrations.

FIFTEEN,

being a multiple of *five*, partakes of the significance of that number, also of the number *three* with which it is combined, 3×5.

Five is, as we have seen, the number of *grace*, and *three* is the number of *divine perfection*. *Fifteen*, therefore, specially refers to acts wrought by the energy of Divine grace.

Deity is seen in it, for the two Hebrew letters which express it are י, *Yod* (10), and ה, *Hey* (5). These spell the ineffable Name of יה, *Jah*, who is the fountain of all grace. The number *fifteen* is thus made up, by addition, $10 + 5$; but as the Jews would not, by the constant use of these two letters, profane the sacred name, two other letters were arbitrarily used for this number, and a different and artificial combination was thus formed—ט (*Teth*) = 9, and ו (*Vau*) = 6. The number $9 + 6$ would thus represent the number *fifteen*, but without any significance.

Fifteen being $8 + 7$ as well as 3×5, it may also include a reference to resurrection, as being a special mark of the energy of Divine grace issuing in glory.

A few examples may suffice:

The Ark was borne by the Flood *fifteen* cubits upwards, Gen. vii. 20.

Hezekiah's reprieve from death was *fifteen* years, 2 Kings xx. 6.

The Jews were delivered from death under Esther on the *fifteenth* day of the month (ix. 18, 21). This is specially significant, as we have seen (p. 222), that their sentence to death was connected with the number *thirteen*.

Bethany, where Lazarus was raised, and from whence the Lord ascended, was *fifteen* furlongs from Jerusalem, John xi. 18.

Paul's ship anchored safely in *fifteen* fathoms on the 14th day, after *thirteen* days of toil and trial, Acts xxvii. 21.

On the *fifteenth* day of the first month was the feast of unleavened bread, Lev. xxiii. 6; and

On the *fifteenth* day of the seventh month was the feast of Tabernacles (*v.* 34).

SEVENTEEN

stands out very prominently as a significant number. It is not a multiple of any other number, and therefore it has no factors. Hence it is called one of the *prime* (or indivisible) numbers. What is more, it is the *seventh* in the list of the prime numbers.

The series runs 1, 3, 5, 7, 11, 13, 17, etc. *Thirteen*, it will be noted, is also a prime number, and is therefore important; but it is the *sixth* of the series: hence it partakes of the significance of the number 6, and is indeed an intensified expression of it.

In like manner *seventeen* being the *seventh* of the series, it partakes of and intensifies the significance of the number *seven*. Indeed, it is the combination or *sum* of two perfect numbers—*seven* and *ten*—*seven* being the number of *spiritual* perfection, and *ten* of *ordinal* perfection.

Contrasted together the significance of these two numbers is clear; and when united in the number *seventeen* we have a union of their respective meanings, *viz.*, spiritual perfection, plus ordinal perfection, or *the perfection of spiritual order.*

We see a beautiful illustration in

ROMANS VIII. 35-39,

which concludes the first great division of that all-important Epistle, and sums up the blessings of those who are dead and risen in Christ. First we have a series of *seven*, then a series of *ten*. The *seven* are marked off by being put in the form of a question, while the *ten* are given as the answer to it.

"Who shall separate us from the love of Christ? Shall

1. Tribulation,
2. Or distress,
3. Or persecution,
4. Or famine,
5. Or nakedness,
6. Or peril,
7. Or sword?

as it is written, For Thy sake are we killed all the day long; we are accounted as sheep for the slaughter. Nay, in all these things we are more than conquerors through Him that loved us. For I am persuaded, that.

8. Neither death (1),
9. Nor life (2),
10. Nor angels (3),
11. Nor principalities (4),
12. Nor powers (5),
13. Nor things present (6),
14. Nor things to come (7).
15. Nor height (8),
16. Nor depth (9),
17. Nor any other creature (10),

shall be able to separate us from the love of God which is in Christ Jesus our Lord."

Thus is set forth the spiritual and eternal perfection of the believer's standing in Christ.

By forming the conclusive answer to the question, and giving us the positive assurance (though in a negative form), it seems as though the number *ten* is of more weight than *seven* when thus used together. It is so in 2 Chron. ii., where, in *v.* 7, Solomon sends to Hiram for a cunning workman, and *seven* particulars are specified; and in *v.* 14 a man is sent and his qualifications are enumerated in *ten* particulars. A more important illustration will be found in

Hebrews xii. 18–24,

where the Old Dispensation and the New are thus contrasted:

"Ye are not come

1. Unto the mount that might be touched,
2. And that burned with fire,
3. Nor unto blackness,
4. And darkness,
5. And tempest,
6. And the sound of a trumpet,
7. And the voice of words . . .

but ye are come

8. Unto Mount Zion (1).
9. And unto the city of the living God (2).
10. The heavenly Jerusalem (3),

11. And to an innumerable company of angels (4),
12. To the general assembly (5),
13. And church of the firstborn which are written in heaven (6),
14. And to God the judge of all (7),
15. And to the spirits of just men made perfect (8),
16. And to Jesus the Mediator of the New Covenant (9),
17. And to the blood of sprinkling that speaketh better things than that of Abel (10)."

Here again the blessings of the New Covenant are seen to be higher than those of the Old, both in number and in importance. The Old were *spiritual* (7), but the latter are more so, for they are doubly the manifestation of Divine grace, *ten*, or 2 × 5.

Psalm lxxxiii. 6–11

gives us the *ten* and the *seven* in a different order. Verses 6–9 give us a confederation of *ten* enemies for the purpose of making Israel extinct, and "to cut them off from being a nation"; while *vv.* 10 and 12 give us an enumeration of *seven* enemies which the Lord had destroyed in the past, with the prayer that He would do to the confederacy of the *ten* what He had done to the *seven* in the past.

The commentators agree that no such confederacy can be found in the past history of Israel, so that we are shut up to the conclusion that the Psalm is *Proleptic*, and speaks of a yet future confederacy of which the later Prophets speak more particularly.

Verses 6–9: The *ten*-fold confederation:—

1. Edom.
2. The Ishmaelites.
3. Moab.
4. The Hagarenes.
5. Gebal.
6. Ammon.
7. Amalek.
8. The Philistines.
9. Tyre.
10. Assur (Assyria).

Then follow, in *vv.* 10–12, the *seven* enemies which had been destroyed in days of old:

11. Midianites (1), Judg. vii. 8.
12. Sisera (2), Judg. iv. 5, 21.
13. Jabin (3), Judg. iv. 5, 21.
14. Oreb (4), Judg. vii. 25.
15. Zeeb (5), Judg. vii. 25.
16. Zebah (6), Judg. viii. 5.
17. Zalmunna (7), Judg. viii. 5.

The number *seventeen* (not the word merely) has a significance of its own, and therefore an importance which must be taken into account wherever it appears in the Word of God by itself or as a *factor*.

It forms a great factor in the number 153 (see pp. 273, 274).

NINETEEN

is a number not without significance. It is a combination of 10 and 9, and would denote the perfection of *Divine order* connected with *judgment*. It is the *gematria* of Eve and of Job.

TWENTY

is the double of *ten*, and may in some cases signify its concentrated meaning. But its significance seems rather to be connected with the fact that it is one short of twenty-one, $21 - 1 = 20$; that is to say, if 21 is the three-fold 7, and signifies Divine (3) completion as regards spiritual perfection (7), then *twenty*, being one short of 21, it would signify what Dr. Milo Mahan calls *expectancy*, and certainly we are not without illustrations in support of it:

Twenty years Jacob *waited* to get possession of his wives and property, Gen. xxi. 38, 41.

Twenty years Israel *waited* for a deliverer from Jabin's oppression, Judg. iv. 3.

Twenty years Israel *waited*. for deliverance through Samson, Judg. xv. 20; xvi. 31. But his work was never much more than "begun," Judg. xiii. 25.

Twenty years the Ark of the Covenant *waited* at Kirjath-jearim, 1 Sam. vii. 2.

Twenty years Solomon was *waiting* for the completion of the two houses, 1 Kings ix. 10; 2 Chron. viii. 1.

Twenty years Jerusalem *waited* between its capture and destruction; and

Twenty years Jeremiah prophesied concerning it.

TWENTY-TWO,

being the double of *eleven*, has the significance of that number in an intensified form,—*disorganization* and *disintegration*, especially in connection with the Word of God. For the number *two* is associated with the *second* person of the Godhead, the living Word.

It is associated with the worst of Israel's kings,—Jeroboam (1 Kings xiv. 20), and Ahab (1 Kings xvi. 29), each reigning 22 years.

Eleven, we have seen, derives its significance by being an *addition* to Divine order (10), and a *subtraction* from Divine rule (12). These are two of the three ways in which the written Word of God can be corrupted—the third being *alteration*. "The words of the LORD are pure words"—words pertaining to this world and therefore requiring to be purified (see p. 169). But these words have been altered, taken from, and added to by man. Is there anything in this which connects it with the fact that the letters of the alphabet (Hebrew) are *twenty-two* in number? Does it point to the fact that the revelation of God in being committed to human language and to man's keeping would thereby be subject to disintegration and corruption?

TWENTY-FOUR,

being a multiple of *twelve*, expresses in a higher form the same signification (as 22 does of 11). It is the number associated with the heavenly government and worship, of which the earthly form in Israel was only a copy. We are told that both Moses and David ordered all things connected with the Tabernacle and Temple worship by direct revelation from God, and as a copy of things in the heavens, Heb. viii. 5; 1 Chron. xxviii. 12, 19. And the sevenfold phrase (in Exod. xl.) "as the LORD commanded Moses" witnesses to the Divine ordering of all. It was so with the *twenty-four* courses of priests in the earthly Temple; these were formed on the "pattern of things in the heavens." Why is it necessary for us, when God tells us anything, to conclude that it means something else? Why, when, in Rev. iv., we read of the *twenty-four* heavenly elders, are we to assume they are anything but what we read, viz., the leaders of the heavenly worship? Why seek to make them redeemed men, or the symbolical representation of redeemed men? Why not leave them alone? It is by such additions as these to what is written that the people of God are divided up into so many schools and parties.

Those who regard them as representing the redeemed have done so on the supposed authority of Rev. v. 9; but they have been misled by some scribe who, in copying Rev. v. 9, altered certain words either to make the passage conform to Rev. i. 5, 6 (which is somewhat similar), or to support this very view. Thus it has been handed down that these *twenty-four* elders were redeemed, and are therefore glorified human beings.

But it is now known that the ancient and true reading was very different. That reading is given in the Revised Version thus:—"And they sing a new song, saying, Worthy art Thou to take the book, and to open the seals thereof; for Thou wast slain and didst purchase unto God *men* * of every tribe,

* The word ἡμᾶς (*heemas*), "us," goes out, with the authority of Lachmann, Tischendorf, Alford, Westcott and Hort, the Revisers, and the Codex A. It is true that the authorities are divided as to this word, but as they are *unanimous* as to the other changes in the verse, this word *necessarily* must go out as the result.

and tongue, and people, and nation, and madest them * to be unto our God a kingdom † and priests: and they reign ‡ upon the earth."

Thus the ancient and true reading takes away all ground for making these elders redeemed men, and leaves them the angelic leaders of the heavenly worship.

TWENTY-FIVE,

being the square of five (5^2 or 5×5), expresses the essence of the signification of *five, i.e. grace,* whether used alone or occurring as a factor in larger numbers. The same may be said of

TWENTY-SEVEN,

being the cube of three.

TWENTY-EIGHT

is a multiple, and therefore has the significance of *seven.* Being also the product of 4×7 it partakes of the significance of 4. See pp. 194, 195.

TWENTY-NINE

is the combination of 20, the number of *expectation,* and 9, the number of *judgment.*

THIRTY,

being 3×10, denotes in a higher degree the perfection of Divine order, as marking the right moment. CHRIST was *thirty* years of age at the commencement of His ministry, Luke iii. 23. As did the Levites, see Num. iv. 3.

JOSEPH, His type, was the same age, Gen. xli. 46.

DAVID also, when he began to reign, 2 Sam. v. 4.

THIRTY-ONE.

The Hebrew expression of this is אל, *El,* the name of God, and its signification as a number or factor would be *Deity.*

* The word ἡμᾶς (*heemas*), "us," must be changed for αὐτοὺς (*autous*), "them," with all the critical authorities.

† The word βασιλεῖς (*basileis*), "kings," must be changed for βασιλείαν (*basileian*), "a kingdom," with all the critical authorities.

‡ The word βασιλεύσομεν (*basileusomen*), "we shall reign," must be changed for βασιλεύουσιν (*basileuousin*), "they reign," with Lachmann, Tregelles, Alford, Westcott and Hort, the Revisers, and Codexes A and B. Or, for βασιλεύσουσιν (*basileusousin*), "they shall reign," with Griesbach, Scholz, Tischendorf, Tregelles in margin, and Sinaitic Codex.

FORTY

has long been universally recognized as an important number, both on account of the frequency of its occurrence, and the uniformity of its association with a period of *probation, trial,* and *chastisement*—(not *judgment,* like the number 9, which stands in connection with the punishment of enemies, but the chastisement of sons, and of a covenant people). It is the product of 5 and 8, and points to the action of *grace* (5), leading to and ending in *revival* and *renewal* (8). This is certainly the case where *forty* relates to a period of evident *probation.* But where it relates to *enlarged dominion,* or to *renewed or extended rule,* then it does so in virtue of its factors 4 and 10, and in harmony with their signification.

There are 15 such periods which appear on the surface of the Scriptures, and which may be thus classified:—

Forty Years of Probation by Trial:

Israel in the wilderness, Deut. viii. 2–5; Ps. xcv. 10; Acts xiii. 18 (the third 40 of Moses' life, 120 years).

Israel from the crucifixion to the destruction of Jerusalem.

Forty Years of Probation by Prosperity in Deliverance and Rest:

under Othniel, Judg. iii. 11,
under Barak, Judg. v. 31,
under Gideon, Judg. viii. 28.

Forty Years of Probation by Prosperity in Enlarged Dominion:

under David, 2 Sam. v. 4,
under Solomon, 1 Kings xi. 42,
under Jeroboam II. See 2 Kings xii. 17, 18; xiii. 3, 5, 7, 22, 25; xiv. 12–14, 23, 28,
under Jehoash, 2 Kings xii. 1,
under Joash, 2 Chron. xxiv. 1.

Forty Years of Probation by Humiliation and Servitude:

Israel under the Philistines, Judg. xiii. 1.
Israel in the time of Eli, 1 Sam. iv. 18.
Israel under Saul, Acts xiii. 21.

Forty Years of Probation by Waiting:

Moses in Egypt, Acts vii. 23.
Moses in Midian, Acts vii. 30.

Forty Days.

There are *eight* of such great periods on the surface of the Bible:

Forty days Moses was in the mount, Exod. xxiv. 18; and to receive the Law, Exod. xxiv. 18.

Forty days Moses was in the mount after the sin of the Golden Calf, Deut. ix. 18, 25.

Forty days of the spies, issuing in the penal sentence of the 40 years, Num. xiii. 26; xiv. 34.

Forty days of Elijah in Horeb, 1 Kings xix. 8.

Forty days of Jonah and Nineveh, Jonah iii. 4.

Forty days Ezekiel lay on his right side to symbolize the 40 years of Judah's transgression.*

Forty days Jesus was tempted of the Devil, Matt. iv. 2.

Forty days Jesus was seen of His disciples, speaking of the things pertaining to the kingdom of God, Acts i. 2.

---

* Thus 40 becomes a number closely connected with *Judah*, as 390 (Ezek. iv. 5) is the number of separated *Israel*. The significance of this will be seen (on p. 215), for 40 is a multiple of 8, and 390 is a multiple of 13. It may also be noted that 65 (5 × 13) is the number of Ephraim, while 70 is specially connected with Jerusalem.

FORTY-TWO

is a number connected with Antichrist. An important part of his career is to last for 42 months (Rev. xi. 2; xiii. 5), and thus this number is fixed upon him. Another number of Antichrist is 1260, and this is 30 × 42.

Its factors are *six* and *seven* (6 × 7 = 42), and this shows a connection between man and the Spirit of God, and between Christ and Antichrist:

> *Forty-two* stages of Israel's wanderings mark their conflict with the will of God.
>
> *Forty-two* young men * mocked the ascension of Elijah to Elisha, 2 Kings ii. 23, 24.

Being a multiple of *seven*, it might be supposed that it would be connected with spiritual perfection. But it is the product of *six* times *seven*. *Six*, therefore, being the number of *Man*, and of man's *opposition* to God, *forty-two* becomes significant of the working out of man's opposition to God.

There may be something more in the common phrase about things being all "*sixes and sevens*." They are so, indeed, when man is mixed up with the things of God, and when religious "flesh" engages in spiritual things. See under "Six and Seven," pp. 158-167.

In Gematria

it is a factor in the number of Nimrod's name, which is 294, or 42 × 7. It will be often found as a factor in the Antichristian names. See under the number *Thirteen*.

It does not often appear as a separate number, but when it is thus seen as a *factor* of another number, it always imparts its significance to it.

FIFTY

is the number of jubilee or deliverance. It is the *issue* of 7 × 7 (7^2), and points to deliverance and rest following on as the result of the perfect consummation of time.

---

* See note on p. 203.

FIFTY-ONE.

This is the number of Divine revelation,
for there are 24 books in the Old Testament,
and 27 books in the New Testament.

making 51 in all.

This is, of course, reckoning the Divine separation of the books, as exhibited in the MSS., which form our *only* authority, and not reckoning according to man's manipulation of them; for both Jewish and Gentile fancies and reasonings make quite a different and conflicting number. See pp. 25, 26.

SIXTY-FIVE,

being a multiple of *thirteen* (13 × 5 = 65), is specially associated with Ephraim (see Isa. vii. 8), and marks the apostasy of that Tribe. This apostasy, which began in Judg. xvii., afterwards extended to the Ten-Tribe kingdom, which is frequently spoken of therefore under the name of "Ephraim."

"Within three-score and five years shall Ephraim be broken that it be not a people."

SEVENTY

is another combination of two of the perfect numbers, *seven* and *ten*. We have seen something of the significance of their *sum* under the number *seventeen*; their *product* is no less significant.

As compared with the *sum* of two numbers, the *product* exhibits the significance of each in an intensified form.

Hence 7 × 10 signifies *perfect* spiritual order carried out with all spiritual power and significance. Both *spirit* and *order* are greatly emphasised.

The Seventy Nations

which peopled the earth are set forth with a particularity which shows the importance of the fact (see Gen. x.).

The Seventy Souls of Genesis xlvi.

are marked not only by the perfection of spiritual truth, as seen by the multiple of 7, but by the perfection of Divine order, as seen in the multiple of 10, *seventy* being 7 × 10.

We stop not to notice the number given in Acts vii. 14, which is different because it refers to a different classification, viz., "all his kindred," which amounted to 75. In Gen. xlvi. 26, God is speaking of another class, viz., only those "which came out of his loins"; these were *seventy* in number.

This number is made up in a remarkable manner, distinguishing the descendants of Leah and her maid from Rachel and her maid,* the latter being a more marked multiple of 7:—

The Children of Leah ... ... 33 (3 × 11)
(Only 32 are *named*, because one, viz., Jochebed,† the mother of Moses, though conceived, was not born till Egypt was reached (Num. xxvi. 59), and therefore could not be *named* here.)

---

* The gematria of their names is just as remarkable. See pp. 210, 211.

† The *gematria* of her name is 42 (6 × 7), for though of Divine calling she was very human.

The children of her maid Zilpah ...	16	(4 × 4)
Together (though not separately) making a multiple of 7 ...	— 49	(7 × 7)
The children of Rachel	14	(2 × 7)
The children of her maid Bilhah ...	7	
	— 21	(3 × 7)
Making separately and together a multiple of seven	70	(7 × 10)

These *seventy* built up the nation of Israel. See Gen. xlvi. 27; Exod. i. 5; and Ruth iv. 11.

Seventy elders furnished Israel's great Tribunal, Exod. xxiv. 1; Num. xi. 16, afterwards called the Sanhedrim. See below, under the next number (120).

Seventy disciples sent out by the Lord prefigure the mighty host which followed them (Luke x. 1, 17) in spirit and in power.

It is the number specially connected with

JERUSALEM,

for the city kept its sabbaths *seventy* years, while Judah was in Babylon, Jer. xxxv. 11.

And *seventy sevens* were determined upon it to complete its transgression, and bring in everlasting righteousness for it, Dan. ix. 24 (see pp. 5, 6, 7).

ONE HUNDRED AND TWENTY

is made up of *three* forties (3 × 40 = 120). Applied to *time* therefore it signifies a *divinely* appointed period of probation, Gen. vi. 3.

Applied to *persons* it points to a divinely appointed number during a period of waiting, Acts i. 15.

It is a *factor* also in the number of those who returned from Babylon, 42,360, being 120 × 353.

It is also a *factor* of the number of the men who went up out of Egypt, 600,000, being 120 × 5000.

It is a *factor* also of the 144,000 who will be sealed from the Twelve Tribes of Israel to go unscathed through the great tribulation, 144,000, being 120 × 1200.

The unanimous voice of Jewish tradition agrees with the Talmud * that "the Great Synagogue" (Neh. x. 1–10) consisted of 120 members. "It was called 'Great' because of the great work it effected in restoring the Divine law to its former greatness, and because of the great authority and reputation which it enjoyed." Its greatest work was in completing the Canon of the Old Testament. The Great Synagogue lasted about 110 years, from B.C. 410–300, or from the latter days of Nehemiah to the death of Simon the Just. It then passed into the Sanhedrim, when its whole constitution was changed.†

* *Jerusalem Beracholh*, ii. 4; *Jerusalem Megilla*, i.; *Bab. Meg.* 17*b*

† See *Kitto*, vol. iii., p. 909.

ONE HUNDRED AND FIFTY AND THREE.

This is a number which has taxed the ingenuity of some of the greatest of Bible students, and that from the earliest times. All have felt there must be something deeply significant and mysterious in this number, from the solemn way in which it is introduced in John xxi. 11,—"Simon Peter went up and drew the net to land full of great fishes, one hundred and fifty and three."

Other miracles are parables in their lessons, and Augustine* has pointed out the comparison and contrast between the two miraculous draughts of fishes, one at the beginning and the other at the end of Christ's ministry (after His resurrection). He and other Commentators see in this number some connection with the saved, as being definite and particular down even to the last one, making up not a large round number, but a smaller and odd number, 153. They saw in this a proof of the fact that the number of the elect is fixed and pre-ordained.†

Jerome also sees there is some deeper meaning in the number, and says that there are 153 *sorts* of fish, *i.e.*, all kinds of men enclosed in the Gospel net.

Other more surprising suggestions have been made, but they are all the outcome of fancy.

The utmost that can be said is that had it been the round number 150, there would have been an absence of all definiteness, but as it goes beyond and gives the three by which the 150 is exceeded, it does seem to convey the impression that we have here, if these fishes are a symbol of the saved, an illustration and confirmation of our Lord's words, recorded in the same Gospel, "of all that He (the Father) hath given Me I should lose nothing" (John vi. 39), and "those that Thou gavest Me I have kept, and none of them is lost" (John xvii. 12).

When we come to the way in which the significance of this number has been estimated, we find a variety of modes. Augustine and Gregory the Great both start with the fact that

* *Tractates on the Gospel according to St. John*, cxxii.

† So Trench, *Notes on the Miracles*, p. 194.

17 is the *sum* of 10 and 7. For the significance of the number 17 (see p. 258). But they deal with the 17 in different ways.

Gregory simply *multiplies* 17 by 3 and again by 3 (*i.e.*, 17×3^2), and thus arrives at 153.

Augustine, on the other hand, employs *addition*, and takes the *sum* of all the digits up to and including 17 as amounting to exactly 153. He says,* "For if you add 2 to 1, you have 3, of course; if to these you add 3 and 4, the whole number makes 10; and then if you add all the numbers that follow up to 17, the whole amounts to the aforesaid number [153]; that is, if to 10, which you had reached by adding all together from 1 to 4, you add 5, you have 15; to these add 6, and the result is 21; then add 7, and you have 28; to this add 8, and 9, and 10, and you get 55; to this add 11, and 12, and 13, and you have 91; and to this again add 14, and 15, and 16, and it comes to 136; and then add to this the remaining number of which we have been speaking, namely 17, and it will make up the number of fishes." †

Bishop Wordsworth arrives at his result in a different manner. He uses two numbers, and employs both multiplication and addition. First he takes the square of 12 (which he holds to be the Church number), and then he *adds* the square of 3 (the number of the Godhead), and points out that $12^2 + 3^2 = 153$, or $(12 \times 12) + (3 \times 3)$.

We might give yet another contribution to these various modes as the result of our investigations in numbers, and say that $153 = 9 \times 17$, and see in this number all judgment (9) exhausted for the people of God (17) in the person of their Surety.

All, however, agree in the great and blessed fact that "Salvation is of the Lord." Divine alike in its source, its agency, and its results.

The same Divine character is stamped upon this miracle and its lessons by the number of disciples who were present when it was wrought. There were *seven*. And the seven is divided into 3 and 4 as usual—3 being named, and 4 unnamed.

---

* *Tractate on John*, cxxii.

† We should express this, now, more scientifically, and say, $1 + 2 + 3 + 4 + 5 + 6 + 7 + 8 + 9 + 10 + 11 + 12 + 13 + 14 + 15 + 16 + 17 = 153$.
And Gregory's we should express thus: $(10 + 7) \times (3 \times 3) = 153$.

The one lesson that remains is true, namely, that the whole number of the redeemed are saved by the power of the Triune God.

We may condense all this by calling 153 simply,

THE NUMBER OF THE SONS OF GOD!

The expression בני האלהים (*Beni Ha-Elohim*), "Sons of God," occurs in *seven* different connections! *

Now the gematria of this expression is exactly 153. Thus:

ב	=	2
נ	=	50
י	=	10
ה	=	5
א	=	1
ל	=	30
ה	=	5
י	=	10
ם	=	40
		153

In Greek, the expression exhibits in another form the same phenomena, the gematria being 3213, or $3 \times 7 \times 153$.

It is very remarkable, in connection with this, that in Job ii. 1 we have "*Beni-ha Elohim* with Satan among them." The gematria of this phrase is 1989, and the two factors of this number are 153 and 13 ($13 \times 153 = 1989$).

The word συγκληρονόμοι (*sungkleeronomoi*), "joint-heirs" (Rom. viii. 17), amounts to 1071, the factors of which are 153 and 7 ($153 \times 7 = 1071$).

The expression συγκληρονόμοι Χριστοῦ (*sungkleeronomoi Christou*), "joint heirs with Christ" (Rom. viii. 17), amounts to 2751. Now the factors of 153, as we have seen, are 9 and 17, and the number 2751 is three times the *nine* hundred, plus *seventeen*, viz., $3 \times (900 + 17) = 2751$.

The expression κτίσις θεοῦ (*ktisis Theou*), "the creation of God," is 1224, or 8×153.

* One of them is slightly different, בני אל־חי (*Beni El-hai*), "sons of the living God." Thus the *human* and *divine* element is seen in the *six* and *seven* (see p. 164).

In the record of the miracle itself there are some remarkable phenomena:—

The word for "fishes" ἰχθύες (*ichthues*), is by gematria 1224, or 8 × 153.

The words for "the net" are τὸ δίκτυον, and by gematria this also amounts to 1224, or 8 × 153, for it is unbroken, and carries the precious freight from "the right side" of the ship safely to the shore, and "not one is lost."

Quite a new thought has recently been given by Lieut.-Col. F. Roberts, who finds that amongst the multitudes who received direct blessing from Christ there are recorded exactly 153 special individual cases! We append his list, with one or two alterations: and if any names appear to be missing, it will be found on examination that there is good reason for omitting them; *e.g.*, Nathanael is the same as Bartholomew; while Matthias, and Barsabas (Acts i. 23), Joses, Barnabas (Acts iv. 36), Stephen, though they with many others may have received blessing from Jesus Himself, and probably did, yet *it is not so stated.* Of course Zacharias, Elisabeth, John the Baptist, Joseph, Simeon, and Anna, are not included, as they were all in blessing before the birth of Jesus.

The following is the list:

1.	The leper	Matt. viii.	2	...	1
2.	Centurion and servant ...	—	5	...	2
3.	Peter's wife's mother ...	—	14	...	1
4.	Two possessed with devils	—	18	...	2
5.	Palsied man and bearers (Mark ii. 3)	— ix.	2	...	5
6.	Jairus and his daughter ...	—	18	...	2
7.	Woman with issue of blood	—	21	...	1
8.	Blind men	—	27	...	2
9.	Dumb man	—	32	...	1
10.	Eleven Apostles	— x.	2	...	11
11.	Man with withered hand ...	— xii.	10	...	1
12.	Blind and dumb devil ...	—	22	...	1
13.	Brethren of the Lord ... (Acts i. 14)	— xiii.	55	...	4
14.	Syrophœnician woman and daughter	— xv.	22	...	2
15.	Lunatic child and father ...	— xvii.	14	...	2

16. Blind men (leaving Jericho) *	Matt. xx. 30	...	2
17. Simon the leper	— xxvi. 6	...	1
18. Mary (sister of Lazarus. See Nos. 32 and 47) ...	— 7	...	1
19. Centurion	— xxvii. 54	...	1
20. Salome (mother of Zebedee's children) ...	— 56	...	1
21. Mary (mother of James, and wife of Cleopas) ...	— 56	...	1
22. Mary Magdalene	— 56	...	1
23. Joseph of Arimathæa ...	— 57	...	1
24. Man with unclean spirit ...	Mark i. 23	...	1
25. Man, deaf and dumb ...	— vii. 32	...	1
26. Blind man	— viii. 22	...	1
27. Son of the widow of Nain	Luke vii. 12	...	1
28. A woman, a sinner ...	— 37	...	1
29. Joanna and Susanna ...	— viii. 3	...	2
30. A disciple—" follow Me "	— ix. 59	...	1
31. The seventy disciples ...	— x. 1	...	70
32. Martha	— 38	...	1
33. Woman with infirmity ...	— xiii. 11	...	1
34. Man with dropsy	— xiv. 2	...	1
35. The ten lepers	— xvii. 12	...	10
36. The blind man (approaching Jericho) †	— xviii. 35	...	1
37. Zaccheus	— xix. 2	...	1
38. Malchus ... ... (John xviii. 10)	— xxii. 51	...	1
39. Penitent thief	— xxiii. 43	...	1
40. The two disciples at Emmaus	— xxiv. 13	...	2
41. Nicodemus	John iii. 1	...	1
42. Woman of Samaria ...	— iv. 4	...	1
43. Nobleman and sick son ...	— 46	...	2
44. Impotent man (Bethesda)	— v. 1	...	1
45. Woman taken in adultery	— viii. 11	...	1

* Bartimeus being one of them (Mark x. 46), these two being healed as Jesus *left* Jericho.

† The blind man (No. 36) was healed (Luke xviii. 35) "as He was come nigh unto Jericho," and therefore is additional to the two who were healed as He was leaving Jericho (No. 16). See Matt. xx. 30; Mark x. 46.

46. Man born blind	John	ix.	...	1
47. Lazarus	—	xi.	...	1
48. Mary, mother of Jesus ...	—	xix. 25	...	1
				153

We give the above not as an alternative solution, but as an *additional illustration*, believing that all may be true; and at any rate, that all contribute to, and increase the cumulative evidence in support of the same great and blessed fact, that it is true of the Lord's people as it is of the stars, "He calleth them all by their names" (Ps. cxlvii. 4). The book of Exodus is the book in which we first hear of redemption (Exod. xv. 14), and the Hebrew and divinely canonical name for this book is "THE NAMES," because His people are redeemed by name!

This is the lesson of the 153 great fishes.

TWO HUNDRED.

Twenty is the number of *expectancy* as we have seen (p. 262). Here we have it *tenfold* (20 × 10).

The significance of this number is suggested by John vi. 7, where we read, "Two hundred pennyworth of bread is NOT SUFFICIENT for them."

And so we find this number stamping various things with *insufficiency*.

Achan's 200 shekels were "not sufficient" to save him from the consequences of his sin (Josh. vii. 21). This shows us *the insufficiency of money* (Ps. xlix. 7-9).

Absalom's 200 shekels weight of hair were "not sufficient" to save him, but rather caused his destruction (2 Sam. xiv. 26; xviii. 9). This shows us *the insufficiency of beauty*.

Micah's graven image was purchased for 200 shekels (Judg. xvii. 4 and xviii.), and led to the introduction of idolatry into Israel and the blotting out of the Tribes of Dan and Ephraim from the blessing of Rev. vii., showing us *the insufficiency of mere religion*.

Ezra's 200 "singing men and women" (Ezra ii. 65), were "not sufficient" to produce "peace with God," true spiritual worship, or joy in the Lord. Only God's word rightly ministered can lead to this (Neh. viii. 5-9). This shows *the insufficiency of external things in the worship of God*, and the impossibility of worshipping God with the *senses*. True worship, which alone God will accept, "MUST" (John iv. 24) be spiritual.

THREE HUNDRED AND NINETY.

This is the number of Israel (Ezek. iv. 5), being 13 × 30; as 65 (5 × 13) is the number of Ephraim (Isa. vii. 8); as 40 (5 × 8) is the number of Judah (Ezek. iv. 6); and 70 (7 × 10) is the number of Jerusalem. See further under these numbers respectively, and under 8 and 13 also.

As a matter of chronology it was 390 years from the division of the Tribes to the Captivity, and thus the duration of the separate kingdom of Israel was 390 years, as referred to in Ezek. iv. See p. 215.

FOUR HUNDRED

is the *product* of 8 and 50, and is a divinely perfect period.

From the fulfilment of the promise to Abraham in the birth of Isaac to the Exodus was a period of 400 years. Stephen mentions it as dating from "his seed" (Acts vii. 6), and God dates it from the same point when He says to Abraham, "thy seed" (Gen. xv. 13).*

It is popularly confounded with quite a different period of

FOUR HUNDRED AND THIRTY

years, which, though it has the same point as to its termination, does not commence at the same point.

From the call of Abraham, or the "promise" made to him at that call (Gen. xii. 3), unto the Exodus was 430 years. This covers the whole period of the "sojourning"; not of Abraham's "seed," as in Gen. xv. 13* and Acts vii. 6, but of Abraham himself. This is what is mentioned in Gal. iii. 17 as the period from the "promise" to the "Law." It is referred to also in Exod. xii. 40, where the "sojourning" is the nominative case (or subject) of the verb, while the sentence, "who dwelt in Egypt," is merely *a relative clause*, defining parenthetically an important point concerning them.

FOUR HUNDRED AND NINETY.

This is the period of the 70 sevens referred to under the head of Chronology (pp. 5, 6). We need not therefore further enlarge on it here beyond pointing out the spiritual significance of the number itself as being *seven* times *seventy*.

Daniel was praying, and he was concerned about the

---

* The structure of this verse rescues it from the way in which it is sadly misunderstood :—

A | "Know of a surety that thy seed shall be a stranger in
  | a strange land that is not theirs,
  B | and shall serve them ;
  B | and they shall afflict them
A | four hundred years."

The structure places B and *B* in a parenthesis. A and *A* cover the whole time of the *sojourn*, while B and *B* refer to the service and sojourn during a parenthesis of unnamed length within that time. The structure of Acts vii. 6 is exactly the same.

70 years prophesied of by Jeremiah (Dan. ix. 2 and Jer. xxv. 11, 12; xxix. 10). And the answer meant that though those 70 appointed years were about to end in restoration and blessing, another period of *seven times* 70 *years* had been determined (ix. 24–27), and they would commence from the very "decree" (Neh. ii.) which should end the former 70 years. And these should run their course, marked by certain incidents, before the full and final restoration of Daniel's "city" and "people" should be accomplished.

The number 490 marks the product of spiritual perfection (7) with regard to the working out of Jerusalem's number (70). For 7 times 70 is 490.

SIX HUNDRED AND SIXTY SIX

is "the number *of a name*" (Rev. xiii. 17, 18). When the *name* of Antichrist is known its gematria will doubtless be found to be the number 666. But this number has, we believe, a far deeper reference to and connection with the secret mysteries of the ancient religions, which will be again manifested in connection with the last great apostasy.*

Many names may be found, the numerical value of whose letters amounts to 666. We have a list of about forty such *gematria*. Most of them are ridiculous, inasmuch as instead of the *gematria* being confined to Hebrew and Greek (which have no Arabic or other special signs for *figures*), the principle is extended to names in English, French, and other modern languages, on the assumption that they would have been spelt in exactly the same way; whereas we know that names both of persons and places are not simply transliterated in various languages.† It is absurd therefore to attempt to take words from the modern European languages which use Arabic figures.

Gematria is not *a means* by which the name is to be discovered; but it will be a *test* and a *proof* by which the name may be identified after the person is revealed.

If six is the number of secular or human perfection, then 66 is a more emphatic expression of the same fact, and 666 is the concentrated expression of it; 666 is therefore the trinity of human perfection; the perfection of imperfection; the culmination of human pride in independence of God and opposition to His Christ.

The number, however, has to be *computed* (ψηφίζω (*psecphizō*), *to reckon*, *to calculate*, not merely to count or enumerate). See Rev. xiii. 18. Therefore it is not to be known by *gematria* merely, though, as we have said, that will be one of the factors in the calculation, just as the letters in the word Jesus amount to 888.

---

* See *The Computation of* 666, published by James Nisbet and Co.

† Take "Venice." This is the English spelling. But the French is *Venise*; the German is *Venedig*; while the Italian is *Venezia*.

But 666 was the *secret symbol* of the ancient pagan mysteries connected with the worship of the Devil. It is to day the secret connecting link between those ancient mysteries and their modern revival in Spiritualism, Theosophy, etc. The efforts of the great enemy are now directed towards uniting all into one great whole. The newspapers, worldly and religious, are full of schemes as to such a union. "Re-union" is in the air. The societies for the re-union of Christendom, and the Conferences for the re-union of the Churches, are alike parts of the same great movement, and are all making for and are signs of the coming Apostasy. During this age, "Separation" is God's word for His people, and is the mark of *Christ;* while "*union*" and "re-union" is the mark of *Antichrist.*

The number 6 was stamped on the old mysteries. The great secret symbol consisted of the three letters SSS, because the letter S in the Greek alphabet was the symbol of the figure 6 (see page 49). $\alpha = 1$, $\beta = 2$, $\gamma = 3$, $\delta = 4$, $\epsilon = 5$, but when it came to 6, another letter was introduced! Not the next—the sixth letter (ζ, *zeta*)—but a different letter, a peculiar form of S, called "*stigma*" (ϛ). Now the word στίγμα (*stigma*), means *a mark*, but especially a mark made by *a brand* as burnt upon slaves, cattle, or soldiers, by their owners or masters; or on devotees who thus branded themselves as belonging to their gods. It is from στίζω, *to prick*, or *brand with a hot iron.* Hence it came to be used of *scars* or *wound-prints*, and it is thus used by Paul of his scars, which he regarded as the tokens of his sufferings, the marks which he bore on his body for the sake of his Lord and Master, and marking him as belonging to the one who had bought him (Gal. vi. 17).

This letter is becoming familiar to us now; and it is not pleasant when we see many thus marked (ignorantly, no doubt) with the symbolical "S," "S," especially when it is connected, not with "salvation," but with *judgment*, and is associated with "blood and fire," which, in Joel ii. 30, 31, is given as one of the awful signs "before the great and terrible day of the Lord come."

Apostasy is before us. The religion of Christ has, in the past, been *opposed* and *corrupted*, but when it once comes, as it has come in our day, to be *burlesqued*, there is nothing left but judgment. There is nothing more the enemy can do before he proceeds to build up the great apostasy on the ruins of true religion, and thus prepare the way for the coming of the Judge.

It is remarkable that the Romans did not use all the letters of their alphabet, as did the Hebrews and Greeks. They used only *six* letters,* D, C, L, X, V, and I. And it is still more remarkable, and perhaps significant, that the sum of these amounts to 666:—

1. D	= 500	} 600		
2. C	= 100			
3. L	= 50	} 60		} 666.
4. X	= 10			
5. V	= 5	} 6		
6. I	= 1			
	666			

In each of the three pairs there is an addition of *one*, for $6 = 5 + 1$. It is the grace of God superseded by the corruption of man.

It will be seen from this that the number 666 is very far-reaching, and is filled with a meaning deeper, perhaps, than anything we have yet discovered. One thing, however, is certain, and that is, that the triple 6 marks the culmination of man's opposition to God in the person of the coming Antichrist.

Further illustration of the significance of this number is seen in the fact that

The Duration of the old Assyrian Empire

was 666 years before it was conquered by Babylon.

Jerusalem was Trodden Down

by the Roman Empire exactly 666 years from the battle of Actium, B.C. 31, to the Saracen conquest in A.D. 636.†

There are Three Men

which stand out in Scripture as the avowed enemies of God

* One thousand was represented by CIↃ, hence the m, and later the letter M.

† See *The Witness of the Stars*, by the same author, pp. 177 to end.

and of His people. Each is branded with this number *six* that we may not miss their significance :—

1. GOLIATH, whose height was 6 cubits, and he had 6 pieces of armour; * his spear's head weighed 600 shekels of iron (1 Sam. xvii. 4–7).
2. NEBUCHADNEZZAR, whose "image" which he set up,† was 60 cubits high and 6 cubits broad (Dan. iii. 1), and which was worshipped when the music was heard from 6 specified instruments ‡, and
3. ANTICHRIST, whose number is 666.

In the first we have *one* six connected with the pride of fleshly might.

In the second we have *two* sixes connected with the pride of absolute dominion.

In the third we have *three* sixes connected with the pride of Satanic guidance.

THE TALENTS OF GOLD

brought to Solomon in a year were 666 (1 Kings x. 14). But this perfection of money-power was only "vanity and vexation of spirit" (Eccles. ii. 8, 11; compare 1 Tim. vi. 10).

As to the triple number 666, we have already seen (page 121) that while one figure (6) is significant, two figures (66) are still more so; and *three* figures (666) seem to denote the concentration or essence of the particular number.

We see further examples of this in

Jesus, 888, the *dominical* number;
Sodom, 999, the number of *judgment;*
Damascus, 444, the *world* number;

---

* In Eph. vi. 14–18, the Christian's armour has a *seventh* piece—"*Prayer.*" See under "*Seven.*"

† We must distinguish the "image" which he set up, from the "man" of whom he afterwards dreamt. The proportions are not the same. The height of a man is to his breadth not as 10 : 1. Some have therefore thought that this "image" may have been an obelisk. But as the word for "image" denotes a form or likeness, it may have been like the form of a man standing on a pedestal of which the height was included. The pedestal being probably 24 (6 × 4) cubits, and the image 36 (6 × 6).

‡ The numerical value (by gematria) of the words in Dan. iii. 1, which describe the setting up of this image is 4662. The very figures are significant, but still more so are the factors of this number. 4662 = 7 × 666.

The beast, 666, the number of *man;*
"Verily, verily, I say unto you," 888;
The Lord God made, 888; etc., etc.

"The children of Adonikam" who returned from the Captivity (Ezra ii. 13) numbered 666. Adonikam means *the lord of the enemy*. This is suggestive, even though it may be vague.

The number 666 has another remarkable property. It is further marked as the *concentration* and essence of 6 by being the *sum* of all the numbers which make up the *square of six!* The square of six is 36 (6^2, or 6×6), and the sum of the numbers 1 to 36 = 666, *i.e.*, $1 + 2 + 3 + 4 + 5 + 6 + 7 + 8 + 9 + 10 + 11 + 12 + 13 + 14 + 15 + 16 + 17 + 18 + 19 + 20 + 21 + 22 + 23 + 24 + 25 + 26 + 27 + 28 + 29 + 30 + 31 + 32 + 33 + 34 + 35 + 36 = 666$.

They may be arranged in the form of a square with six figures each way, so that the sum of each six figures in any direction shall be another significant *trinity* = 111.

6	32	3	34	35	1
7	11	27	28	8	30
19	14	16	15	23	24
18	20	22	21	17	13
25	29	10	9	26	12
36	5	33	4	2	31

GEMATRIA.

It is remarkable that the numerical value of the "SONG OF MOSES" (Exod. xv. 1–18) is 41392, which is the product of the significant factors $13 \times 2 \times 8 \times 199$.

On the other hand, if we compare "the Song of Moses and of the Lamb," in Rev. xv. 1–5, the remarkable value is 9261, which has the remarkable factors $3^3 \times 7^3$.

CONCLUSION.

We have now come to the end of our survey of number as used by God in His works and in His Word, and we have seen that all is perfect.

Our apprehension and interpretation of the phenomena may be marked with many imperfections, and we are conscious that after all we have but touched the fringe of this great and important subject.

One thing, however, is certain, and that is, that we have, in the Scripture of Truth, a revelation from God absolutely without error, and whatever difficulties we may encounter in seeking to understand it, they are all the outcome of our own infirmities.

Of another thing we are also certain, that the Written Word cannot be separated from the Living Word, nor the spiritual meaning of the one understood without a living union with the other.

It may be said of the Word of God, as it is written of the New Jerusalem (Rev. xxi. 23),

"THE LAMB IS THE LIGHT THEREOF."

ADDITIONAL MISCELLANEOUS ILLUSTRATIONS.

Many illustrations have been added while this work has been passing through the press.

A few others are now given, which have been found since the work has been printed.

THREE.

Three multitudes miraculously fed:—(1) 2 Kings iv. 42, 43; (2) Matt. xv. 34, 38; (3) Mark vi. 38, 44.

Three times Abraham called the "Friend of God":—(1) 2 Chron. xx. 7; (2) Isa. xli. 8; (3) James ii. 23.

Three times the word "Christian" is found in the New Testament:—(1) Acts xi. 26; (2) Acts xxv. 28; (3) 1 Pet. iv. 16.

FOUR.

Four times "Eve" mentioned in the Bible by name:—Gen. iii. 20; iv. 1; 2 Cor. xi. 3; 1 Tim. ii. 13.

SIX.

Six times our Lord was asked for a sign:—

1. The Pharisees, Matt. xii. 38; Mark viii. 11.
2. The Sadducees, Matt. xvi. 1.
3. The Disciples. Matt. xxiv. 3: Mark xiii. 4; Luke xxi. 7.
4. The people, Luke xi. 16.
5. The Jews, John ii. 18.
6. The people, John vi. 30.

Six persons bore testimony to the Saviour's innocency:—

1. Pilate, Luke xxiii. 14.
2. Herod, Luke xxiii. 15,
3. Judas, Matt. xxvii. 4.
4. Pilate's wife, Matt. xxvii. 19.
5. The dying thief, Luke xxiii. 41.
6. The centurion, Luke xxiii. 47.

SEVEN.

Seven miracles wrought by Christ on the Sabbath day:—

1. The withered hand, Matt. xii. 10.
2. The unclean spirit, Mark i. 21.
3. Peter's wife's mother, Mark i. 29.
4. The woman, Luke xiii. 11.
5. The man with dropsy, Luke xiv. 2.
6. The impotent man, John v. 8, 9.
7. The man born blind, John ix. 14.

"The last day" mentioned *seven* times in John's Gospel:—John vi. 39, 40, 44, 54; vii. 37; xi. 24; xii. 48.

NINE.

Nine persons "*stoned.*"

1. The blasphemer, Lev. xxiv. 14.
2. The Sabbath-breaker, Num. xv. 36.
3. Achan, Josh. vii. 25.
4. Abimelech, Judg. ix. 53.
5. Adoram, 1 Kings xii. 18.
6. Naboth, 1 Kings xxi. 10.
7. Zechariah, 2 Chron. xxiv. 21.
8. Stephen, Acts vii.
9. Paul, Acts xiv. 19.

Nine widows are specially mentioned:—

1. Tamar, Gen. xxxviii. 19.
2. Woman of Tekoah, 2 Sam. xiv. 5.
3. Hiram's mother, 1 Kings vii. 14.
4. Zeruah, 1 Kings xi. 26.
5. Woman of Zarephath, 1 Kings xvii. 9.
6. The poor widow, Mark xii. 42.
7. Anna, Luke ii. 37.
8. Widow of Nain, Luke vii. 12.
9. The importunate widow, Luke xviii. 3.

Nine instances of people afflicted with *blindness*:—

1. The men at Lot's door, Gen. xix. 11.
2. Isaac, Gen. xxvii. 1.
3. Jacob, Gen. xlviii. 10.
4. Samson, Judg. xvi. 21.

5. Eli, 1 Sam. iv. 15.
6. The prophet Ahijah, 1 Kings xiv. 4.
7. The Syrian army, 2 Kings vi. 18.
8. King Zedekiah, 2 Kings xxv. 7.
9. Elymas, Acts xiii. 11.

Nine were afflicted with *leprosy* in O.T.:
1. Moses, Exod. iv. 6.
2. Miriam, Num. xii. 10.
3. Naaman, 2 Kings v. 1.
4. Gehazi, 2 Kings v. 27.
5-8. The four lepers at Samaria, 2 Kings vii. 3.
9. Azariah, 2 Kings xv. 5; 2 Chron. xxvi. 21.

TEN.

The observance of *ten* passovers are recorded:
1. In Egypt, Exod. xii.
2. In the wilderness, Num. ix. 5.
3. Plains of Jericho, Josh. v. 10.
4. Hezekiah's, 2 Chron. xxx. 1.
5. Josiah's, 2 Chron. xxxv. 1.
6. Ezra's, Ezra vi. 19.
7. When our Lord was twelve years of age, Luke ii. 41.
8. John ii. 13.
9. John vi. 4.
10. Matt. xxvi. 2.

Ten deaths occasioned by women:—
1. Sisera, Judg. iv. 21.
2. Abimelech, Judg. ix. 52, 53; 2 Sam. xi. 21.
3. Sheba, 2 Sam. xx. 1, 21, 22.
4. The harlot's child, 1 Kings iii. 19.
5. The prophets of the land, 1 Kings xviii. 4.
6. Naboth, 1 Kings xxi. 9, 10.
7. The son boiled by his mother, 2 Kings vi. 29.
8. The seed royal, 2 Kings xi. 1; 2 Chron. xxii. 10.
9. Haman's ten sons, Est. ix. 13, 14.
10. John the Baptist, Matt. xiv. 8.

Ten instances in the Old Testament of younger sons being preferred before the elder:—Abel, Shem, Abraham, Isaac, Jacob, Judah, Joseph, Ephraim, Moses, David.

ELEVEN.

Eleven kings and rulers offended with God's servants for telling them the truth :—

1. Pharaoh, Exod. x. 28.
2. Balak, Num. xxiv. 10.
3. Jeroboam, 1 Kings xiii. 4.
4. Ahab, 1 Kings xxii. 27.
5. Naaman, 2 Kings v. 12.
6. Asa, 2 Chron. xvi. 10.
7. Joash, 2 Chron. xxiv. 21.
8. Uzziah, 2 Chron. xxvi. 19.
9. Jehoiakim, Jer. xxvi. 21.
10. Zedekiah, Jer. xxxii. 3.
11. Herod, Matt. xiv. 3.

Joseph was eleven years in Potiphar's house :—

He was 30 years of age when he stood before Pharaoh (Gen. xli. 46)		30
He was 17 years old when sold (Gen. xxxvii. 2, 36)	17	
He was 2 years in prison (Gen. xli. 1) ...	2	
	—	19
		11

THIRTEEN.

Thirteen famines are recorded in the Scriptures :—(1) Gen. xii. 10; (2) Gen. xxvi. 1; (3) Gen. xli. 54; (4) Ruth i. 1; (5) 2 Sam. xxi. 1; (6) 1 Kings xviii. 1; (7) 2 Kings iv. 38; (8) 2 Kings vii. 4; (9) 2 Kings xxv. 3; (10) Neh. v. 3; (11) Jer. xiv. 1; (12) Luke xv. 14; (13) Acts xi. 28.

FOURTEEN.

Fourteen times in the Book of Proverbs the expression occurs "the fear of the Lord" :—Prov. i. 7, 29; ii. 5; viii. 13; ix. 10; x. 27; xiv. 26, 27; xv. 16, 33; xvi. 6; xix. 23; xxii. 4; xxiii. 17.

SEVENTEEN.

Seventeen Angelic appearances are recorded in the Gospels and Acts :—

1–3. Three to Joseph, Matt. i. 20; ii. 13, 19.
4. To the Lord in the wilderness, Matt. iv. 11.

5. In Gethsemane, Luke xxii. 43.
6. On the stone at the sepulchre, Matt. xxviii. 2.
7. Within the sepulchre, Mark xvi. 5.
8. To Zecharias, Luke i. 11.
9. To Mary, Luke i. 26.
10, 11. Two to the Shepherds, Luke ii. 9, 13.
12. At the pool of Bethesda, John v. 4.
13. To the disciples, Acts i. 11.
14. To the disciples in prison, Acts v. 19.
15. To Cornelius, Acts x. 3.
16. To Peter in prison, Acts xii. 7.
17. To Paul, Acts xxvii. 23.

TWENTY.

Twenty dreams are recorded :—
1. Abimelech, Gen. xx. 3.
2, 3. Jacob, Gen. xxviii. 12; xxxi. 10.
4. Laban, Gen. xxxi. 24.
5, 6. Joseph, Gen. xxxvii. 5, 9.
7, 8. The butler and the baker, Gen. xl. 5.
9, 10. Pharaoh, Gen. xli. 1, 5.
11. The man in Gideon's army, Judg. vii. 13.
12. Solomon, 1 Kings iii. 5.
13, 14. Nebuchadnezzar, Dan. ii. 3; iv. 5.
15. Daniel, Dan. vii. 1.
16, 17, 18. Joseph, Matt. i. 20; ii. 13, 19.
19. The wise men, Matt. ii. 12.
20. Pilate's wife, Matt. xxvii. 19.

TWENTY-ONE

times in the Book of Kings it is said that Jeroboam the son of Nebat "made Israel to sin":—1 Kings xiv. 16; xv. 26, 30, 34; xvi. 19, 26; xxi. 22; xxii. 52; 2 Kings iii. 3; x. 29, 31; xiii. 2, 6, 11; xiv. 24; xv. 9, 18, 24, 28; xvii. 21; xxiii. 15.

INDEXES.

INDEX OF SUBJECTS.

*** *Add.* signifies the Addenda, pp. 288–292.

A

B

C

T

U

V

W

Y

Z

INDEX OF TEXTS

MORE OR LESS EXPLAINED AND ILLUSTRATED, OMITTING MERE REFERENCES.

*** *n* signifies Note.

LONDON:
EYRE & SPOTTISWOODE, LTD.,
His Majesty's Printers,
DOWNS PARK ROAD, HACKNEY, N.E.

WORKS BY E. W. BULLINGER, D.D.

A CRITICAL LEXICON AND CONCORDANCE TO THE ENGLISH AND GREEK NEW TESTAMENT. Indispensable to Ministers, Teachers, and Bible Students. Fifth Edition, Revised to date (1907), large 8vo., 1,034 pp. Price 15/-, or $3·65.

LONGMANS & CO., 39, PATERNOSTER ROW.

This Work is specially designed for those who have little or no knowledge of Greek. It shows at a glance the literal meaning of the Greek word, in every passage, by a mere reference to the English word which translates it.

Professors, Divines, and Ministers of various Denominations, and Editors of Leading Papers, unite in hearty approval and commendation.

The following are published by EYRE & SPOTTISWOODE (BIBLE WAREHOUSE), LTD., 33, PATERNOSTER ROW, LONDON, E.C.:—

FIGURES OF SPEECH USED IN THE BIBLE: Being an explanation of 217 Figures of Speech, illustrating some 8,000 passages of Scripture which are obscured by defective translation. 1,104 pages, five Appendices, and seven Indexes, 20/- net, or $5.

THE WITNESS OF THE STARS: Showing how the Ancient Signs and Constellations were designed for "signs and seasons" to record and preserve the prophecy of Gen. iii. 15, for 2,500 years before the revelation from God was written in the Scriptures of Truth. With 41 coloured plates and five engravings. Handsomely bound, suitable for presents. Second Edition. Price 7/6 or $1·85.

NUMBER IN SCRIPTURE: Its Supernatural Design and Spiritual Significance. Demy 8vo. Second Edition. Price 7/6 or $1·85.

***"THE CHIEF MUSICIAN"; or STUDIES IN THE PSALMS AND THEIR TITLES.** (With Illustrations.) A work in 4 Parts:—

Part 1.—THE TITLES

Part 2.—THE SELAHS.

Part 3.—THE SONGS OF DEGREES.

Part 4.—THE 15 SONGS OF THE DEGREES. A New Translation, with the Structure, and Notes. Price 6/- or $1·50 net.

THE APOCALYPSE; or "THE DAY OF THE LORD." Small 8vo., 750 pages. Price 5/- or $1·25. With Analytical Table of Contents, Appendix, and Four Indexes.

In this Work the Apocalypse is treated not as a book to be interpreted by man, but as God's own Interpretation of the Future to us; and of what is to take place in "the Day of the Lord."

The same in GERMAN. Price 6 marks. D. B. WIEMAN, Barmen; or GRUBÉ'S VERLAG, Tellstrasse 19, Düsseldorf.

THE BOOK OF JOB: Part 1.—THE OLDEST LESSON IN THE WORLD. Part 2.—A NEW TRANSLATION: Rhythmical, Idiomatic, and Critical, with brief Explanatory Notes. Price 5/- Cloth, and 7/6 Morocco, or $1·25 and $1·85.

***HOW TO ENJOY THE BIBLE; or "THE WORD" AND THE "WORDS," HOW TO STUDY THEM.** With Four Indexes. Price 5/- or $1·25. This Work is published at this low price on account of the receipt of Special Donations contributed for that purpose by friends desirous of its being put within the reach of most Bible students.

A KEY TO THE PSALMS. A new and unique Work, displaying each Psalm to the eye, so as to exhibit the perfection of its plan, the symmetry of its structure, and the scope of its teaching. By the late Rev. THOMAS BOYS. Edited by Dr. BULLINGER from the Author's unfinished MS., with an Introduction; and an Appendix showing the Structure of the Book of Psalms as a whole. Price 5/- or $1·25.

THE CHURCH EPISTLES (Romans to 2 Thess.): Their Importance, Order, Inter-Relation, Structure, Scope, and Interpretation. With Four Indexes. Second Edition, Revised, Price 3/6 or 85 cents.

* Books marked thus (*) are New Works, published December, 1907.

Published by Eyre & Spottiswoode (Bible Warehouse), Ltd.,
S 12547. 33, Paternoster Row, London, E.C. X

*THE GIVER AND HIS GIFTS: or THE HOLY SPIRIT AND HIS WORK. The Work contains 210 pages, and gives the use and usage of *pneuma* in the New Testament, with a complete list and exposition of the 385 passages in which the word occurs; together with Appendixes and Indexes. Price 2/6 or 65 cents.

TEN SERMONS ON THE SECOND ADVENT. Preached at Oxford Fifth Edition. Price 2/- or 50 cents, Cloth, gilt lettered. Cheap Edition, Cloth, cut flush, 1/- or 25 cents.

In JAPANESE, with additional matter on the Mystery. Cloth, 50 Sen. (1/-); Paper Covers, 35 Sen. (9*d*.).

FIFTEEN POINTS preliminary to the Study of THE APOCALYPSE, showing its future fulfilment in "THE DAY OF THE LORD." 132 pp. Price 1/- or 25 cents.

SUNDAY SCHOOL LESSONS. A Series for Five Years. Price 1/- or 25 cents. for each separate series; or 9*d*. (18 cents.) each for Sunday Schools. 4/- or $1 the complete set.

THE MASSORAH: Being an account of the Preservation, Translation, and Transmission of the Hebrew Text; containing a large amount of interesting information. With three Photographic *facsimiles* of Ancient Manuscripts. Price 1/- or 25 cents.

THE DIVINE NAMES AND TITLES. This Pamphlet contains the principal Divine Names, with their signification, usage, and occurrences. Price 1/- or 25 cents.

*THE TWO NATURES IN THE CHILD OF GOD. Cloth, 1/6; Paper Covers, 1/- or 25 cents.

In GERMAN: (Die Zwei Naturen im Kinde Gottes.) M 0.75; geb. 1.25 M. Grubé's Verlag, Düsseldorf.

*HEBREWS XI. Ready early in 1908 (D.V.)

*THE VISION OF ISAIAH: Its Structure and Scope, showing its Unity and Integrity as a whole. A standing refutation of the theories of the Higher Critics. Price 6*d*. or 12 cents.

"THE MYSTERY." Price, Leatherette, gilt lettered, 1/- or 25 cents. Paper Covers, 6*d*. or 12 cents. Third Edition.

In GERMAN: (Das Geheimnis.) Grubé's Verlag, Düsseldorf. 35 M.

In JAPANESE: with the Ten Sermons (above), Price, Cloth, 50 Sen. (1/-); Paper Covers, 35 Sen. (9*d*.).

THE STRUCTURE OF THE TWO EPISTLES TO THE THESSALONIANS, arranged like the *Key to the Psalms*, on two large sheets, folded in envelope. Second Edition. Price 6*d*. or 12 cents.

"THE SPIRITS IN PRISON." An Exposition of 1 Pet. iii. 17—iv. 6, in the light of the whole Epistle. Fourth Edition, 6*d*. or 12 cents.

CHRIST'S PROPHETIC TEACHING IN RELATION TO THE DIVINE ORDER OF HIS WORDS AND WORKS. Demy 8vo., Paper Covers, 32 pages. Fourth Edition. Price 6*d*. or 12 cents.

THE RICH MAN AND LAZARUS: or the "Intermediate State." Second Edition, Revised. Price 6*d*. or 12 cents.

THE OLDEST LESSON IN THE WORLD: giving (in a connected form) the great objects of the whole book as exhibiting "the End of the Lord." Price 6*d*. or 12 cents., Paper Covers. Cloth, gilt, 1/6 or 36 cents.

"THE NAMES AND ORDER" OF THE BOOKS OF THE OLD TESTAMENT ACCORDING TO THE HEBREW CANON Second Edition. Price 6*d*. or 12 cents.

*THE TWO PRAYERS IN EPHESIANS I. & III. Price 6*d*. or 12 cents.

*THE KNOWLEDGE OF GOD. Price 6*d*. or 12 cents.

*"THE LORD'S DAY." (Rev. i. 10.) IS IT A DAY OF THE WEEK? or "THE DAY OF THE LORD?" Being a Paper read at a meeting of the "Prophecy Investigation Society" of London, in November, 1906. Price 6*d*. or 12 cents.

*Books marked thus (*) are New Works, published December, 1907.

Published by Eyre & Spottiswoode (Bible Warehouse), Ltd.,
33, Paternoster Row, London, E.C.

WORKS BY E. W. BULLINGER, D.D.

*THE TRANSFIGURATION: The Historical Interpretation. The Spiritual Application and Practical Conclusions. Price 6*d.* or 12 cents.

"ALSO": A Bible Study on the usage of the word "also" in the New Testament. Second Edition, corrected. Price 4*d.* or 8 cents.

*"SHEOL" AND "HADES." The Biblical meaning and usage of these words. Price 4*d.* or 8 cents.

HOLINESS: God's Way better than Man's. Price 3*d.* or 6 cents. In GERMAN: Heiligung und Heiligkeit. 10 M.

THE IMPORTANCE OF ACCURACY IN THE STUDY OF HOLY SCRIPTURE. Ninth Edition. Price 3*d.* or 6 cents.

*"LEAVEN." Its Scripture usage and Interpretation. Price 3*d.* or 6 cents.

*"THE LORD'S PRAYER." Its Dispensational Place, and Interpretation. Price 3*d.* or 6 cents.

*"THE PAULINE EPISTLES": The Dispensational teaching of their Chronological order. A sequel to "The Church Epistles." Price 3*d.* or 6 cents.

*PARATHĒKĒ; or "THE GOOD DEPOSIT": A sequel to "The Pauline Epistles." Price 3*d.* or 6 cents.

*"THE SONS OF GOD" in Gen. vi, and other Scriptures. Price 3*d.* or 6 cents.

THE STRUCTURE OF THE BOOKS OF THE BIBLE. This is intended as a sequel to the work on *The Names and Order of the Books of the Old Testament.* Is shows the nature and supernatural design of this order, and affords a strong corroborative proof of the authenticity of the Canon of Scripture. Price 2*d.* or 4 cents.

THE NAME OF JEHOVAH IN THE BOOK OF ESTHER Its occurrences in Four Acrostics, with their Lessons. Fourth Edition, Price 2*d.* or 4 cents

"THE KINGDOM" AND "THE CHURCH." Sixth Edition, Revised and Enlarged. Price 2*d.* or 4 cents.

*"THE GOSPEL OF THE KINGDOM": As set forth in the Parables of the Sower, the Dinner, and the Great Supper. Price 2*d.* or 4 cents.

THE ZIONIST MOVEMENT: Being a paper read at the "Prophecy Investigation Society" of London, April 22nd, 1904. Price 2*d.* or 4 cents.

*THE CHRISTIAN'S GREATEST NEED; or "THE SECRET OF A HAPPY AND HOLY LIFE." Price 2*d.* or 4 cents.

"THE MAN OF GOD": A Bible Study. Fifth Edition. Price 1*d.* or 2 cents.

"THINGS TO COME": An Epitome of Prophetic Truth. Envelope size. Eighth Edition, Revised. Price 1*d.* or 2 cents. Also in French, German, and Welsh. Price 1*d.* or 2 cents each. In Morocco, gilt, for Presents, 1/- or 25 cents.

FOUR PROPHETIC PERIODS: A Key to the "Things which must Shortly come to Pass." Eighth Edition. Revised. Price 1*d.* or 2 cents.
- "MAN'S DAY." 1 Cor. iv. 2.
- "THE DAY OF CHRIST." Phil. ii. 16.
- "THE DAY OF THE LORD." Rev. i. 10.
- "THE DAY OF GOD." 2 Pet. iii. 12.

THE NEW CREATION AND THE OLD; or, The Ways of God in Grace, illustrated by the works of God in Creation. A Bible Study of Genesis i. in the light of 2 Cor. v. 17. Fifth Edition. Price 1*d.* or 2 cents.

THE INSPIRATION AND AUTHORITY OF HOLY SCRIPTURE. Sixth Edition. Price 1*d.* or 2 cents.

GOD'S PURPOSE IN ISRAEL. Fifth Edition. Revised Price 1*d.* or 2 cents.

THE RESURRECTION OF THE BODY. Fifth Edition. Price 1*d.* or 2 cents.

* Books marked thus (*) are New Works, published December, 1907.

Published by Eyre & Spottiswoode (Bible Warehouse), Ltd.,
33, Paternoster Row, London, E.C.

WORKS BY E. W. BULLINGER, D.D.

"RIGHTLY DIVIDING THE WORD OF TRUTH": Being an Address at the Mildmay Prophetical Conference, 1898. Second Edition. Price 1*d.* or 2 cents.

"THIS IS MY BODY." Being a specimen of the Author's Work on *The Figures of Speech used in the Bible.* Second Edition, Revised. Price 1*d.* or 2 cents.

INTONED PRAYERS AND MUSICAL SERVICES: Are they in Harmony with the Worship of God "in spirit and in truth"? Price 1*d.* or 2 cents.

THE FIG, THE OLIVE, AND THE VINE: An Epitome of Israel's History and Destiny; with special reference to the Dispensational position of the Gospel of John. Price 1*d.* or 2 cents.

RATIONALISM AND ROMANISM IN RELATION TO THE BIBLE: Being an Address delivered at the National Protestant Congress, held in Manchester, October, 1899. Price 1*d.* or 2 cents.

KNOWING CHRIST AFTER THE FLESH: An Exposition of 2 Cor. v. 14-17. Second Edition. Price 1*d.* or 2 cents.

"THE POTTER'S HOUSE." Jer. xviii. 1-4. Its Interpretation and various Applications Second Edition. Price 1*d.* or 2 cents.

THE GREAT CONFLICT OF THE AGES. Being the Author's Address at the Mildmay Conference, 1902. Price 1*d.* or 2 cents.

*JEHOSHAPHAT: or LESSONS FOR OUR TIMES. Price 1*d.* or 2 cents.

*"THE VAIL" of the Tabernacle and Temple, and its Teaching. With special reference to the New Gospel of Humanity. Price 1*d.* or 2 cents. In German (Der Vorhang) 10 Pf.

"MADE MEET." 1*d.* } In German: (Tüchtig Gemacht) 10 Pf.
"BE PERFECT." 1*d.* } Grubé's Verlag, Düsseldorf.

"THE GUILTY BY NO MEANS CLEARED." 1*d.*
In GERMAN: (Der Schuldige mitnichten unschuldig). With "THE VAIL" (Der Vorhang). 10 Pf., Grubé's Verlag, Düsseldorf.

WHERE TO WORSHIP. 1*d.*

THE ROYAL ROAD TO HOLINESS. 1*d.* or 2 cents.

SANCTIFICATION. 1*d.* or 2 cents. In GERMAN: 10 Pf. (Heiligung und Heiligkeit). Grubé's Verlag, Düsseldorf.

THE FALLACIES OF EVOLUTION. 1*d.* or 2 cents.

GOD'S BUILDING. An Exposition of 1 Cor. i.—iii. 1*d.* or 2 cents.

FIFTY ORIGINAL HYMN TUNES. Set to Appropriate Words. Third Edition. Price 2/- or 50 cents.

TWENTY-ONE ORIGINAL HYMN TUNES. Being a Second Series. Price 2/- or 50 cents.

SIXTY-SIX OLD BRETON TUNES. Collected and Transcribed from the lips of Breton peasants; and harmonised in short-score, for the use of the churches of the Breton Evangelical Mission. Cloth, 2/- or 50 cents.

IN GERMAN.

To be obtained at:—GRUBÉ'S MISSIONS VERLAG, TELLSTRASSE 19, DÜSSELDORF, GERMANY.

DIE ZWEI NATUREN IM KINDE GOTTES. (The Two Natures in the Child of God.) 0.75 M. Geb. 1.25 M.

DAS GEHEIMNIS (mit einem Vorworte des Prof. E. F. Ströter), "The Mystery." 35 Pf.

"TUCHTIG GEMACHT." ("Made Meet.") 10 Pf.

HEILIGUNG UND HEILIGKEIT. (Holiness and Sanctification.) 10 Pf.

DER SCHULDIGE MITNICHTEN UNSCHULDEIG. ("The Guilty by no means Cleared.") 10 Pf.

* Books marked thus (*) are New Works, published December, 1907.

Published by Eyre & Spottiswoode (Bible Warehouse), Ltd.,
33, Paternoster Row, London, E.C.